GUNS, CASH AND ROCK 'N' ROLL

Steve Overbury worked at Chrysalis Records when punk broke big, during which time he danced with Debbie Harry and loaned money to Billy Idol. He later became a producer, was in a band with Adamski and managed both The Whizz Kids and Shadowfax. Then it was time to get a job and 15 years of writing, editing and designing magazines followed. He lives in London.

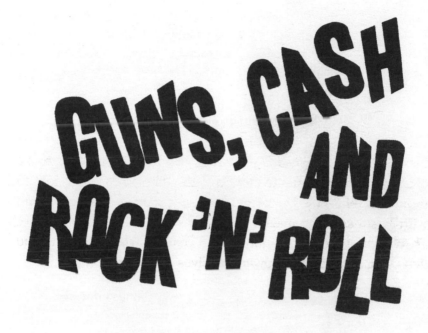

GUNS, CASH AND ROCK 'N' ROLL

THE MANAGERS

STEVE OVERBURY

MAINSTREAM
PUBLISHING

EDINBURGH AND LONDON

First published in Great Britain in 2007 by
MAINSTREAM PUBLISHING COMPANY
(EDINBURGH) LTD
7 Albany Street
Edinburgh EH1 3UG

ISBN 9781845962340

A catalogue record for this book is available
from the British Library

Typeset in Palatino and Horseradish

Printed in Great Britain by
William Clowes Ltd, Beccles, Suffolk

ACKNOWLEDGEMENTS

Many thanks to the following for granting permission to use copyrighted material:

PASSION IS A FASHION: The Real Story of the Clash by Pat Gilbert used by permission of Aurum Press Ltd;

The Lamberts: George Constant and Kit by Andrew Motion, published by Chatto & Windus. Reprinted by permission of The Random House Group Ltd;

Who's Crazee Now? by Noddy Holder, published by Ebury. Reprinted by permission of The Random House Group Ltd;

Black Vinyl White Powder by Simon Napier-Bell, published by Ebury Press. Reprinted by permission of The Random House Group Ltd;

Faber & Faber for permission to use extract from *Money for Nothing: Greed and Exploitation in the Music Industry* by Simon Garfield and *England's Dreaming* by Jon Savage

Animal Tracks – The Story of the Animals: Newcastle's Rising Sons reprinted by permission of Helter Skelter Publishing, copyright Sean Egan;

Omnibus Press for their permission to use extracts from *Peter Grant: The Man Who Led Zeppelin* (2002) and *Hendrix: A Biography* (1972), both by Chris Welch, *Wannabe: How the Spice Girls Reinvented Pop Fame* (2004) by David Sinclair, and *Sex Pistols: The Inside Story* (1987) by Fred Vermorel and Judy Vermorel;

Rogues, Villains and Eccentrics: An A–Z of Roguish Britons Through the Ages by William Donaldson, reproduced by kind permission of Phoenix Press, a division of The Orion Publishing Group;

Plexus Publishing, *Before I Get Old: The Story of The Who* by Dave Marsh and *Rotten: No Irish, No Blacks, No Dogs* by John Lydon with Keith and Kent Zimmerman;

Extracts from *Mr Big* by Don Arden reproduced by permission of Robson and Portico, and imprint of Anova Books Co. Ltd

Stoned and 2Stoned by Andrew Loog Oldham, published by Secker & Warburg. Reprinted by permission of The Random House Group Ltd;

In My Life: The Brian Epstein Story by Debbie Geller, copyright © 2000 by the author and reprinted by permission of St Martin's Press, LLC;

extracts from *A Cellarful of Noise* by Brian Epstein, reprinted by the kind permission of Souvenir Press;

extracts from *Vacant: A Diary of the Punk Years 1976–79* by Nils Stevenson, photographs by Ray Stevenson. Copyright © 1999 Nils Stevenson and Ray Stevenson. Reproduced by permission of Thames & Hudson;

'Song for Nico' Written by David A. Stewart/Marianne Faithfull. Published by BMG Music Publishing Ltd. Used by permission. All Rights Reserved. 'Song for Nico'. Words by Marianne Faithfull and music by Dave Stewart © 2001, reproduced by permission of EMI Music Publishing, London WC2H 0QY.

The author would like to give special thanks to Eric Burdon.

CONTENTS

INTRODUCTION

The music business is a cruel and shallow money trench, a long plastic hallway where thieves and pimps run free, and good men die like dogs . . . There's also a negative side.

– *Hunter S. Thompson* (misquoted)

Back in the days of sweet rationing, when there were only two TV channels in Britain and they both closed down at 11 p.m., back when stereo was mono and Radio 1 was called the Light Programme, a bunch of disparate individuals gazed across the Atlantic and sniffed the air.

They smelt money.

There was an outburst of exuberance in '50s America. You could almost see the lights on the horizon. Sure, the US had suffered its war dead, but it recovered from the deprivations of the conflict far faster than most of the other combatants. After all, it had never been bombed flat. The farmers of the big country dug deep and put food on the table; the production lines hummed with clothes and cars. While bombsite Britons pedalled to work in shades of grey, the Americans hauled ass down to the soda shop in a pink Cadillac.

Guns, Cash and Rock 'n' Roll

Tom and Jerry was on the TV. Teenagers had just been invented, or classified as a bona fide subculture at any rate. Boys chewed on Bazooka Joe, greased out their quiffs and cleaned their nails with switchblades; girls teased up beehives, talked dirty and sang into their hairbrushes. They ripped up the seats in the cinemas and the record shops were mobbed. Elvis was king.

And he wasn't the only rocker in town – others rocked, too: Jerry Lee Lewis, Chuck Berry, Bo Diddley, Gene Vincent and Eddie Cochran. The old crooners slunk off, dried up and dead, their records remaindered. The new hip kids didn't even see them go; they were preoccupied, straining at the leash, rushing into the future – all sex and swagger. Rock and roll turned you on.

In 1957, John Lennon formed his first group. The following year, Eveready produced its first batteries for use in personal transistor radios and Billy Fury was signed on the spot by Britain's first pop impresario, Larry Parnes, because he had that rock and roll 'look'. The 51st State was starting to grow some modest rock and roll talent of its own. Soon skiffle king Lonnie Donegan, Adam Faith, Marty Wilde and Cliff Richard were shaking the cobwebs out of the UK music charts. They aped their American heroes, and they learned their lessons well, but few of them could sell outside the UK. Acker Bilk's 'Stranger on the Shore' and 'Telstar' by The Tornadoes were among the only British contributions to the USA's Billboard Hot 100.

It wasn't until 1964 that the situation changed, but when it did, it changed for good. The Beatles lit a touchpaper that launched the opening salvo of the British invasion and for more than 30 years British bands (led by British managers) pushed and jostled into, and often disproportionately dominated, the American charts.

The Beatles, like Elvis, had good songs, good looks and oozed talent but, as everyone knew (especially Colonel Tom Parker and Brian Epstein), that wasn't quite enough. Both acts had needed grooming, promoting, managing. There were many would-be kings or Beatles. Anybody who could play the spoons was having a crack at the big time. It was vital to stand out. Packaging paid off.

Introduction

Some decided that if they didn't have the wherewithal, if they couldn't be the king themselves, then perhaps they could be a kingmaker, a Svengali, the power behind the throne, like Tom Parker. They cottoned on to the fact that although Elvis was nominally the king, he and Parker shared the throne. Tom was the king, too – the king of the cash. He was on a 50 per cent cut of the action.

The British music business suddenly became terribly attractive, sometimes fatally attractive, to a mishmash of dodgy end-of-the-pier entertainers, ex-Butlins redcoats, college dropouts, failed public schoolboys, spivs, hustlers, hucksters, whores, blowhards, thieves, liars, drunks, junkies, the deluded, the damned, the venal, the violent and the insane. Yet at the heart of this motley crew, like pearls in bad oysters, were some of the finest, most outstanding minds of our times: world-class entrepreneurs, Machiavellian schemers, eccentrics, adventurers, buccaneers, dreamers and big-time litigants.

Britain had always been a place of entrepreneurs, a busy hive of money-making activity, but the Second World War had snuffed much of that spirit. While we'd historically been good at rather unglamorous things, such as heavy engineering, agriculture and insurance, an ambitious young man leaving school in the late '50s or early '60s had relatively few career options available to him; it was either the professions, the trades or the army. Most resigned themselves to buying a Burton suit, clocking in at the local factory for a few quid a week and having nothing to look forward to but 50 years on the treadmill and a gold watch at the other end, if they got there. Showbiz came from over the sea.

But there was now a new cash machine on the horizon – the music machine – and a tiny gang of men (and they were all men) ate the rulebook for breakfast. Undaunted by the scale of the challenge (getting British records into the American charts was no easy task), un-awed by the size of the venues (Shea Stadium held 55,000 people) and unimpressed by the fees (The Beatles would regularly turn down offers of $1 million to re-form for a one-night concert), they embarked, in the wake of the Epstein vanguard, on a piratical conquest of the world. In the context of pop managers, words like pirate and buccaneer are hard to resist, as are militaristic terms like 'invasion' and 'raid'. Glitz and glamour were a definite draw, but money was the motivator.

This seemed like a classic extract from the tale of the American Dream – the little guys take on the big guys and win – but it was deliciously twisted: the '60s Brit Pack took on the might of the American entertainment industry, played them at their own game and saw victory time after time. It was a slim volume indeed, but it might have been called the 'British Dream'.

Colonel Parker, it is often said, was the greatest artist manager of all time; he was a genius who cared for nothing except Elvis's health and wealth, they say. Others portrayed him as a cigar-chomping Disney villain with the ethics of a hyena and the powers of Rasputin.

But the figures reveal the truth. On Elvis merchandising, Colonel Tom made 80 per cent while Elvis made only 20 per cent. He was a genius all right. He may also have been a murderer, which is something you couldn't accuse any of the managers in this book of . . . although some got close.

They certainly were not angels: lawlessness and danger pervaded the business. Because of his predilections, Brian Epstein was frequently violently assaulted by strangers in toilets; Stones manager Andrew Loog Oldham liked to point guns at people; Led Zeppelin's Peter Grant dished out judicious beatings hither and thither, while those in his entourage did far worse. Then there was Don Arden . . .

What have the managers in this book got in common? Well, a good few were low academic achievers with a lot to prove. Some were homosexuals, some were Jewish; one was Jewish and homosexual. Several wanted to be performers of various kinds. Most of them were slavish fans of their acts. Nearly all were/are determined to the point of obsession. Some acquiesced to their charges, others were tyrants. Bands are rarely democracies: they usually behave like a rapacious chimp troupe.

Introduction

How would one go about advertising for a band manager? What essential qualities should a candidate have? Does a band really need a manager in the first place? After all, these days there is a piece of software that cheerfully aims to do the whole job for you. Indie Band Manager promises that, in return for $39.95, it will 'help bands look more professional, reach more fans, get more press, book better gigs, sell more CDs and be more organised'.

'All we need,' a band might think, 'and no 25 per cent commission to pay either.' But can it drive a van? Can it dangle a competitor from a balcony? How would it deal with a crack-head drummer on a four-day bender with a shark in the hotel wardrobe, a bedful of groupies and the police at the door?

The very best managers have been resourceful enough to turn their hands to just about anything – jacks of all trades and masters of some: money, law, promotions, deal negotiation, the press, stage management, sound mixing, make-up and hair, marketing, psychiatry, procuring, lighting, transport, substance abuse, security, sales and social work – to be Samaritan, a sheepdog and a shark.

Andrew Loog Oldham and Kit Lambert could also produce their artist's music. Steve O'Rourke and Lambert produced movies (Malcolm McLaren still does). Loog Oldham and Simon Napier-Bell are now successful writers. But the killer skill is, and always was, being able to make people pay up when they didn't really want to.

And lest we forget, whatever talents they possess, even the best manager in the business is nothing without a talented act – although, in 2007, many would argue that artists are getting by with considerably less of it than their forebears.

Why did any of the remarkable impresarios in this book want to be band managers in the first place? What was the fascination? Often on-call 24 hours a day, pandering to the whims of a bunch of dissolute adolescents with a heightened sense of their own talent and value: what was the draw?

Power and the pursuit of power has a lot to do with it.

Jeffrey Archer, who thankfully didn't take up an instrument, was nevertheless keen to be associated with those who did – specifically The Beatles (Ringo is reported to have called him 'a nice enough fella but the kind of bloke who would bottle your piss and sell it'). Tony Blair was briefly a lead singer and guitar player. Why? Was it because he harboured ambitions to be a serious musician? Not for a moment. It was because our future leader perceived that being in a hit band was a short cut to the money and fame he lusted after, and with money and fame comes status and power. Tony, apparently, demonstrated some form but not enough, so ultimately he had to seek his thrills elsewhere. Since, of course, he has become the biggest manager in town, but there remains a lurking suspicion that deep down he would have preferred to have been on the road with Ozzy Osbourne – at least once.

Pop music is a door opener. It was, and is, one of the fastest conceivable ways of making lots of money legally: a mid-range band can potentially earn more money than a drug baron or a firm of corporate lawyers. A top-of-the-range band could make off with the riches of a pharaoh.

Essentially a band is a gang; us against the world and, unless the act is Jools Holland's orchestra, it aims to be a small, effective unit, a mighty atom, with its manager (gang boss) at its head. A touring band could be, if a tad romantically, likened to a bunch of bandits: fast-moving raiders with a mission, its members watching one another's backs. If successful, the gang could make more money than a car plant: at its peak, Swedish band Abba had earnings greater than Swedish car manufacturer Volvo. That was the scale of it. Yet Abba had no factories, no plant, machinery or employees, bar a couple of lorry-loads of equipment and a ragbag crew of roadies.

A band on tour could also be compared to a funfair and it was no doubt useful to Colonel Tom Parker that as a young man he had been a 'carny', a roustabout. The funfair nips in, sets up, does the show, grabs the loot and legs it, leaving little trace of its presence save perhaps for a few teenage girls worrying about missing their next period – all very appealing to the inner hunter-gatherer. And at a time when few of us had been further than a daytrip to Calais, British bands didn't only have British dates on the tour schedule, they went international – TWA.

The thrilling key to it all is the nature of the product. Pop music and pop bands are not baked beans, despite the packaging, no matter how economists then and now try to denigrate the phenomenon. People don't clamour for baked beans. They don't work themselves into screaming froths of excitement, pee their pants and then pass out over cans of beans, or food of any description. Pop music inspires quasi-religious devotion and sex-like passions, and people will tear the house down trying to get at product like that. No wonder everyone wants to be in the pop business.

Like any gold rush, oil strike or dot-com scheme, pop has an intoxicating allure and has long attracted itinerants who've flooded to its cause. Among the first wave were men who kick started the Swinging '60s and earned incalculable sums of money for themselves, their clients and the country. Along the way, they delivered some of the best bands and enduring music that the world will ever know. These men could definitely run a piss-up in a brewery.

1

DON ARDEN

Animals, Small Faces

I always wanted to be in show business. When you stood next to Don Arden, you were.
— *Andrew Loog Oldham*

You won't find Don on Robert Stigwood's Christmas card list. You won't find him on Lynsey de Paul's either or those of any of the ex-members of The Nashville Teens, come to that. He's not down on the list of any of the remaining Small Faces, not even his own daughter, Sharon Osbourne's – not for 20 years anyway. If Don ever read Dale Carnegie's book *How to Win Friends and Influence People*, then he completely rejected its message in favour of his own less friendly alternative.

'Don't mess with Don.'

Don Arden really created our perception of what constitutes a pop group manager. The requisite mix of Svengali and mobster, essential to survive let alone prosper in the rough-and-tumble music business, he inspired so many others who were to follow him, including his protégés Led Zeppelin manager Peter Grant and the Stones' Andrew Loog Oldham. Don was a big talker with a quick temper, and a notorious penny pincher who kept the Small

Faces on twenty quid a week when they had top-ten records and who fought protracted court cases over years for a few thousand pounds. The legend was that if you robbed Don or threatened to steal one of his bands, then you had better watch out. You had better take regular peeks over your shoulder and out of your office window in case a carload of toughs turned up to pass on a message from their boss in no uncertain terms. Arden did nothing to dispel the notion of him as a London mafioso or the rumour that he would use henchmen with guns or even his own fists whenever he felt slighted.

'Don't mess with Don.'

On Arden's own website, he lauds himself with alternatives to Don: 'Don't mess with the Godfather of Rock' and 'Don't mess with the Al Capone of Pop'. Originally, though, it was 'Don't mess with Harry Levy', the name he was born with in 1926 in Cheetham Hill, Manchester. Now that's notorious gangland, and Don was forced to keep his fists at the ready and grow up quickly. As he says in his autobiography, *Mr Big*, 'I was one of those guys who came out of the womb fighting.'

Don's dad was a hard nut called Lazarus, who worked in a raincoat factory. His mother looked after the house and dreamed about being in the theatre. Don would impress the local kids by winning the rat-catcher competitions that they regularly held as a substitute for gang fights. 'I made a point of carrying the dead rats down to show the other kids, who would act very strangely when they saw me coming, swinging them by their tails,' he writes. 'A strange mixture of repulsion and admiration and . . . something else: fear.'

Don left school aged 14 and at the outbreak of the war was doing stand-up comedy. He'd trained himself to sing down the garden in the house's outside toilet. 'I'd sit there for an hour singing my head off,' he remembers. He refused to be evacuated to the countryside and stayed on to entertain the troops.

He had a lot of success for a kid (he'd lied about his age) and at a time when his father was making £5 a week, Don was making £8. But he'd have made a good deal more if he'd had a telephone to take bookings. The solution: 'I used to commandeer a public telephone box just down the road from us and use that as my office.' He was undertaking a crash course in dealing with booking agents and theatre managers that would stand him in good stead in later years. The telephone-box office was such a runaway success that he had to get business cards made up with the number printed on them.

Tough guy Don was then called up into the army himself and had to tough out the war. He conceived of a survival strategy that entailed pretending he was crazy. This required him to take to his bed and only speak odd words now and then. 'I spent the latter part of my so-called army career either appearing on the stage or lying in my bed in the hospital. I wasn't sure which was the greater acting job.'

After he was demobbed, Don returned to the stage and between 1946 and 1953 worked the variety circuit, using as his agent, amongst others, Joe Collins, the father of Jackie and Joan. In his act, he would sing the songs of the great tenor Enrico Caruso and then do a quick Edward G. Robinson routine. He topped up his wages doing Al Jolson impressions for Jewish clubs at the weekends, and at some point he was one of the Black and White Minstrels. 'By 1948,' he says, 'I was getting £350 per show, which was berserk money in those days. Star money.'

It's hard to imagine the aggressive impresario as a comedian, but he is remembered by his old management adversary Peter Walsh as 'a tremendously funny man', which, when considering what later occurred between Arden and Walsh, is a very charitable statement.

Don's uncompromising attitude and uncertain temper prompted him to quit the boards and launch a new career as a show-business agent. He'd already had many backstage altercations: on one occasion, he floored a theatre manager and, on another, a lighting engineer, and he'd lost his job both times. He didn't often need to hit anyone, though, as the mere sight of him could be enough to win the argument. 'I'd see guys staring at my physique – big barrel chest and big muscled arms and legs – and I knew what they were thinking: "God, look at that guy, you'd have to hit him with a hammer to knock him out."'

Again using his Jewish connections, Don began organising Hebrew folk-song contests and putting together his own shows. However, there was soon to be a far more exciting and profitable musical prospect.

When the '60s arrived, Don enrolled all the burgeoning American rock and roll stars to perform in the UK. He couldn't stand any of the 'lite' British rock and roll versions, stating that he considered Cliff Richard to be 'a pathetic imitation of the real thing . . . I could never understand how someone like Cliff Richard was allowed near a stage.' He is equally disparaging of the Larry Parnes stable of acts. '[Larry] used to say Billy Fury could hold his own with Eddie Cochran, and that was exactly what he did – stood there onstage, holding his own cock. Billy Fury wasn't fit to wipe Eddie Cochran's arse for him.'

Arden started running tours with Chuck Berry, Bo Diddley and Gene Vincent and even got to tread the boards again himself, acting as a warm-up act, cracking jokes and bursting into song to get the audience in the right frame of mind for his bands.

His tight purse strings and knock-down bartering methods were by this stage legendary. If he owed you £1,000 and you went and asked for it, he would try everything conceivable to avoid paying you. Great old music business lies like 'The cheque's in the post' or 'Oh, I'm sorry, but the banks are shut now' originate with old-school managers like Don. At best, you might emerge with half the debt; at worst, you'd get a thick ear. It's down to Don that, to this day, Chuck Berry won't play anywhere in the world without getting his entire fee paid up front. Don is unrepentant about the animosity shared between him and Chuck: 'I hated him from the moment I met him,' he says.

Arden liked Gene Vincent, though, and has often claimed that Vincent was the best performer he ever worked with. But the American rocker's career wasn't in any great shape back home in the USA, despite his success in Britain, and he began to spend a lot of time in the UK. Arden's mate TV producer Jack Good put Vincent on television and Don put him on the road. Together they honed the Vincent bad-boy image, with the greased quiff and leather suit.

When the singer moved to the UK, Don decided he should be his manager and they enjoyed a successful, if tempestuous, relationship. Vincent was a troubled man. A few years earlier, he'd been involved in a motorcycle crash that had left him with steel braces in his legs and he hadn't easily come to terms with his fall from favour in the US. He had developed a taste for booze and pills and his angry alcoholic outbursts were bad for business.

Johnny Rogan claims in *Starmakers and Svengalis* that Don resolved decisive action was necessary and convinced a Harley Street doctor to put Vincent to sleep for a few days while he was fed intravenously in an attempt to wean the star off his addictions. Regardless of the validity of this claim, Vincent soon hit the bottle again in a big way. His booze-fuelled rages against his dying career once led the Virginia wild man to pull a knife on his manager. That didn't scare Don; he'd seen knives before.

One of the minders Arden used for Gene was Peter Grant. It seems that he and his old employee crossed swords and Don isn't bashful about speaking ill of the dead. The late Grant was, he says, 'a chancer I knew from the fringes of showbiz' and 'a three-hundred-pound bag of shit'. The bad-mouthing continued when, in his book, Don refuted the accepted story that Grant had once been a wrestler. 'What crap! Peter Grant could barely wrestle his own dick out of his trousers.' Although this could just be manager-on-manager professional jealousy still raging on after all these years, it's likely that the harsh words are more to do with the influential role Grant played in The Animals giving Don the two-finger salute and clearing off to join one-time Rolling Stones manager Allen Klein's stable.

Whatever the row was about, the fearsome duo was at the time trying and failing to keep Vincent on the rails. Arden attempted to get Gene psychiatric help, but it didn't work out. A bitter acrimony grew between singer and manager, and they split. An irked Don felt that the artist still owed him some money, so their parting was by no means the end of the affair. Don, or any of his bag men, would frequently turn up at Vincent gigs and make strenuous efforts to collect what they thought was due.

Don undoubtedly learned from his miscreant star – one thing, certainly. 'Gene always carried at least one gun with him wherever he went,' he wrote, 'a habit I would also acquire for a period some years later.'

Arden was touring other American acts such as Jerry Lee Lewis, Little Richard and Sam Cooke during this period, but the times were a-changing and Don showed himself uncharacteristically out of step in losing around £100,000 on one of the tours. It seemed American acts were no longer the rage; the stars of the British beat boom had taken over and Arden set about finding himself one.

Arden had seen The Beatles when he had promoted bands in Hamburg's legendary Star Club. They were the future, he somewhat belatedly reasoned: the glory days of the old rock tours were over. 'The Beatles had killed everything,' he says. 'People who had been stars all their lives suddenly became milkmen.'

Don figured he should be managing bands now, not just booking their tours and filing their petrol receipts. Management was where the money was. He needed a band that was going places. The Beatles had Brian Epstein, a man Don alleges he liked but in the same breath accuses of being 'a lower-middle-class poof who longed for respectability . . . I could have taken The Beatles from him, of that I have no doubt . . . but I didn't want to do that to the boy. I already owned a Rolls-Royce and I didn't need to take anything from the likes of him.' The Stones were being guided by their wunderkind manager Andrew Loog Oldham, who Don had briefly employed as a publicist. But The Animals had only Mike Jeffery.

The Animals were all from Newcastle and so was their somewhat shady manager, a man Don succinctly dubs 'a small-time know-nothing shithouse'. Jeffery needed an agent in London to get his act gigs in the town that mattered; Arden brought The Animals to the capital and put them on at one of the city's chicest clubs, the Scene, where they raised the roof with their earthy bluesy songs.

The Animals became overnight stars and Arden signed them to him as their exclusive worldwide agent. He claims to have introduced them to Mickie Most, who produced 'House of the Rising Sun' for them. (Arden also claims in his autobiography that he helped Mickie Most get a work permit to come to the UK from his native South Africa, gave him work as a performer and subsequently convinced him to retire from the stage and become a producer, but you can only be so many places at the same time and perhaps a pinch of salt or two might not go amiss in his account. 'Mickie may have been a useless prick onstage,' he says, 'but it turned out he was something of a genius in the studio.')

'House of the Rising Sun' was a worldwide number 1 hit and Arden was raking it in touring the band. Inevitably, however, there were skirmishes with Jeffery. Suddenly, Allen Klein, who would later play a part in the break-up of The Beatles, was The Animals' American manager, and a thwarted Arden, who had no official management contract, figured he'd quit while he was ahead, sold out his agency rights and moved on.

The Animals had more big hits such as 'Don't Let Me Be Misunderstood' and 'We Gotta Get Out of This Place' without any help from Arden, who, nearly 40 years later, remains bitter about the band leaving him. 'I knew that without me they'd be dead,' he says scornfully. 'They had a couple more hits in the UK, but The Animals never really did anything again in America and by 1967 the band was finished. As far as I'm concerned, they got what they deserved.'

Whatever part Peter Grant played in The Animals' defection, Don never forgave him. He figured that Grant had seen an opportunity to make some fast money and had brokered a deal with Klein.

He also reckons it was built out of envy: Grant's wife had less jewellery than 'Paddles', Arden's wife. 'She never hid how pissed off she was that Paddles and I were so much better off than she and Peter were,' he says. 'She'd look at my wife's jewellery and get on to Grant about it. I used to hear her.' Did The Animals ever know that their destinies once hinged on the caprices of two women bickering about jewellery?

Arden likewise sees treachery in the actions of Mickie Most, who allegedly claimed the master tapes for 'House of the Rising Sun' and sold them to Allen Klein for $150,000. It hardened his heart. 'After all I had done for that boy,' he says. 'I learned another valuable lesson: help and trust alone did not command loyalty. Only fear and loathing could do that.'

Don's next plan was his most audacious yet – to get Elvis to come to Britain. He knew that Colonel Tom Parker was deeply averse to his boy ever leaving the States, not because Parker was an illegal immigrant, as the rumour goes, nor because of his involvement in the murder of a woman in his native Holland, but because the rewards were so great over there, so why should he bother? What incentive was big enough to persuade the indolent Colonel to go through the hoop-la of a foreign tour? Money was no good: Arden calculated that he just couldn't compete in cash terms. But what about royalty? That's royalty, not royalties.

Don calculated that the best way to get the Colonel off his ample backside was to put in a request for Elvis to play a charity concert hosted by royalty. He would get the King to perform for a duke – more specifically, the Duke of Edinburgh at one of his award ceremonies. After much lobbying of both Buckingham Palace and the Elvis camp, the Colonel agreed to do the gig, but only if the Duke personally invited Elvis.

Don writes: '[Parker] just wanted Elvis to go on American TV with that letter in his hand. You can picture the scene he had in his mind: Elvis looking solemnly into the camera and drawling, "I got this letter today from little old England, from the husband of the Queen. They want to know if I can go over there and help them . . ."'

Don's power play fell at the final fence but, he says, 'I came closer than anybody back then to making it happen.'

One door closed, but Don soon had another one open. His radar picked up The Nashville Teens, who had also slogged through an apprenticeship at the Star Club in Hamburg. He signed them to Decca Records. It was a rotten deal, according to Johnny Rogan in his book *Starmakers and Svengalis*, worth only seven-eighths of a penny per record sold – and that's pre-decimalisation pennies. There were six members of the band, which would mean that if they were to make a mere £1,000 each, they would have to sell a staggering 1,500,000 records.

The Nashville Teens would have to have sold millions of records to raise enough even to buy a new van. However, that was all academic since the band had only one big hit, 'Tobacco Road', followed by a string of flops. So nobody made any money.

The rotten deal wasn't entirely Don's fault, outrageously small royalty payments were the norm in those days – even the mighty Beatles earned only one-eighth of a penny more.

The band realised something was wrong, but they weren't suspicious of Don, to the extent that they used his solicitor, David Jacobs, to make enquiries into why whatever little money there was wasn't finding its way into their pockets. Jacobs did do a bit of research, but the investigations were curtailed with his sudden death.

Arden's talent as an agent and The Nashville Teens' considerable experience of playing live was to be their temporary salvation. They toured constantly and were picking up pretty good money for the times – around £350 a gig. (Don was creaming off a third of this, but, even so, they were making a living.) There were still money problems, however, since all the cash had to go through Arden's ledgers before the band saw a penny. It was at this stage that the band found themselves on the wrong end of Don's robust bartering methods.

In *Starmakers and Svengalis*, the band's singer/bass player, Ray Phillips, claims, 'We had to go up and barter for the money. If we were owed a grand, he'd say, "Would you settle for £600?" We'd be sitting in the office waiting for some money to get to a gig. He'd keep us waiting till the banks closed. "Oh, I've got no money now. I've got some here – would you settle for that?" Little did you know, that was it – you were paid off.'

Pianist John Hawken, another band member, describes in *Starmakers and Svengalis* how he foolishly decided to challenge the might of Don when he went to the Carnaby Street office to collect £120 he thought he was due. He was offered only £20. He should have acted grateful and disappeared, but John was wound up and skint and had the temerity to demand the lot. Worse, he raised his voice. In a flash, Arden had the musician pinned up against the wall with his hands around his neck, yelling, 'I've the strength of ten men in these hands!' Then, the story goes, warming to his psycho act, Don dragged Hawken to the second-floor office window, saying, 'You're going over, John, you're going over!'

Hawken wriggled free and fled, leaving a chuckling Arden to muse on the negotiation tactic he had just invented: if you can't get your way, hang them out of the window.

Next up were the Small Faces. Arden's son, David, had known the band's singer/songwriter Steve Marriott at stage school, and when Kit Lambert, The Who's big-time manager, went up against Don in a race to sign the hot new act, Arden played his ace by calling on David's friendship with Marriott. Don crossed the line first.

When the band arrived for the deal-signing, he couldn't help but notice they were covered in cuts and bruises. There had been a fight and Marriott had had a bottle stuck in his face. Ronnie Lane had been clumped on the head with an iron bar. Many managers might have been put off by the unpleasant sight of a hacked-up band of East End brawlers in the office, but Don thought it was hugely amusing; in fact, he was smitten. 'At that time, on the first hearing, I thought it was the best band in the world,' he said. He had found his Beatles.

Kenny Jones, the Small Faces drummer, recalls: 'He was kind of a Jewish teddy bear, I suppose. You liked him immediately because he was enthusiastic and he talked about what he could do and what he couldn't do and whenever he said, "I'll do this, I'll do that," he did and it came true.'

One of Don's first stunts was to telephone the band and tell them that he had secured them a part in a Brigitte Bardot movie and that they should get togged up because a *Daily Mirror* reporter was coming over to talk to them about it. Thrilled, the band rabbited on to the journalist about St Tropez, sand, sea and sex and he went home happy, but they'd all been had. Don later explained that there was no movie; it was just a way of getting the band in the national press. 'I couldn't tell you beforehand,' he said. 'You might have blown it.'

The Small Faces' first release was the rousing 'Whatcha Gonna Do About It?', which showcased the mighty Marriott larynx and charted at number 14. The song was written for them and at first the band objected to doing it, but Arden persuaded Marriott, saying, 'Do what you're told, sonny, and play the fucking song.'

'Whatcha Gonna Do About It?' might well have gone into the charts under its own steam, but we'll never know because Don gave it a shove and bought it in – blatant chart hyping was rife in those days. It still is, of course, but it's become a much subtler affair. Back then, the record companies would find out which record shops were providing sales statistics to the chart compilers and those shops would be offered singles at a knock-down rate. Further sweeteners might be an offer like, 'You take these 50 singles by this unknown band and we'll give you 50 Beatles albums.' More obvious was to just hand over a bagful of money to a DJ.

Interestingly, if you put the phrase 'chart hyping' into the Yahoo search engine, a site about Don usually comes up in the first few pages. He remains devoid of remorse: 'I knew that for certain sums any record I was associated with could be elevated to the charts. It got to be a habit. I paid out anything from £150 to £500 a week to people who manipulated the charts and who in turn shared the cash with people organising other charts so as to ensure they tallied . . . Neat little swindle, wasn't it? Of course, the Small Faces had no idea what went on.'

It is true that the Small Faces were oblivious to Don's efforts to get them in the charts. It's also true that they were oblivious of much else besides. According to keyboard player Ian McLagan, they were up to their ears in spliffs, LSD and leapers from the word go. The band would often do TV appearances and gigs stoned or drunk or both, and had little interest in how their affairs were being managed.

In McLagan's book, *All the Rage*, he explains that when he first joined the band, he was put on a weekly salary of £30, which, at first, he was more than happy to accept. Later, he complained to Don that he wanted to be put on the same wages as the rest of the band. Arden complied and McLagan's wages dropped to £20 a week, which was what the other members were getting. Ian remains unamused by his old manager. In turn, the old manager remains unimpressed by McLagan, referring to him as 'a Scottish lad who got lucky'.

Arden was even less impressed by Ronnie Lane: 'Ronnie . . . was an unpleasant guy and I'd quickly grow to hate him. He was an evil little man with a massive head on this tiny body and deathly pale skin. He was supposed to be Stevie's best pal, but you could tell he was nobody's friend really.'

Eventually, all the band members started moaning about being broke all the time. Don said in his own defence that what the Small Faces lacked in credit balances at the bank, he'd more than made up for by bankrolling the hedonistic rock star lives they were leading. The band shared a West End house; they had a Jaguar Mk 10 and a chauffeur on standby; and, the bit the band liked best, they had accounts at all the finest mod shops on Carnaby Street, where they could buy up-to-the-minute handmade clothes seven days a week. They reckoned they spent £12,000 on clothes in 1966.

'Just to prove that the Al Capone of the pop world has a soft spot,' Don said, 'let me tell you, I felt these kids should have at least one year of enjoying the very best in life.'

Too stoned to take their manager on, it was eventually left to the band members' parents to confront Arden about the apparent big hole in their sons' finances. His way of fobbing off the irate parents was pure Arden magic. He diverted their attention to the Small Faces' prolific drug use and, without really saying it, implied that the band was seriously into heroin and cocaine and that that was where all the money had gone.

Now chastened, the parents left quietly, considerably more concerned about their errant sons' health than their wealth.

Soon, there was no option: the band started looking around for new managers. That hit Arden's paranoia button. On one occasion, he heard that Brian Epstein had visited the West End house and smoked some dope with the band, who were sure that Brian was after one of them. Don figured that Brian had been after them all. He rang Epstein to warn him off.

Don then starred in the most notorious chapter in the annals of the music business. He heard a whisper that someone in rival impresario Robert Stigwood's office was sniffing around the Small Faces. Don was having none of it and felt that an extreme reaction was called for. 'I had to stop these overtures – and quickly. I contacted two well-muscled friends and hired two more equally huge toughs. And we went along to nail this impresario to his chair with fright. There was a large ornate ashtray on his desk. I picked it up and smashed it down with such force that the desk cracked – giving a good impression of a man wild with rage. My friends and I had carefully rehearsed our next move. I pretended to go berserk, lifted the impresario bodily from his chair, dragged him onto the balcony and held him so he was looking down to the pavement four floors below. I asked my friends if I should drop him or forgive him. In unison, they shouted: "Drop him." He went rigid with shock and I thought he might have a heart attack. Immediately, I dragged him back into the room and warned him never to interfere with my groups again.'

A traumatised Stigwood had never personally contacted the Small Faces, but now he never would. The word was out: 'Don't mess with Don.'

The police called round to ask Don questions about the incident but got short shrift. Arden had received quite a number of police visits over the years – about chart rigging and the more flamboyant behaviour of some of his artists. He reserves a special contempt for the boys in blue, saying, 'The police as an institution detested and feared the new rock and roll culture.' He has a point. These were the days when rock and roll was considered anti-establishment, something that should be stamped out. 'All they wanted to do was bag a showbiz celebrity,' he adds. 'I think they were just pigs, as the hippies said . . . My attitude was: you do your worst and I'll do mine and we'll see who's still standing at the end.'

'Am I for real, though?' asks Don in *Mr Big*, before answering his own question. 'Ask anybody who has ever received an unexpected visit from me how "real" it felt . . . There have been enough of them over the years and I'm sure they'd be glad to tell you about it – the ones that aren't dead!'

In the event, the band did break from Don. They moved to Andrew Loog Oldham, who purportedly gave Arden £25,000 for them. The legend goes that Arden requested the money be paid in used notes and delivered in a brown paper bag, but Don stoutly refutes this. 'Complete and utter bollocks,' he says. However, whatever the fee and whatever the denomination of the notes, the band was paying back the buyout fee for years. It was out of the frying pan and into the fire for the Small Faces.

On Ian McLagan's website (www.macspages.com), the keyboard player gives an ironic 'thanks' to both Don and Loog Oldham for some royalties he seems convinced they failed to pay.

There are many references to Don in McLagan's *All the Rage*. In the final pages, he baldly wrote, 'Don Arden is retired and lives in Los Angeles, where if the earthquakes, smog and general violence don't get him, then there's no justice.'

Sometime in 1967, the Small Faces tried to get a sum of around

£4,000 of royalties owed by Don's company, Contemporary Records. They got a judgment in their favour and Arden assured the court that his company had sufficient funds to pay the debt. The following week, his solicitor wrote to say that there were not sufficient funds after all and that Arden could only pay the debt at the rate of £250 a month. The band reluctantly accepted, but after receiving just £500 the payments stopped. The Small Faces had no alternative but to issue a petition to wind up the record company. Drawn-out litigation ensued and it wasn't until 1977 that the band finally got its money, ten years after the original order. Arden's talent for dragging out court cases rivalled Dickens's *Jarndyce* v *Jarndyce*.

Oddly, Small Faces drummer Kenny Jones maintains not altogether negative feelings about Don. 'Without Don,' he says, 'the Small Faces might not have existed; without his sort of vision at that time, be it short-lived or what. The fact is we became known and we got a breakthrough because of Don. So, if you think of it like that, and I think all of us are prepared to swallow what went on, leave it, fine, it's history. We all learned from each other, he gave us our first break, fine, fair enough, you know, leave it. I've got good and bad memories, but mainly I think of Don with affection, surprisingly enough.'

In fact, Arden's reputation seemed to attract bands rather than deter them. Perhaps they fancied the association with the kind of manager who was known to dangle business opponents from their own office windows.

The Move had had a run of hits, but by the early '70s their career was flatlining. The age-old remedy, change of management, was the considered option and they signed to Don after leaving Tony Secunda (Don refers to Secunda as 'another schmuck who won the lottery'). The trouble was to start immediately.

The band came across at the time of 'Goodbye Blackberry Way'. When Don got the band to sign on the dotted line and with a hit in the offing, Secunda, who had an ongoing drug problem, saw red. Arden claims in *Mr Big* that Secunda was even trying to get him killed. 'So I had him warned off,' says Don. 'Once it became clear that if anything happened to me, he would be dead himself within the hour, he decided to see sense and never bothered us again.' With the memory of an elephant, though, Don was never in the business of forgiving and added, 'I never stopped hating him, though. I still hate him now, even though he's dead . . . He committed suicide in the end and I like to think he did it because he finally realised what a bastard he was.'

Peter Walsh, the powerful manager who had handled Brian Poole and the Tremeloes and Marmalade, once sent a minion to ask The Move if they fancied moving from Don's company to his. The Arden reaction was typically swift.

'He didn't hang anybody out of a window in my office,' says Walsh in *Starmakers and Svengalis*. 'He just came in and beat up a guy that was working with me called Clifford Davis, who was then managing Fleetwood Mac. He slapped him around the face a little and threatened what he would do if he didn't lay off The Move . . . I don't know why he came around when he did. I was out at lunch, fortunately, so he got Davis and gave him a good going over. When I came back, it had all finished.'

Don remembers the confrontation differently. Davis had (foolishly) been smoking a cigar at the time: 'I took the cigar out of his mouth with my right hand and grabbed him by the back of the head with my left, all in one easy movement. Then, holding him tight, I drilled the lit end of the cigar into the middle of his forehead. He struggled, of course, but I was too strong, too intent upon my work, and I held him there for a long time until he went limp. I wanted to see if I could actually penetrate his forehead with that thing . . . I felt so good I dismissed my driver and decided to walk home. Stuff like that made you feel alive.'

Walsh contacted the police. 'I got police protection against him . . . In fact, if anything, Don Arden was my protector because the police warned him, and this came from very high up at Scotland Yard, that if anything happened to me he would be dragged in immediately and, whether it was him or not, he would be charged.'

Don affirms that the police were keen to get him at whatever cost and this story would seem to bear out that theory.

Around this time, Andrew Loog Oldham needed some money, so he and his old partner in crime, Arden, went on a cash hunt. This is how Andrew recalls it in his autobiography, *Stoned*: 'I was in England in '70 or '72 and Don Arden and I both needed some quick cash, so we had Gered Mankowitz take a group photo of some interesting-looking friends from the art and photography world and called them Grunt Futtock.

'Then we had a guy who used to work for me at Immediate write up some anal fictitious bio. Then we gathered a few old pals and clients – Roy Wood, Peter Frampton, Steve Marriott, Andy Bown – and engineer Alan O'Duffy. Don Arden threatened to break their legs, so they all made the record for nothing. Then Don sold the record to EMI as the next best thing since sliced bread and Don and I went shopping.'

Don doesn't recall that there was a band at all. In his account, they approached a friend of Don's called Freddie Bienstock, who worked for music publisher Carlin, and played a tape that he thought Andrew had knocked up in the studio one night when he was drunk. When they realised two big names, Loog Oldham and Don, were behind it, they couldn't wait to hand over £10,000.

Arden's friendship with Bienstock was put under considerable strain when the truth came out: 'I last saw Freddie in the early '90s and he was still upset with me over it. We bumped into each other somewhere and started chatting and I noticed that he was a bit cool. I said, "What's the matter with you, you old c***?" He's Viennese and he said in his accented English, "Well, you know, Don, I like you, but sometime I remember, you sold me a group that did not exist."'

The Move tried various singles and various looks, but it wasn't until the act transmogrified into the Electric Light Orchestra that things really got going. ELO floundered for a while, and disagreements plagued the band, but when Roy Wood left and formed Wizzard everything changed.

Both bands became frequent visitors to the *Top of the Pops* studio and Don, at last, started making big bucks. When Wizzard eventually flagged in the mid-'70s, ELO shifted into overdrive: the band started playing stadium gigs in the States and selling millions of albums. It seems that throughout their relationship the band and its manager remained on cordial terms and that there were few bust-ups – presumably because there was more than enough money to go round. With ELO at their zenith, the idea that Don's Contemporary Records could be wound up for a mere £4,000 became ludicrous.

But that didn't mean Arden had calmed down or changed his ways. An incident at an ELO gig in Spain when he had a run-in with the local police chief and shook the man by his lapels saw him carted off to prison. The band had to pay his bail and whisk him out of the country.

When Don had tried to get the band off the Warner label, he ran into a brick wall. The label, as represented by Mo Austin, dug in its heels. Don continues the story: 'Then something funny happened: Warner's offices in Greek Street burned down. Arson was suspected, though never proved. But within two or three days of that their whole attitude changed and suddenly ELO were free to go . . . they thought it was I who had set fire to their building. Did I do it, though? Well, I was away in America at the time and so I couldn't have, could I? Of course not . . .'

A final ELO curiosity concerns the name of one of their albums. They released their first album entitled *The Electric Light Orchestra* in the UK and shipped the masters over to the States for release. Presumably, there was no cover with the record so a secretary from the American record company apparently telephoned Don to ask him what the name of the album should be. There was no answer from Don's phone, so she wrote on the pad 'No Answer' and that is the reason why ELO's first release in the USA is entitled *No Answer* despite the fact that there is no track of that name on the album nor is the expression used in any of the lyrics. So the pop myth goes. . .

Where there's a hit, there's a writ, and the saga of Lynsey de Paul, another of Don's artists, ended with her needing to go into therapy and reaching 'rock bottom'. De Paul's recording advance was paid late and she felt the relationship between her and Arden had broken down.

'Personally, I found her a nightmare,' said Don, who gave daughter Sharon the job of being Lynsey's tour manager, thinking the two women might get along better than he and she had. 'Big mistake,' says Don. 'The two of them fought like cat and dog.' The relationship soured to the point that Sharon peed into Lynsey's suitcase.

In the pattern of many previous deals, de Paul wanted to be free of her contract. It all ended up in the High Court, where Arden prepared for a long haul. But as time went by, and the costs mounted, it was the petite de Paul who cracked first. She collapsed twice in 1977 and began to consider suicide as the only escape route out of her bitter travails. 'It was a time in my life that I'll never forget,' she said in *Starmakers and Svengalis*. 'I'll never forgive him. And if anybody was near suicide, and if ever I was near, it was then, because it was awful.'

A vexed settlement wasn't reached for two years and even then Arden's company retained the rights to Lynsey's existing material, including unreleased material. During this period, she released 'Rock Bottom'. These days, Lynsey appears on TV and is an authority on self-defence for women.

About this time, the BBC's *Checkpoint* programme started an investigation of Arden's 'colourful' business practices and Don was doorstepped by a burly Roger Cook. In time-honoured fashion, Don went straight on the offensive, saying, 'I'll take you with one hand strapped up my arse. You're not a man, you're a creep.'

He continues: 'If I had walked into a restaurant any time over the next ten years, say, and Roger Cook had happened to be there, I'd have gone for him immediately, no question. I would have got hold of him and I wouldn't have let go until he died in my hands.'

In the late '70s, Arden's children, David and Sharon, joined the company. Don was building his dynasty, but the kids had inherited Dad's genes and there were storms ahead. At that time, ELO was one of the biggest-selling bands in the world and Don was living high on the hog. He had bought Howard Hughes's old house in Beverly Hills and he was throwing a lot of parties. When the next-door neighbours complained about the noise, he bought their house, too. 'I may have been rich before,' he said, 'but I was now mind-blowingly filthy stinking rich.'

But the trouble didn't stop. Don had taken over Black Sabbath, their previous management having folded, and one of the old managers, Patrick Meehan, had an affair with Sharon. Meehan got on the wrong side of Don soon enough and naturally received a visit from Arden senior at his office – without having made an appointment, needless to say. Don explains: 'I pulled a gun from my jacket pocket and laid it very carefully on the table. There was nothing in the gun: I had taken all the bullets out in case somebody made a grab for it. But they didn't know that . . . I looked at young Meehan and said, "This is just a warning to tell you to leave my daughter alone. From this moment on, you don't know her, you don't speak to her, you never say her name again. Do you understand? Otherwise, the next time you see me I'll be pointing that gun at your head. This is what I do to slags like you who upset my family – I kill them."'

The cops were called and it went to court, but Don got off.

The next time they met was at the Midem music trade festival in Cannes and the encounter became a full-on bar brawl. Don then arranged for some Mob mates to give Meehan a sleep-with-the-fishes warning which, unsurprisingly, seemed to do the trick.

That year, Don printed up the office Christmas cards with a picture of himself on the front holding a gun, with the seasonal message: 'Here's an offer you can't refuse.'

Black Sabbath had a bit of success but then asked Ozzy Osbourne to leave. His boozing had made him unreliable and the rest of the band said that he wasn't contributing much to the music. Arden sided with Ozzy and he and the band parted ways. Cast adrift, Ozzy moved into the Arden family house, where he stayed for a year while Don tried to get him back on track. However, it wasn't a totally teetotal experience. 'You'd agree to have "just the one" with him,' complained Don, 'and the next thing you knew you'd been slumped there for five hours and he'd pissed himself three times and set fire to the carpet.'

The close proximity of Ozzy to Don's daughter had inevitable consequences. The couple courted, were married and Sharon asked her father if she could take over as Ozzy's manager. Don says he handed her the management contract as a wedding present, but he then found out that she wanted to take Ozzy away from Don's Jet label. It all went to court, father and daughter in a rancorous head-to-head. Sharon was forced to buy Ozzy out of his contract for $1 million. She and Don didn't speak for 20 years as a consequence.

Sharon told the *Daily Mirror*: 'My family cut me off dead because of money. People said, "Oh, your dad must have been worried when you married Ozzy." But he didn't give a shit. Ozzy was his cash cow. And Dad knew I'd take him with me.'

When she could, Sharon took Ozzy to another record label. The reverberations continued. Don claims that she tried to run him down in her car one day.

In 1986, Don and David Arden found themselves being charged with kidnapping, blackmail, torture and the assault of Don's company accountant, Harshad Patel. It was alleged that Arden had imprisoned Patel for 24 hours in a dispute over £100,000. Patel claimed he had been beaten up by the two men.

David was sentenced to two years' imprisonment, with one year suspended. Don, who had been watching events unfold from Los Angeles, was then subjected to extradition proceedings. In 1987, it was his turn to stand in the dock at the Old Bailey and listen to a string of accusations from Patel. This time he claimed that Don had attacked him with a hat stand and then pulled a gun from a briefcase and threatened to shoot him. Furthermore, Arden was accused of forcing the accountant to write some cheques before his car keys were taken from him and he was sacked. Don admitted that he cracked the accountant across the nose with the butt of a gun.

It was also alleged that once, when Patel had been asleep at home, a 'heavy' had appeared and dragged the accountant to Arden's Wimbledon home, where he was assaulted by Don, occasioning a fractured rib. On a further occasion, Patel claimed he was taken to the office and assaulted and threatened by Don and that David had made suggestions that Muslims knew how to deal with thieves by cutting their hands off.

David denied this charge. Arden senior also vigorously denied all charges and was cleared by the jury.

And now he's the Grandfather of Pop – a guest in episodes of *The Osbournes*, seen tiptoeing round the dog shit with his son-in-law, Ozzy, and chatting with his grandchildren, Kelly and Jack, just like a regular old geezer despite the fact he hadn't met them before 2002. Sadly, Don suffers from Alzheimer's disease, but it's a given that the one-time Godfather of Rock won't go down without a fight.

Meanwhile, Don's son David was recently negotiating taking over the *Queen Mary*, although it's not an act of piracy. He and his business partner were attempting to take a lease on the cruiseliner, which is moored at Long Beach, California. They planned to turn it into 'a cultural and entertainment centre for Long Beach', the previous owners having gone bankrupt.

Don's rapprochement with his daughter was a long time coming and the intervening years hold unpleasant memories for Sharon. She had returned to her father's house to tell her parents that she was pregnant with her and Ozzy's first child. As she stepped through the door, Arden's dogs attacked her and, as a consequence, she has said, she lost the baby. She told the *Daily Mirror*:

> He didn't set them on me, to be truthful. Because I had been living
> in America and not in England, the dogs didn't know me. Three of

them went for me and just tore me apart. My mother found me and she wasn't sympathetic at all – her husband came first in her life.

I ran next door to my brother, who called an ambulance and got me to hospital. My parents, though, didn't give a shit.

Her mother died without ever seeing her grandchildren. Sharon didn't even attend the funeral.

In business, by inaugurating Ozzfest, by turning her family life into a soap and by judging on the *The X Factor*, she has made considerably more money than her father. Her autobiography was a bestseller and she has had chat shows on prime-time TV on both sides of the Atlantic. Sharon, however, disagrees with the suggestion that she might be a chip off the old block despite the fact that her brother refers to her as 'Don in a skirt'. She told *The Guardian*: 'The best lesson I ever had was watching him fuck his business up. He taught me everything not to do.'

What is clear is that Sharon is no pushover either and prefers direct action. In her own autobiography, she explains, 'The music business in those days was a boys' club fuelled by cocaine and sexual favours. These were the days of payola and Mafia involvement, and the standard currency if you were a woman was a blow job, but men soon learned that Sharon Arden was more likely to kick them in the balls than suck their dick.'

That's an Arden, all right!

2

BRIAN EPSTEIN

Beatles

Sayest thou that the man diligent in his business shall stand before kings.
                                    – the rabbi at Brian's funeral

It was Frank Sinatra who was the first to be greeted by screaming girls every time he showed his face or sang a note. But that had been a cheat. The story goes that the first-ever devoted bobby-soxers had been paid to yell themselves sick at Ol' Blue Eyes. It turned out to be a sound investment on Sinatra's manager's part – a handful of girls screaming for a few dollars soon became thousands of girls screaming for free.

The bobby-soxers screamed for Frank but not for Bing; they screamed for Elvis but not for Deano; they did it for James Dean but not for Rock Hudson; but of all the teenage idols, they screamed the loudest and the longest for The Beatles.

And once they started screaming in 1962, they didn't stop for eight years, whether at a concert, airport, opening or screening. They screamed before the band went onstage and kept it up all the way through the show until long after the band were offstage, in the car and nearly home. In an inchoate, passionate jet stream of devotion, the girls (and not just a few

40

of the boys) were feeling the weightlessness of utter emotional abandonment.

Beatlemania.

A contemporary observer of the phenomenon, the consumer capitalism expert Vance Packard, offered an interesting if somewhat stuffy analysis: 'The subconscious need that [The Beatles] fill most expertly is in taking adolescent girls clear out of this world. The youngsters in the darkened audiences can let go all inhibitions in a quite primitive sense when The Beatles cut loose. They can retreat from rationality and individuality. Mob pathology takes over, and they are momentarily freed of all civilisation's restraints.

'The Beatles have become peculiarly adept at giving girls this release. Their relaxed, confident manner, their wild appearance, their whooping and jumping, their electrified rock 'n' roll pulsing out into the darkness makes the girls want to jump and then scream. The more susceptible soon faint or develop twitching hysteria. (One reason why Russia's totalitarian leaders frown on rock 'n' roll and jazz is that these forms of music offer people release from controlled behaviour.)'

It's a touching story that once, at a Beatles concert, the buttoned-up Brian Epstein let the guise slip for a few moments, went to the back of the hall and, when he thought no one was looking, screamed along with all the girls. It wasn't really anything to do with his girliness or his homosexuality, just that Brian was an out-and-out Beatles fan and had been since moment one (although it's sometimes said that he didn't care much for popular music). He was just letting go; he wanted to feel what the girls felt and give himself up at the Beatles altar, to surrender to the sheer unadulterated joy the band seemed so easily able to engender.

'I find all large gatherings of fans immensely exhilarating and thrilling,' he said in his autobiography, *A Cellarful of Noise*, published by Souvenir Press. 'I can think of no warmer experience than to be in a vast audience at a Beatle concert. I hope Beatles crowds continue to scream themselves hoarse in a frenzy of exaltation.'

Andrew Loog Oldham talks about one of the first times he saw

The Beatles play, in his book, *Stoned*:'I stood at the back of the stalls beside Brian Epstein, who'd been slightly apprehensive about the lukewarm receptions his boys had been getting"down south". This night, though, there was a tangible sense of mad hysteria rising all over the theatre, and with the arrival of The Beatles onstage, it rose to a frenzy and took on a life of its own.

'The kids broke all the backstage windows. It was pandemonium. Onstage, you could not hear The Beatles for the roar of the crowd, and the roar I heard was the roar of the whole world. You could hear something without seeing it, in the same way as you can have an experience that is beyond anything that you've had before. You don't have to be clever, you only have to be a member of the public. The noise that night hit me emotionally, like a blow to the chest. The audience that evening expressed something beyond repressed adolescent sexuality. The noise they made was the sound of the future. Even though I hadn't seen the world, I heard the whole world screaming. The power of The Beatles touched and changed minds and bodies all over the world. I didn't see it – I heard and felt it. When I looked at Brian, he had the same lump in his throat and tear in his eye as I.'

Here the prophet of pop zeroes in on the essence of The Beatles – although nobody, not even them, could change the world with a few well-crafted pop songs. But they sure kick-started the start of the change.

Worship brings belief, with belief comes power, and with power comes cash.

Brian Epstein had been an unremarkable student at a range of schools. Learning bored him and he would attempt to counteract the drudgery of it by drawing pictures of dancing girls beneath his desk. He was expelled from Liverpool College at the age of ten for 'inattention and being below standard'; aged sixteen, he asked to be taken away from school altogether. He had one ambition: 'A dress designer was all I wanted to be,' he said, but he was to be immediately thwarted. His parents felt that young Brian would be better placed in the family's expanding furniture business than the risky rag trade.

Epstein & Son was built by Brian's father, Harry, and his grandfather, Isaac. It sold furniture and musical instruments, and the legend goes that a young Paul McCartney played his first tunes on a piano supplied by Epstein's.

A spell of national service broke what it seemed would be an inevitable destiny – a life as a 'settled, soon-to-be-stolid furniture salesman'. An 'incident' severed the relationship between him and HM Armed Forces, however, and what should have been a two year stint in uniform was over before one year was up.

Brian is vague about the exact nature of the mysterious 'incident' but described in his autobiography how he had contrived to be moved from the base at dreary Aldershot to the bright lights of London's Regent's Park, and how he had been availing himself of the pubs, theatres and clubs in the evenings. 'I used to enjoy off-duty life in the West End for I had a lot of relatives in London,' he said. 'On this particular night, I had myself brought back to camp in a large car. It slid gently to a halt outside the barracks' gate. I marched into camp wearing – rather pompously, I'm afraid – a bowler, pin-striped suit and, over my arm, an umbrella.'

This rather cheeky but seemingly trivial act led to the always well-dressed Epstein being accused of impersonating an officer. He was examined by a psychiatrist, who referred him to a succession of other 'specialists', who recommended, somewhat mysteriously, that he be discharged from the army on 'medical grounds'. This would seem to have been a massive overreaction on the part of the army to a bit of dressing up; however, other reports of the evening's events, while conceding that he may well have impersonated an officer, allege that he was probably doing so when importuning in a public toilet.

That he returned to the family business and pretty quickly confessed his homosexuality to his parents and brother, Clive, is surely a clue. Dad and Clive were apparently shocked, while his more pragmatic mum, Queenie, was sympathetic. It was a courageous thing to do in mid-'50s Britain, but it also sounds uncharacteristic of the outwardly reserved, staid Brian. A plausible reason for his daring confession may have been that he had to act quickly to pre-empt being roughly outed by the army.

It seems Brian felt enormous guilt over his homosexuality and sensitivity about his Jewishness. An excerpt from his diaries published in Debbie Geller's book *In My Life* confirms the turmoil he was feeling: 'It was after I left the army that I found out about the existence of the various rendezvous and homosexual "life". My life became a succession of mental illnesses and sordid unhappy events, bringing great sorrow to my family. My loneliness throughout has been acute. I found myself unable to concentrate on my work and unable to live in peace with my family. I tried psychoanalysis with a psychiatrist, but I was so embarrassed by the arrangement that every time I visited him (two or three times a week) I had to go to my father and request three guineas to pay him. I could not proceed for very long.'

Epstein, despite his self-loathing and outward disdain for the homosexual life, couldn't help himself and was inexorably drawn to the town's theatrical set – elegant actors, designers and writers – who he hoped could offer the kicks that his job in furniture sales failed to provide and who might help counter the drabness of those pre-Beatles days in Liverpool. He had entered the gay demi-monde. When he subsequently expressed an interest in acting and passed an entrance exam for RADA, the family allowed him to once again leave the business and make a foray down to London for the course.

He learned the plays fast but merely knowing your way around the scripts wasn't really enough. Acting is about body language as much as it is about the English language and despite asking a fellow thespian for coaching, poor Brian just couldn't loosen up. He was stiff, stilted, wooden. And his mind wasn't entirely concentrated on the higher arts either. The big city held many diversions: there were concerts, parties and restaurants to go to. There were also sexual encounters with males and females, but eventually something made him turn against it all. Deciding he didn't really like acting or actors after all, he returned to Liverpool. 'The narcissism appalled me,' said the dandy.

Early in 1957, Brian was at Swiss Cottage station using the toilet facilities. He saw a young man watching him and became convinced that the man was gay. In the way that these things are done, he walked around for a while, sneaking glances at the young man, then spoke briefly to him. The young man was then joined by another. Brian was confused and excited, but soon he was just plain arrested and was up before Marylebone Magistrates' Court the following morning, accused of 'persistently importuning for immoral purposes'. He pleaded guilty to avoid the publicity of a hearing.

'Through the wreckage of my life by society, my being will stain and bring the deepest distress to all my devoted family and few friends,' he lamented in his diaries. Yet he couldn't resist the very kinds of encounters and dangerous liaisons that often led to violence, blackmail, the police and more shame.

He was attacked and beaten in a public toilet in Derby by a man dressed as a builder. The 'builder' stole Brian's wallet, money and watch, and then attempted to blackmail him. Epstein was forced to confess to the police and the man was eventually caught after a police 'sting' operation. But even then, Brian's guilty secrets remained safe, for in the resultant court hearing an embarrassed but undoubtedly relieved Epstein was referred to throughout as 'Mr X'. For years, however, Brian lived in dread that the man might try to find him when he was released from prison.

He'd been lucky. Although the Wolfenden report, published in 1957, recommended that male homosexual behaviour in private by consenting adults over the age of 21 should be decriminalised, homosexual sex in a public place was still an imprisonable offence and if the ever-prurient press had got a whiff of lurid stories of toilet trading and sodomy among the Liverpool upper-middle classes, he might well have been destroyed. It would be a further ten years before the Sexual Offences Act partially decriminalised acting male homosexuality. Brian had died a few months beforehand.

Future NEMS (North End Music Stores) boss and Epstein friend, Geoffrey Ellis, commented on Brian's street encounters with young men: 'When he lived in London – and perhaps particularly when he visited America – and he was fascinated by the American homosexual scene in the '60s – he behaved sometimes in a way which was very dangerous and he was conscious of this. In some ways, he sought out danger. It gave him a thrill, but of course led him into many very awkward situations from time to time. I think deep down he didn't want to be a homosexual but paradoxically he enjoyed his homosexual experiences very much.'

A curious aside is that Epstein's quest for danger may well have been what drove him to develop a very curious passion for bullfighting. In the early '60s, he started popping down to Spain for the big events and collecting posters. There, he met Orson Welles, a fervent fan of the 'sport'. Later, he was even to manage bullfighter Henry Higgins, 'the English Toreador'.

In 1957, while Brian was trying to stay out of trouble by developing the NEMS record shop, which the family had opened as an adjunct to the furniture store, and reacquainting himself with the prices of sideboards and sofas, John Lennon and his friend, Pete Shotton, were starting a band called the Black Jacks with a plan to play skiffle music and American renditions of rock and roll songs at local venues. A few weeks later, Lennon was introduced to Paul McCartney by another friend, Ian Vaughn. They were the perfect complement – wide-eyed McCartney, acerbic Lennon – in nature, look and music.

Oddly, a good description of the Lennon/McCartney relationship is provided by Dr Jonathan Miller in a biography of Peter Cook by Harry Thompson. He draws a parallel with it and the relationship between Cook and Dudley Moore. At the time, Peter and Lennon had become close friends. 'Peter and John Lennon had become drawn to each other because of their profound similarities, both being sharp, cynical, witty and the brains of their respective writing partnerships. Dudley and Paul McCartney were in each case the housewives' choice of the duo, their wholesome, sympathetic and in some ways greater mainstream appeal providing a slight source of irritation for their more caustic and dominant partners. In each case, however, the relationship was symbiotic; both Peter and John Lennon knew deep down that they performed better with their sidekicks than without.'

This is brilliantly distilled by Ian MacDonald in his book, *Revolution in the Head*. Ian has McCartney as 'melodic, consonant' and Lennon as 'harmonic, dissonant'. 'A classic clash between truth and beauty,' he writes.

When John started his course at Liverpool College of Art, Paul was at the Liverpool Institute High School for Boys with George Harrison. Paul's route to school was the same as John's. On the bus, they became friends, swapped music stories and began plotting. A few months later, George was introduced to a sceptical Lennon, who finally caved in to George's persistent pleadings to join John's band, now called The Quarrymen.

Various line-ups were tried, but within two years The Beatles were an entity, albeit with Pete Best on drums and Stu Sutcliffe on bass. Their then manager packed them off to Hamburg for their legendary stint at the Star Club.

It's easy to underestimate how influential and just how damned exciting this period must have been for them. While their repressed stuffed-shirt future manager was knocking out leather three-piece suites, the Brylcreemed Beatles were wearing leather suits and doing three gigs a night, boozing, dropping pills, going to transvestite bars and getting their legs over.

George remembered those days in an interview on Australian radio: 'In Hamburg, we were living right in the middle of St Pauli, which is right in the middle of the Reeperbahn district in Hamburg. All the club owners were like gangsters, and all the waiters had tear-gas guns, truncheons, knuckle-dusters. They were a heavy crew. Everybody around that district was a homosexual, pimp, hooker. You know, being in the middle of that when I was 17 [laughs] . . . It was good fun.'

There were wild scenes. George got deported for being underage and having no work permit. He was punched for calling a German acquaintance a Nazi. The Beatles had a dispute with a club owner. There was a fire and the police arrested Pete and Paul, who spent a night in the cells. There were also girls – and one in particular: the exotic black-clad photographer Astrid Kirchherr, who bewitched John Lennon and then led Stu Sutcliffe away to her bed. He was never to return.

'[George] was a little boy,' she said. 'They were all so young and I was so different. I was a few years older, I had my own flat, my own car, my own career. They hadn't met anyone like me before. I was quite nice to look at, so they thought, "Wow, yeah," and jumped at the chance when I invited them back to my flat. In some ways, I was more like a mother figure. When George was being deported for being underage and not having a work permit, I looked after him, drove him to the airport. When the others spent a night in jail for setting fire to some place, I took them bread and cared for them. They were my friends.'

They did their first recordings in Germany, laying down backing tracks for Tony Sheridan on behalf of songwriter/composer Bert Kaempfert and knocking off a version of 'My Bonnie (Lies Over the Ocean)'.

Back home in Liverpool, The Beatles rehearsed at the Cavern Club. The band's exploits in Germany had been chronicled by Bill Harry in his *Mersey Beat* magazine and he approached Epstein to sell copies of it in his up-and-coming record shop. It was in *Mersey Beat* that Brian read about The Beatles – talent on his own doorstep. Could this, at last, be what he had been looking for?

When The Beatles returned to Germany, they had a new manager. The Beatles had become tight – musically and as friends. They'd been given the Star treatment.

Don Arden thinks that if The Beatles had not done their time in Hamburg, they would never have made it as big as they did: 'That time at the Star Club, months and months at a stretch, that's what I think developed them. That youthful exuberance, that cheerful defiance, that sense that a bomb had just gone off and no one knew what might happen next – all of those things that characterised the early Beatles hits, to me, had nothing to do with Liverpool. That was the sound of Hamburg and the Star Club at its giddy height.'

Brian's record shop had by now become a substantial part of the Epstein family empire. It was constantly packed with kids eager for the new sounds, particularly the latest releases by American artists. Liverpool was a big port and was full of sailors who would regularly travel to the USA. Consequently, they were very knowledgeable about American artists like Fats Domino, Ray Charles and Jerry Lee Lewis. It seems that Brian developed a knack for spotting the next big thing and would order records accordingly. He took pride in his nascent talent-spotting abilities. This and the increasing buzz about 'the best band in town' drove him to the Cavern for the historic lunchtime session.

Epstein fell for The Beatles and they, in turn, fell for this smooth, charming man with expensive clothes, a gold watch and, most importantly, a big car.

Paul McCartney explains in Debbie Geller's book: 'The big impressive thing about Brian was his car. He had a bigger car than anyone we knew. He had a big Zephyr Zodiac and we were really impressed. We knew people in Ford Populars. I had a Ford Classic, but Brian had a big Zodiac, so there was obvious wealth there. So he was quite different from everyone else . . . My dad, when he heard about Brian wanting to manage us, said, "This could be a very good thing." He thought Jewish people were very good with money.'

John Lennon agreed, saying later in the *New York Times*: 'Show business is an extension of the Jewish religion.'

The band was also switched on enough to know that Brian was gay. It was a positive thing, they thought; there were lots of homosexuals in show business. It might be the very entrée they needed.

Rejecting The Beatles' rough look (one that Brian must secretly have loved), he packaged the band in more respectable mohair suits, Chelsea boots and had the mop-top haircuts first devised by Astrid Kirchherr trimmed. The Beatles didn't mind. In an interview for *Hit Parader* magazine in 1975, Lennon said:

> Everybody wanted a good suit, you know. A nice, sharp black suit, man . . . We liked the leather and the jeans, but we wanted a good suit, even to wear offstage. 'Yeah, man, I'll have a suit!' So if you wore a suit, you'll get this much money . . . All right, I'll wear a suit. I'll wear a fucking balloon if somebody's going to pay me. I'm not in love with the leather THAT much. Wear a suit, you'll get more money.

The leather jackets were ditched (although, paradoxically, Epstein could then often be seen wearing leather himself) and The Beatles were suited and booted and cleared for take-off – Brian had found his *raison d'être*.

Shawn Levy in his book *Ready, Steady, Go!* says it was 'an instance of absolute kismet. In The Beatles, Brian had found a medium to express his sense of daring and flamboyance while still maintaining his discretion and reserve.'

'Brian wanted to be a star himself,' adds Beatles producer George Martin, 'and he couldn't do it as an actor, so he did it as a man who was a manipulator, a puppeteer. The Beatles were smart-ass, sexy, rough-and-tumble and extrovert – everything, in short, that Brian wished for himself (and it can't be avoided saying, that he sought in sexual partners).'

Epstein wanted to go shopping for record contracts while the band did gigs – often at the prodigious rate of 30 a month – but first he needed the security of a contract for himself. He struck a deal with The Beatles in early 1962 and in the light of some of the catastrophic deals he did later, it stands out. It was a five-year contract that pegged his commission at 10 per cent for any monies up to £1,500 per year and 15 per cent of any monies above that. At the end of 1962 – a year that saw Ringo join the band, Lennon get married, the band get a deal with Parlophone and record 'Love Me Do' – there was a revised contract which hiked his percentage up to 25 per cent. It's a testament to the band's affection for Brian that he was able to get a higher royalty for himself after the band had seen some success, a feat rarely accomplished by other managers in the music business.

The Parlophone deal was lousy and, while all record deals were lousy at the time, this one was a stinker. Even George Martin, a dyed-in-the-wool EMI man, called it 'pretty awful'. And he should know – he was on the other side of the negotiating table from Brian. There was no advance at all and they would receive only 1p (pre-decimalisation) per single and half that for overseas sales. For some bizarre reason, a twelve-track album was to be considered as six cuts. The record company would have three one-year options on the deal: if they took the first, the band's royalties would go up by a quarter of one penny, and if they exercised the second option then the royalty would go up by a halfpenny per single.

But Epstein had had to struggle to get the deal in the first place – The Beatles weren't only and famously turned down by Dick Rowe at Decca: EMI, Pye, Philips, Columbia, HMV and Oriole also rejected the band of the century – so he shouldn't perhaps be blamed too much for the niggardly royalties. The Beatles, however, started to sell huge numbers of singles right from the off and he should have swiftly renegotiated their royalty rate upwards. He did so eventually, but only after his own contract with The Beatles had come up for renewal and he needed to offer them a sweetener.

Understandably, McCartney and Lennon came to be furious about the paucity of their deal, particularly when they found out what the Rolling Stones were earning. When Allen Klein renegotiated their deal with Decca, the Stones got a £3 million advance and a higher royalty rate. They were earning far more than The Beatles, although they were selling far fewer records. However, in 1963, despite their dismal royalty rate, rumour has it that a staggering £5 million passed through Epstein's hands.

The extraordinary thing was that although Epstein had snapped up a band that everyone was now confident would be bigger than any before it, he seemed eager to give them away to almost anyone he met. And there must be many who deeply regret they didn't leap at the chance.

In 1963, Adam Faith's booking agent, Joe Collins, was apparently offered a share in their management. The following year it was the turn of Lew Grade. However, when Brian offered to sell the band to the boss of ATV, John Lennon found out and warned him, 'If you sell, we'll never play again.'

Most bizarrely, The Beatles might at one point have been taken over by comedians Mike and Bernie Winters, who weighed up the proposition but opted to work on their act instead. Even Little Richard, who sometimes used to play on the same bill as them at the Star Club, reckons he was offered a 50 per cent share of what would become the hottest band in the world, but gamely admits he turned them down because he couldn't see how they would make it to the big time.

The next deal Brian negotiated was, in the long run, even more disastrous than the EMI record deal. He needed a company to collect the band's songwriting royalties and somehow he found his way to Dick James, a small-time publisher who, it was rumoured, may have been on the brink of going out of business. James, briefly famous for singing the theme tune to TV series *The Adventures of Robin Hood*, managed to get The Beatles onto the *Thank Your Lucky Stars* music show and Brian was impressed enough by that one act to commit Lennon and McCartney's entire song catalogue to him. Northern Songs was formed in 1963; James and his partner held 50 per cent of the shares, Epstein and The Beatles held the remainder. The poorly performing company turned itself around and published seven number 1 songs that year. Dick James became the biggest publisher in town on the back of the deal.

In Epstein's defence, after the deal was done Dick James worked his backside off for The Beatles and should be given some credit. However, years later he was to be sued by Elton John over a contract which the court considered so unfair that James was ordered to pay compensation in the millions.

Don Arden had known Dick James back in the days when they appeared as performers on the same bill. In Loog Oldham's *Stoned*, Arden talks of the infamous deal with typical candour:'Dick used to wear these fucking terrible wigs that he bought from Woolworths, the worst wigs you've ever seen in your life. We all used to stand on the side of the stage making fun of him when he came on singing these love songs. Despite this, he managed to be quite well known.

'Epstein told me that while he was trying to do business, Dick sat eating sandwiches out of a brown paper bag. Unbelievably, he gave him The Beatles' first album for nothing. Epstein had just done this deal with EMI; I think he'd signed for eight or ten years. Epstein was the kind of guy who, if you stuck by him in the beginning, stuck by you. Dick James got The Beatles for nothing; he was more or less a fucking doorman, if you really want to know. He was a guy on his own, just starting up.'

Two years later, Northern Songs went public against The Beatles' wishes and the shareholding changed: James and his partner now held 23 per cent more than the individual shareholdings of John and Paul, who owned only 15 per cent each. In 1969, James and his partner sold their part of the company to Lew Grade's ATV without alerting The Beatles to the deal and thus preventing them from putting together a rival bid themselves.

There then followed a period of protracted wrangling as first ATV, then The Beatles, tried to gain full control of Northern Songs. The Beatles, believe it or not, were experiencing difficulties raising cash – some say it was because of Lennon's antipathy to banks and those very businessmen who might have been able to help them.

The deal went against The Beatles. Incredibly, ATV took control of the publishing of The Beatles, and Lennon and McCartney no longer owned their own songs. The wrangling continued, but eventually an agreement was struck that brought Lennon and

McCartney to the table to sign contracts with ATV directly.

But that was far from the end of the matter. ATV was gobbled up by Associated Communications Corporation, which itself was taken over by the corporate raider Robert Holmes à Court, who, in 1985, sold ATV Music to Michael Jackson for $47.5 million.

McCartney, of course, finds this situation very irksome for many reasons, one small example of which is that when he wanted to print the lyrics to 'Eleanor Rigby' in the programme for his 1989 world tour, he found he had to pay Michael Jackson for the privilege. Another humiliation occurred when Jackson allowed a Beatles track to be used in a Nike TV ad for which Jackson is said to have received $250,000. At the time, George Harrison said, 'Unless we do something about it, every Beatles song is going to end up advertising bras and pork pies.'

If he couldn't gain control of his own back catalogue, McCartney thought, he'd damn well get control of somebody else's, and when Buddy Holly's publishing rights came on to the market in 1976, he snapped them up in a deal which has given him an asset that might possibly be worth as much as $600 million.

As a postscript to this deal, it seems that Michael Jackson's recent woes may include an inability to pay the instalments on the loan he originally raised to buy ATV. If he defaults, then The Beatles catalogue may well go under the hammer yet again and potential bidders would surely find themselves up against the purchasing power of one Sir Paul McCartney and maybe one Mrs Yoko Ono Lennon, guardian of her late husband's legacy.

The band's next deal is often cited as the worst. It involved The Beatles' merchandising rights. Inevitably, The Beatles' incredible success attracted gold-diggers: Brian was approached by many and various companies, often American, who wanted licences to manufacture items with The Beatles' name and picture on them. These he had been granting on an ad hoc basis, but it was a very time-consuming and unsatisfactory way of doing things. Someone had to take charge and Epstein delegated the mess to his (and Don Arden's) solicitor, David Jacobs. Jacobs ran into one Nicky

Byrne at a party. Yes, Nicky said, he would love to have a crack at it, and immediately set up a consortium of English businessmen who persuaded Epstein's lawyer to grant them the rights for all Beatles merchandise, which they would sell on. In return, Byrne would pay The Beatles 10 per cent of the profits and retain 90 per cent for his partners. Epstein, perhaps unaware of the huge amounts that would be made, or possibly too busy to give the matter his full attention, agreed.

Byrne had struck pay dirt. It is now generally recognised that the 10/90 percentage split should have been totally the other way round.

There was a torrent of licensing applications, including that of a Texan businessman who had met John Lennon on a flight and offered the stunned Beatle $3 million for the rights to open 'Beatleburger Palaces'.

With an eye for a fast buck, an American company wrote asking if The Beatles would let them sell their bath water at $1 per bottle. A radio station in Vancouver offered to buy The Beatles' hotel beds.

Byrne moved to the States and started making (and spending) millions. Beatle watches, pens, towels, T-shirts, lunch boxes, wigs, magazines, Zippo lighters, ashtrays – you name it – flooded onto the market. Even now, a search of eBay turns up hundreds of categories of Beatles products and many thousands of Beatles merchandised items for sale.

Everyone, it seems, was making money out of The Beatles except The Beatles themselves and inevitably a massive dispute blew up between Byrne's Seltaeb company (Beatles backwards, just like the royalty rates) and Epstein and other companies, who felt that they had the rights to manufacture and sell this or that.

There was also a separate squabble, related in Philip Norman's book, *Shout!*, between Byrne and some of his partners, who alleged at the time that Byrne was squandering huge amounts of money on himself. He'd based himself in a hotel and it was said he kept two limousines on twenty-four-hour call and had a helicopter to ferry businessmen to and from the airport. It was also claimed that he'd run up a bill of $50,000 in personal expenses and used company money to pay his girlfriend's charge accounts.

NEMS sued Seltaeb and Seltaeb counter-sued NEMS. After protracted litigation, a New York court ruled against NEMS and ordered it to pay over $5 million. A worried Epstein needed a new lawyer to sort out the mess. The lawyer asked for a hefty $50,000 retainer, which Epstein paid with his own money, perhaps as a tacit admission of culpability, or at the very least of a degree of negligence in the running of The Beatles' affairs. It's estimated that the spend on Beatles-branded products in the USA in 1964 came in at $50 million. The potential losses worldwide were incalculable. The row rumbled on for years and it was to become Epstein's bête noire. Clearly, his eye was not always on the ball.

However, Epstein was undoubtedly stretched. There were many demands on his time. As well as attempting to direct The Beatles, he was developing his 'stable' of artists, having taken on Gerry and the Pacemakers. The chirpy Gerry was to have three consecutive number ones, the first of which was 'How Do You Do It?', a track that George Martin had originally found for The Beatles but which they had rejected. Number ones from Billy J. Kramer and the Dakotas and then cloakroom assistant at the Cavern Club, Cilla Black, followed.

George Martin, The Beatles' producer, was at the leading edge of Epstein's charge at the charts, as he explains in Geller's *In My Life*: 'After Gerry, Billy J. Kramer was brought to me, and we started a similar kind of system – finding the songs, recording them and hitting oil. We were striking pay dirt.'

But The Beatles' 'Love Me Do' made it to only number 17 in the charts. The (disputed) story goes that Brian had to buy 10,000 copies of the single to get it in the charts at all.

Another Beatles fable is that Epstein and John Lennon had a homosexual experience on a holiday that the two took in Barcelona. It was given credence in *The Love You Make*, written by Epstein's employee and friend Peter Brown. Lennon told Brown: 'I went on holiday to Spain with Brian . . . which started all the rumours that he and I were having a love affair. Well, it was almost a love affair but not quite. It was never consummated. But we did have a pretty intense relationship. And it was my first experience with someone I knew was a homosexual. He admitted it to me. We had this holiday together because Cyn was pregnant and we left her with the baby and went to Spain. Lots of funny stories, you know. We used to sit in cafés and Brian would look at all the boys and I would ask, "Do you like that one? Do you like this one?" It was just the combination of our closeness and the trip that started the rumours.'

At McCartney's 21st birthday party, a DJ from the Cavern Club, Bob Wooler, is said to have made a pass at Lennon, who gave him a black eye and broke his nose. In another version of the story, Lennon is outraged by a comment Wooler makes about his holiday with Brian.

The Beatles marched on, their sights now firmly on America, a vast market that until then had resisted artists from the UK. Sid Bernstein was to become famous as the promoter of The Beatles' Shea Stadium concert, but in the early months of 1963 he was only a small-time agent. He liked to read the British press and there spotted an article headed: 'Beatlemania sweeps Great Britain.'

'I thought, God, I've gotta get 'em here,' he said.

Keen to be involved in something new, he phoned around and eventually tracked down Brian, who amazingly was still living with his parents. Interviewed for *In My Life*, Bernstein recalls, 'Brian said, "Where would you present them?" I said, "I'd like to present them at Carnegie Hall." . . . I had never been to Carnegie Hall in my life, so I rang them and found out that I needed a $500 deposit. I didn't have it and had to borrow the money from my old friend Abe Margolis, a very successful jeweller. He said, "Who do you want to present?" I said, "I've got a group from England. You wouldn't know them. They're called The Beatles." And Abe said, "Sid, in my last stages of syphilis will I ever be crazy enough to back you with a group with a name like that." But I got the money.'

It was a brave gamble. The Beatles were yet to have chart success in the UK let alone the USA, where Capitol, the American arm of EMI, wasn't keen to even release their records.

Bernstein didn't have to wait long, though. 'Please Please Me' was number 1 in the British charts in March, 'From Me to You' went to number 1 in May (and stayed there for seven weeks), and the *Please Please Me* album hit the number 1 spot two days later. 'She Loves You' was number 1 in September and 'I Want to Hold Your Hand' was number 1 in December.

Epstein acts occupied the number 1 slot for 37 weeks that year.

Capitol was finally persuaded to release Beatles records when Brian phoned Alan Livingston, the label boss. 'I didn't know who he was,' said Livingston. 'I picked up the phone and he said, "Mr Livingston, we don't understand why you don't put out The Beatles' records. Have you heard them?" I told him I hadn't. So he said, "Would you please listen and call me back?" I said, "Sure." And I went downstairs and I heard "I Want to Hold Your Hand". I can't honestly say I knew how big they would be, but I heard something and I saw the look of them. Also I liked Brian just then on the telephone. He was a gentleman and he was persuasive. I called him back and said, "OK, we'll put them out." Brian said, "Wait a minute. I'm not going to give them to you unless you spend $40,000 to promote their first single." Well, that was pretty much unheard of in the early '60s . . . For whatever reason, I said, "OK."'

The money was never spent; there wasn't any need.

Another American who caught the first wave of Beatlemania was Ed Sullivan, who the previous year had been passing through Heathrow at the same time as The Beatles and had been astonished by the spectacle of the screaming girls. He had taken a gamble and booked the unknown band into the top-of-the-bill slot on his show months in advance, then sat worrying that the gamble was going to blow up in his face.

With exquisite timing, 'I Want to Hold Your Hand' was at number 1 in the USA (where it stayed for seven weeks) on 1 February 1964. A week later, The Beatles arrived to a rapturous welcome at

Kennedy Airport. Two days after that, around 75 million people watched them perform on *The Ed Sullivan Show*. Then they played a sold-out Carnegie Hall two days later.

The prescient Bernstein went on to represent many of the bands that flocked to the USA during the so-called 'British invasion' and would become famous as the agent who, in the '70s, regularly offered The Beatles $1 million to get back together.

These were heady days – for the band, for Epstein and for the American record company. It was the norm at Capitol to press up around 5,000 copies of a single for a new artist. They would press perhaps 25,000 copies for an established star. With The Beatles, they'd press a million advance copies for each release and a million copies was never enough. Capitol's other artists would claim that the pressing factory was so full of Beatles product that they couldn't get their own stuff onto the presses.

In April 1964, The Beatles had singles at numbers 1, 2, 3, 4 and 5 in the American charts. They also had singles in nine other slots in the Billboard Hot 100. This phenomenal feat is unlikely to ever be repeated.

Brian started to realise some of the fruits of his labours. NEMS, a one-time provincial family business, now had a staff of about 25 and moved from Liverpool to Argyll Street, next to the London Palladium. He was on the up and building an entertainment empire; rather pompously, he made the cable address of the office 'Nemporer'.

He acquired a West End flat (George and Ringo became neighbours) and he now drove a Bentley, a Mini Cooper and a Jaguar. At home, food was served by Lonnie Trimble, his black American manservant. Dinner guests included Alma Cogan, Lionel Bart and DJ Alan Freeman. On other occasions, guests were bits of 'rough' that Brian brought back to play 'housey housey' with.

One of the bits of rough arrived with Brian from Los Angeles. He was taken on as a NEMS employee on £50 a week plus a clothes allowance, but no one knew exactly what his 'duties' were. Brian also covered numerous living expenses for the young American. He had his 'boys' (as he always called The Beatles), he had money, cars, prestige, a glamorous lifestyle and now he seemed to have found, at last, that for which he had most yearned: a permanent partner. But it wasn't to be – the man was a hustler who, like so many others, and perhaps understandably, seemed to be more interested in the cash and the glitz that surrounded the manager of The Beatles than the manager himself. The story goes that when things went sour, Brian's lawyer warned him off but that he wouldn't go without a pay-off.

Then came another crummy deal. The Beatles wanted a movie, so Walter Shenson, an American producer, was taken on, as was American director Richard Lester. The combined efforts of Lester and Liverpool playwright Alun Owen produced a film commonly credited with being a tour de force. The seminal *A Hard Day's Night* would influence film-makers and pop-video producers for years to come with its pop-art styling, jump cuts, helicopter shots and use of slow motion. And it was very funny, with natural Beatle humour adding to the scripted gags, all embellished by lots of jokey asides, a technique Lester was to employ to good effect in the follow-up, *Help!*, and his two star-studded Musketeers movies of the early '70s.

A Hard Day's Night was cheap to make at £180,000 and took only three weeks to complete. It made a fortune at the box office. When the film opened in Liverpool, a crowd estimated at 150,000 was waiting to see its conquering heroes make their homecoming. Eight months earlier, they had been playing the dingy Cavern Club; now they had a world stage.

The budget for *Help!* was double that of *A Hard Day's Night* but was still negligible. It was shot in colour on location in the West Indies and took 11 weeks to make, but it was still a cheap movie for the biggest band in the world. It's unclear how much money The Beatles got from the films – thousands, maybe a million or two, came in from here and there – however, what is clear is that the box-office takings were many millions and because no one in the Beatles camp read the small print in the contracts, the copyright of the two films reverted to the producer after fifteen years. The remaining Beatles no longer own them: Shenson owns *A Hard Day's Night* and *Help!* lock, stock and barrel.

Even so, the money flowing into NEMS became a deluge. Brian reportedly rang one of the American agents one day and pleaded, 'You've simply got to do something about all that money pouring in. You've got to find a way to stop it.'

The Beatles received MBEs in 1965, but Brian didn't. John said, 'I thought you had to drive tanks and win wars to win the MBE.' Another crack which has been attributed to both Princess Margaret and George Harrison was, 'MBE? Mr Brian Epstein.'

An emboldened Sid Bernstein phoned to ask Brian if The Beatles would do another concert. No Carnegie Hall this time – Sid wanted the 55,000-seater Shea Stadium. Despite the shrieking fans who made the music pretty much inaudible, it was a historic event, with The Beatles, arriving in an armoured car, ushering in the era of stadium rock. They made $180,000 for a 28-minute performance.

Years later, Sid says he was at a Jimmy Cliff concert with John Lennon, who said to him, 'You know, Sid, at Shea I saw the top of the mountain.' Sid replied, 'John, so did I.'

Sid went on to explain the enduring love of The Beatles and their music: 'They are part of the fabric of our souls. They are almost embedded in our genes. We're not going to let them forget that we still love them.'

In 1966, when the band were playing in San Francisco, Brian's bit of rough turned up and a beaming Epstein declared that his lover was a changed man and that they were together again, much to everyone's despair. Later that evening, he disappeared – along with briefcases belonging to Brian and his attorney.

Brian's briefcase contained a large amount of cash and important documents, such as Beatles contracts, but, more importantly, there were also a number of bottles of pills – amphetamines to keep him up and sleeping pills to take him down. Brian asked the attorney to let the matter go, fearful of the consequences, but the attorney made sure the bags and their contents were tracked down and returned, although, allegedly, a lot of cash was missing.

Lennon said,'Brian Epstein's sex life will make a nice "Hollywood Babylon" some day.'

Epstein had had a premonition about this tour even before this episode. He'd had fears about the band's health and its members' states of mind. There had also been concerns about their safety since a number of very flaky people had begun to crawl from the woodwork. He had asked his attorney how much it would cost to call the whole thing off, and on being told that it would be in the region of $1 million, had considered pulling the plug at his own personal expense.

Worried, paranoid and unlucky in love as ever, his senses alternately heightened and then dulled by pills, many believe this was the period when Brian's fantastic powers of calm self-confidence began to fail him. He started to become erratic in behaviour and more prone to mood swings and tantrums. He would sack staff and then immediately reinstate them with choruses of apologies. Yet, despite his erratic behaviour, his employees always showed him incredible affection and loyalty.

Epstein had always been a gambler and perhaps this was a key to his character and some of his reckless business tactics. In the music shop, he and his assistant would bet on the success or failure of the records they bought in, and from the outset he invested considerable sums in the unsigned Beatles – clothes, transport, support staff, haircuts, visits to London, hotel bills, etc. – without any guarantee that the monies would be repaid. In fact, they very nearly weren't.

When he started moving in London's showbiz circles, he and the band would frequent the stylish clubs like the Scene, the Scotch of St James and the Cromwellian, but these see-and-be-seen venues soon palled on Brian and he began to visit the high-class gambling clubs instead. By all accounts, Epstein was a canny gambler, but he was prepared to lose as well.

It is recorded that once, during a card game on a train, he lost £100, a £250 watch and a £100 lighter to Neil Aspinall, then a roadie but now the managing director of Apple Corps. It is also said that Gerry Marsden was present when Brian won £11,000 one evening and then dropped £15,000 the following night.

Brian's friend Peter Brown was a frequent companion on these tours of the casinos and he recalls Brian losing £17,000 (approximately £75,000 in today's terms) in one evening and then swearing Brown to silence. He was embarrassed by the loss.

Brian had by now reversed his days and nights, sleeping all day and gambling or indulging in other activities hidden by the night. He took drugs to balance him out, but they were unbalancing him even more. The dispute over the merchandising wore on and depressed him. He'd bought the Saville Theatre with grand plans for it, but he encountered problems there, too.

Against the wishes of The Beatles and the NEMS staff, he brought in Robert Stigwood to look after some matters outside The Beatles. It's interesting that although he and The Beatles were as close as ever, and there was an enduring affection and trust between them, there were still times when he took on a high-handed, autocratic style and struck deals that they bitterly resented.

During this period, The Beatles gave up touring and looked towards the recording studio for the next stage in their develop—ment – *Sergeant Pepper*. Brian could not easily involve himself in these activities – he had no role in the making of their music – and in reality he had less and less to do. Boredom became a factor, the kind of boredom that drove him to taking drugs, reckless behaviour in casinos and late-night liaisons.

When he was found in bed unconscious, everyone knew it had been a suicide attempt because he had left a note. He survived, but there were more episodes and the writing was on the wall. He checked himself into The Priory a number of times, but its regime was not as strict then as it is now and he would check out when he became bored with the cure.

There were to be dazzling bright spots in the gloom, though: when he finally got his hands on a copy of *Sgt. Pepper's Lonely Hearts*

Club Band, he became extremely excited, thrilled that his boys had finally produced the magnum opus he had always known they would. When, shortly afterwards, he came to renew his contract with The Beatles, ever fair, or maybe just realistic, he talked of getting his management royalty reduced from 25 per cent to 15 per cent.

It's possible that LSD may have been a factor in his malaise. There was certainly plenty of it about and in those days it was strong stuff. Some users were evangelists for it, others were ripped apart; a bad trip could leave you mentally changed and rarely for the better.

A certain hippy dippyness was in the air now, and it even crept into Brian's 'proper' vocabulary, which became peppered with flower and love references. This was 1967 and he was at the epicentre of all things psychedelic. The band was on the verge of the 'All You Need is Love' broadcast, which went out to more than 200 million people, an unprecedented event. All around him was positivity and hope. But his father had just died, so it was obviously a turbulent time for him, an epoch-making time that he was facing alone, as always, despite the throngs of people that surrounded the Nemporer.

And then the party was over. When some friends didn't arrive for a weekend party at his country house, he became bored and drove himself back to London, a little drunk. Two days later, his butler and his doctor kicked in his bedroom door and Brian lay dead in bed with bottles of pills all around him and a plate of chocolate digestives spilled out over the covers.

When the news broke, The Beatles were away with the Maharishi in North Wales. They were with their guru when they lost their mentor. John commented, 'Well, you know . . . We don't know what to say. We loved him and he was one of us.'

McCartney believed that John was scared by the death. 'Reading through some things that John felt and hearing some stuff, I think he thought, "Right, this is it. This is the end. This is the end of The Beatles," and it kind of was. We made a few more albums, but we were sort of winding up. We always felt we'd come full circle and Brian's death was part of that.'

The conclusion must be that he didn't commit suicide but that it had definitely been on his mind. His stalwart PR Derek Taylor said of him in a radio interview: 'He was very funny, very romantic, very sensitive to beautiful things. Other areas in his life caused him some pain. We never knew where he went at night. Sometimes he would get lonely. He had a full address book, but there were times he couldn't reach people and he'd get very depressed and paranoid and think it was all over and it was one of those weekends he died.'

And it's amazing how many things did unravel around the time of his death – as if Brian had been some universal glue of the age itself. Gerry and the Pacemakers split. The Beatles started the road to their split after Robert Stigwood failed in his attempt to take them over. He pulled out of NEMS altogether and NEMS itself sort of withered away. When Allen Klein stepped up to the mark, The Beatles' fate was sealed and there followed years of acrimony and litigation. David Jacobs, the solicitor who set up the Seltaeb deal, was himself dead within the year when he was found hanged at his home.

Marianne Faithfull, who, with Mick Jagger, was one of the band's inner circle, is emphatic that the shockwaves of Brian's death ultimately led to her own problems and a suicide attempt in Australia. She says in her autobiography, *In My Life*, 'The whole thing just changed and it began with Brian's death . . . The Beatles were just fucking around really with the Maharishi, that's all. Brian was much more than a brilliant businessman. He was a spiritual centre.'

John scotched any plans the Maharishi might have had for The Beatles, though. When the guru said they shouldn't mourn Brian's death, he muttered, 'Fucking idiot.'

The meteoric rise of The Beatles is well chronicled. Epstein had done deals on the run or delegated too much; he freely admitted he lacked experience and was, in business terms, naive. It wasn't really a matter of managing The Beatles, since the band's upward course had its own dizzying momentum; it was more a matter of trying to keep the crazy gravy train on the rails.

Maybe if he'd found a caring partner, someone who could have shouldered a bit of the load, things might have been very different. Maybe The Beatles might not have broken up quite so soon, or so frustratingly, with so many people left wanting, knowing that there were many more wonders that The Beatles as a band might have performed.

If Brian had been able to step back from the game for a few minutes to reflect on it all, or if there had been sensible professional advice around him, he might not have done those awful deals. But it's only really in retrospect that The Beatles' business affairs look so bad; at the time, those types of deals were common practice. In any event, as far as the original record deal is concerned, Epstein didn't have much choice.

Brian's charisma and his patrician style meant he wasn't intimidated by the puffed-up pop moguls he encountered: he stared them straight in the eye, their equal financially, intellectually and culturally. The Beatles undoubtedly loved that about their manager. They loved their manager. There just wasn't anyone like him in Liverpool in those days. Above all, he was an ardent fan of The Beatles. Long before they even had a record deal, he always said, as they did, that they would be the biggest band in the world – and it wasn't just blind hope: he meant it and he kept on saying it.

Expert, methodical planner and reckless gambler rolled into one, Ian Macdonald in *Revolution in the Head* extols 'the only honest manager in Britain at that time'.

Jude Law has been thinking it's time for a film about Brian. Fascinated by the fabled manager, he has acquired Epstein's diaries and is reported to have been working on a biopic entitled *Tomorrow Never Knows*, with himself in the lead.

The best band, the best manager: they say he could light up a room when he walked in, and if his boys were with him, people were dazzled. Brian Epstein was truly the Nemporer.

3

ANDREW LOOG OLDHAM

Rolling Stones

Now it's 1966,
Andrew's up to all his tricks.
– *Marianne Faithfull*, 'Song For Nico'

Cometh the hour, cometh the man. Station Hotel, Richmond, West London: 28 April 1963. But then timing was Andrew's thing – finger on the pulse, ear to the ground and all that. And just behind those shades, he kept his beady little eyes on the prize.

He'd always been able to create a space for himself at the centre of things: he put himself about, knew everyone and he was a real grafter, they all agreed. Andrew was the ace face in early Swinging London – possibly its first mod, certainly its second.

Oldham was obsessed with actor Laurence Harvey and in particular Harvey's role as the sleazy agent in *Expresso Bongo*, the first Cliff Richard film. He liked the idea that Harvey may have had some of his side teeth removed to give him a certain gaunt look. Appearances were all to Andrew; rule number one in the Loog Oldham manual – clothes maketh the man.

In the early days, he wore button-down-collar shirts and thin knitted ties with grey flannel suits. Later, he was backcombing his hair mod-style and often opted for a little bit of eyeliner. He was probably wearing make-up before any of the Rolling Stones. His reasoning was, 'Most people speak instead of listen, therefore only remember what they see.'

Then came the trademark shades. He reckons that his mother once told him he had 'eyes like raisins'. It is more likely that he was copying his second role model, Phil Spector. On went the shades and on they stayed.

All the girls and the gays wanted Andrew, like they came to want his prodigy, Mick Jagger. But Jagger's flash was pure Andrew.

Ever the chameleon, Jagger assimilated nuances, affectations, lip-gloss tips and anything else he could scavenge from all around him. Andrew provided a rich seam that was plundered wholesale. Mick hijacked Oldham's mannerisms as deftly as he stole Tina Turner's dance moves. But Oldham himself hadn't arrived fully formed: his radar was constantly sweeping, too. He was cherry-picking as well as Jagger, but always one step ahead.

It's interesting to consider what Loog Oldham's motives might have been in those early days: what set him off on his quest to become pop manager superstar? He obviously liked money and the things that it bought him, but not that much. 'I did not wear that money hat,' he once said – although some of his bands would come to disagree.

He liked clothes, though, and after leaving school went as far as getting himself a job in a clothes shop so he could steal them. He also liked cars – especially his big powder-blue Yankee drophead and later a Rolls-Royce Phantom V, like Brian Epstein's, with its natty little built-in record player – but they were more an extension of Oldham's wardrobe and a tool of the trade than a passion in their own right.

Andrew liked beautiful women and they liked him, too (whether he liked boys as well, he is fashionably vague about – androgyny was in), but he could never be accused of having been a hound (apart from a particularly debauched evening with Rolling Stone Brian Jones that he confesses to, where the two of them were in a hotel room, stripped bare and heavily outnumbered by strumpets).

The list goes on: he liked drugs. By God, he liked drugs, but only much later. In the early days of managing the Stones, he wasn't doing much more than an occasional spliff and a few purple hearts – amphetamines. No one suggested he was a fiend . . . not then anyway.

As far as boozing was concerned, prior to things turning to shit for Andrew in 1967, it barely gets a mention in his book *Stoned*, though it permeates the sequel, *2Stoned*.

So if not a thirst for booze, was it a thirst for power – what Oscar Wilde called 'the one supreme pleasure'? Probably not. A prodigy like Oldham would probably have rocketed up through the ranks of the music business anyway, even without the Rolling Stones, if he'd only sung to the establishment tune, but he had his own song sheet.

So power, drugs, drink, women, cash, fast cars, houses – in the early days, the heady days, they weren't ostensibly the driving forces, although they all came to play their part. What Andrew liked was playing the ace face, which is good because he was it.

Like many of the other great managers in this book, Oldham wanted to be associated with a 'national anthem'. That's what really turned him on. He uses the phrase over and over in *Stoned*. He didn't demand to have written the anthem himself, he just wanted to be involved with the band that did – to be around it, to be part of the genesis of it, to feel the electricity crackles. When he first heard the hacksaw chords of 'Satisfaction', the hairs stood up on the back of his neck.

Oldham had all the qualifications to succeed in rock and roll in the UK, to be the definitive rock band manager – perhaps he defined what those qualifications would always be. He was a hustler with the gift of the gab and he could do it in English and French, too; he was a dandy, he lived in Hampstead; he had experienced a taste of the good life at an early age; he'd mixed with the nobs; he was slightly Jewish (so he says); he left public school with one O level; and he swung both ways (again, so he says). And after working with Don Arden, he saw the usefulness of violence in business and was intrigued by it and those who carried it out.

To varying degrees, you could associate Brian Epstein with quite a lot of the above and there were other similarities between the managers of the two biggest bands in the country, and ultimately the world. They were both into pills and danger. Epstein's idea of fun, in the early part of the evening at least, was just what you would imagine of a man who wore Turnbull and Asser shirts with 24-carat-gold cufflinks: an establishment cocktail party where perhaps a few MPs would mix with some socialites and maybe, Brian hoped, a young man or two, who might return his timid smile.

Another night, you'd see Brian gambling in the chic Clermont Club, where old Etonians frittered away their inheritances, where Lord Lucan and James Goldsmith sat at the bar and the owner, John Aspinall, strolled around with a snow tiger on a lead.

So far, so sophisticated; but there was a sinister subtext. Brian's gambling wasn't just a harmless little flutter: he'd be winning or losing thousands, grinding his teeth down on amphetamines. And later, much later, he would go cruising, on the lookout for a bit of 'rough' and occasionally getting himself beaten bloody, robbed and blackmailed for his trouble.

Andrew also liked a few drinks with friends – a less stuffy but no less glamorous set than Brian's – but then he and his criminal chauffeur would take the Chevrolet Impala careering around Marble Arch on the wrong side of the road, waving a gun around, cranked up on speed.

Different kicks, but they both wound up in rehab.

Oldham was a war baby. He never knew his Texan pilot father, who had been shot down a few months before Andrew was born, or the man he was told was his father anyway, for here the waters get muddy pretty quickly.

His mother, Celia, had known Alex Morris, a wealthy furniture manufacturer, before the war and, according to Morris's daughter,

Alex once had red hair similar to Andrew's, despite the fact he was a Polish Jew. Apparently, there had once been many red-headed Jews in Poland. Celia was also a Polish Jew, with a bit of Russian thrown in, and had arrived in the UK by way of Australia.

Andrew and his upwardly mobile mother lived at various London addresses, ranging from a crummy bedsit on the Edgware Road to an austere but expensive apartment in Hampstead – the assumption is that it was paid for by Alex. Celia worked, but only as an adding-machine operator, so Hampstead flats were not really within her scope. Alex, the sugar daddy, used to drive a Rolls-Royce and would take young Oldham for a ride in it. There were teas at Fortnum and Mason and holidays in the south of France.

Mother and son had an intense relationship, as those in fatherless families often do. When Andrew went out to work – one of his first jobs was with Mary Quant – rumours circulated that he used to knock his mother around. He's since denied them.

Andrew went to a succession of boarding schools, including one in Oxford, which turned out to be a cut-and-run money-making scam for the senior master – something he seems to have found fascinating.

He stood out at school: he ran a sort of mini-nightclub in one of the classrooms for a while and was often in trouble for wearing only versions of the uniform. One of Oldham's wicked wheezes involved Burton, the male outfitter's. It offered a deal where for £12 you could get a suit made and choose from a range of features to add a little originality. Most punters didn't want to look distinctive, they wanted the conservative dull-grey lookalikes that the tailors could knock out with their eyes shut. 'Oldham drove the firm crazy, memorably finagling out of their offer a dove-grey mohair suit with a nipped waist, inverted vents and paisley lining to wear atop draped trousers with slanted pockets,' his school friend, John Douglas, recalled in *Stoned*. 'When he showed up back at school in the get-up, it was immediately confiscated by his housemaster. "I don't know why you bother," the man remonstrated. "You only wore it for one day."

"Yeah," said Oldham, "but what a day."'

He left with that one O level and a report that said, 'Andrew may do well but not here.' He was 16. It was 1960.

John Douglas also remembers him returning to the school once in his chauffeur-driven sky-blue Chevrolet, with Keith Richards lounging next to him. The Chevrolet crashed into the school wall. 'Another time,' John says, 'he drove his Rolls-Royce across the cricket wicket. The final time he returned, it was for the old boys' football match. After scoring a goal for each side, he blacked out. During the evening, he escorted DJ Alan Freeman from dormitory to dormitory, giving out his autograph.'

Oldham blagged the job with Mary Quant's King's Road operation by simply knocking on her door and asking for it. In the evenings, he moonlighted as a waiter at Ronnie Scott's Jazz Club. A formative influence was Peter Meaden, who was quite possibly London's first mod and who dressed in a bottle-green mohair suit with paisley lining, coupled with side-laced suede ankle boots. Peter would later manage The Who and contrive their early mod look.

At some point, Andrew took off to the south of France for a summer, which he financed by begging. 'In my best public-school accent, I vultured the Croisette's circumcised and wealthy,' he says. There, he conned some cash out of Lionel Bart, the writer of *Oliver!*, the musical. Sold on Andrew's story that his allowance from his parents hadn't arrived, Bart took pity on the waif and gave him a few francs before going to have lunch with Pablo Picasso. The two then watched Andrew performing the same scam over and over. Impressed, Bart told Andrew to look him up when he returned to London. They became buddies and workmates.

On the same French trip, Oldham was spotted standing beside the road wearing riding breeches, hard hat and holding a riding crop. He was telling someone that his horse had just thrown him and bolted, and could they run him into the next town?

Back in London, Andrew decided to be a publicist. He employed his customary direct approach and knocked on a door requesting a job. That door belonged to Don Arden.

He says: 'Andrew came into the office and we did a deal on the Sam Cooke/Little Richard tour. I don't know why I thought he could do it, but I did . . . Then Andrew put an article in one of the London papers. It said, "The kids are gonna go crazy, they're gonna rip the seats out of the theatre."'

Granada theatres didn't want their seats ripped out and demanded that Arden sack Oldham or the tour would be cancelled. Andrew had to go, but the mutual respect lingered on.

Phil ('wall of sound') Spector became a profound influence after the pair met. The weirdo-genius producer and London's latest hip young gunslinger hit it off immediately. One was tall and the other short, but in other ways they resembled each other. Andrew wanted to know everything about how to find your way around a recording studio (especially with shades on); Spector basked in the warmth of Oldham's hero-worship, smirked at some of his crazy pop talk and then visited the men's room to check out his eyeliner.

But it was to be another meeting that went further in shaping his destiny.

On 13 January 1963, two weeks before Andrew's 19th birthday, he accompanied one of his acts to the *Thank Your Lucky Stars* studio in Birmingham and witnessed The Beatles make their first-ever TV appearance. He made a beeline for Brian Epstein and demanded a job there and then. Brian was in the centre of a whirlwind; he always needed help.

And what a dream job. Andrew had no trouble getting the band written about. Everyone was talking about The Beatles. Journalists were beating the door down to get at them. He should have been set up for life, but the fates had different plans for him and only weeks later Andrew was in the De Hems pub off London's Shaftesbury Avenue having his now-famous drink with the editor of the *Record Mirror*, Peter Jones, who told him about a group he'd heard a buzz about. The Rollin' Stones, as they were known then, played every week in the Station Hotel in Richmond. Oldham looked at the rail map. He later claimed that if the train from Hampstead hadn't gone directly to Richmond, if he'd had to go through the effort of changing trains, he might have not bothered to go and see the world's greatest rock and roll band at all.

But go he did, and it was love at first sight. 'I'd never seen anything like it,' he says. 'They came on to me. It was a feeling of all the elements falling into the right place and time . . . I heard the anthem of a national sound . . . I saw and heard what my life, thus far, had been for.'

The trendsetter and trendspotter's epiphany was all about timing. 'I knew what I was looking at,' added Oldham. 'It was sex, and I was 48 hours ahead of the pack.'

The Stones looked back at the dapper Andrew, listened to some of his revved-up blarney and decided to give him a whirl, in the process carelessly dumping their previous manager, Giorgio Gomelsky, who never forgave them and tried to fill the gap by taking on The Yardbirds.

Keith Richards remarked that Andrew was 'a fantastic bullshitter and an incredible hustler'. Venerable jazzer, pop commentator and all-round wag George Melly was on the scene. He recalls in his book, *Revolt into Style*, the queues growing longer outside the Station Hotel. 'It was only a matter of time before the right entrepreneur walked in and recognised his chance. Oldham had no reservations . . . He looked at Jagger as Sylvester looks at Tweetie Pie. Oldham was calculatedly vicious and nasty but pretty as a stoat. He had enormous talent totally dedicated to whim and money.'

Another time, Melly was to famously comment on Jagger. Mick was heard explaining away the lines on his face as 'laughter lines', when Melly snorted, 'Surely, Mick, nothing's that funny.'

Gered Mankowitz, who was to regularly photograph the Stones, saw Andrew as 'one of those people who is capable of bringing people together, a catalyst'. He goes on to say: 'He was very stimulating, very funny. Able to be incredibly cruel. Very cutting. He had an enormous talent for hearing the right thing – he had great ears – and understood the nature of the business, understood the nature of the media as it was then. He was an extraordinary bloke.'

Of course, he would first have to resign as Beatles publicist, an act of considerable courage when one considers that all but the deranged could see that The Beatles were going to be the biggest thing ever. He telephoned Brian Epstein to explain and asked him if he wanted to get involved with the new band he had found. Epstein declined the second-biggest band in the world because he was too busy with the first, as well as Gerry and the Pacemakers and Billy J. Kramer.

Having failed to bag the biggest manager in the business as a partner, Andrew lowered his sights. He needed someone who could get gigs and cough up for recording sessions. His choice was Eric Easton, a small-time old-style music agent whose offices Andrew had been sharing. Easton brought considerable music-business ken to the table, but, most importantly, he was an adult. In 1963, Oldham was only 19, two years too young to sign a contract – quite an impediment for the budding teen tycoon. He sat down with Easton and offered him 'the chance of a lifetime'. Easton had just inadvertently won the lottery.

From this point on, Epstein and Loog Oldham were head to head.

The game of Epstein v. Loog Oldham is perfectly illustrated by the different ways the two managers set about carving the images of their respective bands. The Beatles had served a gruelling apprenticeship doing 20 gigs a week in the Star Club in Hamburg. They were rough-rocking hellraisers from Liverpool who wore leather and Brylcreem, who popped pills, smoked fags and played with the *fräuleins*. In short, they were the real thing – working-class heroes. But Epstein had thought it essential to clean up their act and turned them into besuited mop-top popsters who wouldn't fart in front of Grandma or even so much as touch an aspirin without a prescription.

Oldham saw the yin and the yang of all this. He'd tried the Stones out in matching dogtooth jackets, but they'd take them off or purposely leave them at home. Keith Richards wiped chocolate pudding on his, then poured whisky on it. So he turned the game on its head and replaced wholesomeness with bad. Andrew reckoned he could see a yawning gap in the market and a space in the hearts of Britain's teenagers, a latent desire for a new band, a band that came up from the pelvic floor. Where The Beatles had been made sweet and cuddly, they might have lived next door and your mum liked them, Oldham moved his middle-class college boys over to the wrong side of the tracks. Andrew realised early on that the Stones would make great rebels, and fashioned Jagger particularly, but the band took to the plan with considerable enthusiasm. 'They were all bad boys when I found them,' Andrew has said. 'I just brought out the worst in them.'

'The Beatles want to hold your hand. The Stones want to burn your town,' said Tom Wolfe.

Right on the zeitgeist, Andrew came up with the 'Would you let your daughter go out with a Rolling Stone?' slogan. When Bill Wyman was apprehended peeing on a garage forecourt, it was Andrew who spun the tale around the press but made out it had been Jagger who had been the offender. Jagger read the runes and was a willing victim. 'We piss anywhere, man' was the slogan of the moment.

When he wangled them onto music show *Juke Box Jury*, they lounged around, laughing at their own private jokes and looking bored. It was all an act, but the dailies took the bait and thundered that the band was 'an utter disgrace'.

'Not bad for an afternoon's work,' commented the arch media manipulator, adding: 'By the time I got through planting all that negative publicity, there wasn't a parent in Britain that wasn't repulsed by the very sound of their name.'

Easton worked the band all round the country and the reaction was always enthusiasm from the girls and sullen indifference from the boys until three or four numbers in and then the place would start going wild. The pheromones were flying. Keith once spoke of the crowd noise reaching 'a sort of hysterical wail, a weird sound that hundreds of chicks make when they're coming . . . They sounded like hundreds of orgasms at once. They couldn't even hear the music and we couldn't hear the music we were playing.'

Decca was persuaded to sign the Stones. Dick Rowe, the man who would be pilloried for the rest of his life for turning down The Beatles, was now terrified to reject any aspiring Brit beat group and Andrew convinced him his career would end right there and then if he didn't sign the Rolling Stones. He teased out the poor guy's paranoia until his pen hit the paper.

In those days, you were supposed to believe there was intense competition between The Beatles and the Stones, enmity even. In the school playground, you had to choose, either or. You weren't allowed to like both. It was like the old mod or rocker game: Lambretta or BSA, parka or leather?

The reality was the opposite. Lennon recalled in *Rolling Stone*:

That was a great period. We were like kings of the jungle. I spent a lot of time with Brian Jones and Mick Jagger . . . we were in our prime. We created something there . . . we didn't know what we were doing, but we were all talking, blabbing over coffee, like they must have done in Paris . . . me, Eric Burdon and Brian Jones would be up night and day talking about music, playing records, arguing and getting drunk. It's beautiful history.

The Beatles had been to see the Stones. George Harrison had even told Decca to sign them. And the Stones? Well, the Stones worshipped The Beatles, particularly when the Fab Four gave them the hit they so badly needed. The way Oldham remembers it, the band had been trying to write something – anything – in their Tin Pan Alley studio. They had run into a wall and Oldham had taken himself for a walk when who should he see but two of the Fab Four.

'The two beams of light and ale emerged from a taxi in front of Leicester Square Tube station. They were a slightly wobbly John Lennon and possibly slightly tipsy Paul McCartney . . . I hurried in their direction, little thinking that this chance meeting would be yet another signpost to the top of the pops . . . I told them I had nothing to record for the Stones' next single. They smiled at me and at each other, told me not to worry and our three pairs of Cuban heels turned smartly back towards the basement rehearsal . . . Once downstairs, the boys quickly got to work teaching the Stones 'I Wanna Be Your Man'. Yeah, they gave us a hit, which was certainly my oxygen, but more than that they gave us a real tutorial in the reality they were forging for themselves: lesson of the day from John and Paul. I went from downed to reprieved to exalted as the two Beatles ran through their gift for the open-mouthed Stones.'

In and out: Oldham left with John and Paul. Can you imagine how the Stones felt about Andrew at that moment? There they were, in a threadbare studio, songless and witless. Out pops Andrew, who pops back in again only minutes later with the two most famous pop writers the world had to offer. And not only that, he'd persuaded them to let you have a song they didn't need right now. 'Here you go. Play around with that. We're off.' He'd delivered up two gods and then off he went with them just like he was one of them.

Lennon recalled it slightly differently, but with no less significance for the Stones, when he spoke to *Playboy* magazine in 1980:

Paul and I finished that one off for the Stones. We were taken down by Brian to meet them at the club where they were playing in Richmond. They wanted a song and we went to see what kind of stuff they did. Paul had this bit of a song and we played it roughly for them and they said, 'Yeah, OK, that's our style.' But it was only really a lick, so Paul and I went off in the corner of the room and finished the song off while they were all sitting there, talking. We came back and Mick and Keith said, 'Jesus, look at that. They just went over there and wrote it.' You know, right in front of their eyes. We gave it to them. It was a throwaway. Ringo sang it for us and the Stones did their version. It shows how much importance we put on them. We weren't going to give them anything great, right? That was the Stones' first record. Anyway,

Mick and Keith said, 'If they can write a song so easily, we should try it.' They say it inspired them to start writing together.

The Stones' version of 'I Wanna Be Your Man' reached a respectable number 12 and the band turned to bite the hand that had so effortlessly fed them: the Stones' first album was to knock The Beatles' album off the top of the chart and take up residence there for three months.

But The Beatles ran like a river through the '60s. Every youth cultural event in town happened either with them or somehow because of them, and Andrew knew you couldn't take your eyes off them for a moment. When they made the *Hard Day's Night* movie, he was hard on their Cuban heels and became obsessed with making a Stones film. Not for him a jovial day on the road with Wilfred Bramble and the band, though. Andrew had, for some time, been trying to acquire the rights to *A Clockwork Orange*. Loog and the droogs. Mick was to be Alex; the Stones were to be the droogs. In the event, the rights stayed just out of his reach.

> I wouldn't have said any of the Stones as individuals were particularly interesting to talk to whereas Andrew was. He was a major creative force in image and music making . . . Oldham, without doubt, was the most flash personality that British pop has ever had, the most anarchic and obsessive and imaginative hustler of all
>
> Nik Cohn, *Awopbopaloobop Alopbamboom*

There was a good deal of respect from at least one Beatle for Andrew. John Lennon observed his own manager making rotten record deals, genuflecting to old-guard booking agents, like Bernard Delfont and his brother Lew Grade, and generally being sniffy about what he considered to be cheap publicity stunts. Epstein said in *A Cellarful of Noise*, 'I never pulled one stunt to publicise any of my artists.'

Lennon looked wistfully at Loog Oldham – the man who no

longer knocked on doors so much as kicked them down, the man often credited with creating hype and a man The Who's manager Chris Stamp described admiringly as 'a tea leaf gangster'.

Andrew had learned from Spector and his other American friends that, instead of getting a record contract, the smart new thing to do was to get a tape-lease deal. Instead of the record company arranging recording sessions and employing a producer, an independent producer (him) would record the band and then present the record company with finished tapes, thus earning roughly twice what ordinary artists earned.

It was a revolutionary tactic in stuffy old England, where even George Martin was a mere wage slave. Only Mickie Most and a couple of others had the clout and the nous to pull off a tape-lease deal, but surely the old-style record executives would never consider such a thing. Or would they? Andrew bulldozed it through on sheer chutzpah, cheek and charm, and as a consequence the Stones were to make more money per record than The Beatles did for many years.

Ironically, Oldham's own deal with his partner was a shambolic affair and effectively permitted Easton to row him out of the big money for a considerable time. Crafty Easton had signed the band's publishing to a company he had a half-share in, so he was getting even more of a slice of the songwriting than the writers. Oldham allowed himself to be fobbed off; he was naive and wound up in the day-to-day blur of the band – a band of which he thought he was one.

And for a good while, he was certainly part of the inner core. It was an electric relationship. Mick, Andrew and Keith Richards sparkling, working, socialising and living together, although sadly the shift of power was to have the effect of isolating Brian Jones and to set in motion the train of events which would lead to his death. But these were the good times and there was a lot of success. Oldham had made his mark on the Stones. He'd taken them from the back room of a pub to the top of the charts. The record company was now crying out for anything touched by the hand of Jagger, Richards and Oldham. Andrew is credited as producer on some of the Stones' finest material – the anthems he'd so desired, including 'Satisfaction', 'The Last Time', 'Under My Thumb', 'Get Off of My Cloud', 'Lady Jane', 'Play with Fire', 'Out of Time', 'Mother's Little Helper', 'Nineteenth Nervous Breakdown' and 'Paint it Black'.

Spurred on by this succession of triumphs, he was cocky enough to think he could duplicate it and started shopping for other talent over which he could wave his magic wand.

He bumped into one such talent at a party. Marianne Faithfull was an ex-convent girl and a descendant of the Sacher-Masochs, Austro-Hungarian aristocrats. Great Uncle Leopold had written *Venus im Pelz* (Venus in Furs), which not only inspired the Velvet Underground to write the eponymous track but was also the origin of the expression 'masochism'.

'She had this fantastic virginal look,' Andrew was to say. 'At a time when most chicks were shaking ass and coming on strong, here was this pale, blonde, retiring, chaste teenager looking like a Mona Lisa, except with a great body.'

Andrew went into overdrive. He badly wanted this girl, whom he later called 'a siren slut from the top drawer'. Standing with his back to Marianne, he interrogated her then boyfriend, John Dunbar. 'Who is she? Can she act? What's her name?' He'd handed Dunbar a flashy business card and identified himself. 'I'm Andrew Loog Oldham, darling.' In her autobiography, *In My Life*, Faithfull commented, 'He called everyone "darling", especially men – it made them nervous and that gave Andrew an edge. Andrew was all edge; he exuded menace, shock, razor-blade hipness . . . Andrew would say things you only hear in films, like: "I can make you a star, and that's just for starters, baby."'

Only Oldham could get away with that sort of corny shtick – doing a pull routine right in front of her boyfriend's eyes while wearing mascara around his own. A week later, he had her in the studio and produced 'As Tears Go By', a Jagger/Richards/Oldham mini-masterpiece, which he'd inspired by asking the Stones to come up with something that would conjure up 'brick walls, high windows and no sex'. In the car afterwards, Mick tried to get her to sit on his lap.

Kim Fowley, who either recorded with or composed for everyone from John Lennon to Nirvana, recalls Oldham wheeling Marianne around a launch party. 'Andrew controlled the room with her . . . [He] was a great hustler. He was old school Broadway–Beverly Hills. He had his "I'll kill you, I'll charm you, I'll leave you for dead" act.'

'As Tears Go By' made the top ten in the UK and top 20 in the USA. *Billboard* magazine called her 'the greatest discovery of the year'.

Today, there is apparently ongoing affection between Marianne and Oldham, the two old '60s warhorses, but it seems there was a good deal less sentimentality back in the day. Marianne recalls Oldham's reaction to the news that she had overdosed and gone into a coma in Australia: 'Within days of my overdose, Andrew Oldham had issued a greatest hits album of my records, the cover framed with a black border and the title in Gothic letters.'

Andrew then began using the name The Andrew Oldham Orchestra and recorded four albums: *16 Hip Hits*, featuring Mick Jagger, John Paul Jones and Jimmy Page (later to play with Led Zeppelin); *East Meets West*, a tribute to The Beach Boys and the Four Seasons; *Lionel Bart's Maggie May*, an orchestral homage to the composer's stage show of the same name (all in 1964); and *The Rolling Stones Songbook* in 1966, from which the track of Andrew's arrangement of 'The Last Time' was used without permission by The Verve in their 1997 hit 'Bittersweet Symphony'.

This was to cause a 'bitter' and not so 'sweet' dispute between The Verve, Andrew and Allen Klein, who continues to manage the use of the early material. The single 'Bittersweet Symphony' sold a million copies and the riff from The Andrew Oldham Orchestra track, as modified by The Verve, was used in advertising campaigns by Vauxhall Motors and Nike.

Klein sued on behalf of Andrew, Jagger and Richards, and an

agreement was reached whereby Jagger and Richards were entitled to royalties on the Verve track and Klein would collect them. Loog Oldham is now credited as the track's producer, with The Verve's Richard Ashcroft as lyricist.

In late 1964, Oldham demonstrated to all perhaps his greatest strength when the Stones were umming and ahhing over which track to release as a single. He thought 'Little Red Rooster' was the best of the material to hand. His soon-to-be partner in Immediate Records, Tony Calder, who was helping out with the Stones press, thought he'd lost his mind: 'The only person who wanted to put it out was Andrew,' he said. 'What he wanted was a record that he could claim was a piece of art and wasn't an out-and-out attempt at further commercial success. I was against it. I said, "This'll never be a fucking hit; this'll kill them." He said, "No, you don't understand how big they are. This is where we can manipulate the charts and have a career record." We boosted the pre-orders, got a lot of the fans who bought for us in the chart shops ordering before the fucker came out. It came out and went straight into the charts at number 1. I'd just thought it was the greatest mistake ever – you couldn't dance to it, Decca hated it and Eric Easton thought Andrew was nuts. It made the Stones. That they were able to take a blues thing to number 1 took the game to a whole new level. Andrew was able to show the business the band's popularity and translate it into record success. I was staggered. I hated the record.'

OK, there had been a little chart rigging along the way, but every label in London was giving its acts a leg-up in a similar fashion. It's a bit like sport: if all the athletes are on drugs, then it's a level playing field.

The Rolling Stones/Andrew Loog Oldham partnership had a tremendous run, but eventually, inevitably, things got a little frayed. Oldham and Mick – so close that on one occasion Oldham's mother had found them in bed together, sleeping soundly after a night out – began to pull apart. Brian Jones became a liability to the band, as his drug use reached industrial levels. He was often hospitalised and even slept through recording sessions. Andrew wanted rid of him, but it didn't stop him joining the decadent Jones in an orgy in a hotel bedroom. Perks of the manager's job.

He had certainly been ruthless in his aim to shape the perfect band. He'd already been instrumental in the sidelining of the 'sixth Stone', Ian Stewart, whose chunky features, he considered, didn't fit in with the Stones' image. Stewart harboured a grudge ever after, once saying, 'Andrew Oldham? I wouldn't piss on him if he was on fire.'

Then his marriage started going off and on. Black depressions plagued him. Oldham let his composure slip when, rotten drunk, he had taken out a gun in a Chicago hotel and demanded to be let into Mick and Keith's room. Drummer Charlie Watts was summoned; he knocked Andrew out and chucked him in his bed to sleep it off.

Keith and Andrew talked up their mutual 'gun love' thing, then went to Dublin to buy a couple and recklessly returned wearing them in shoulder holsters on the plane.

Violence held a charge for Loog Oldham. He became obsessed with *A Clockwork Orange*. Andrew thought he was Alex – a better Alex than Jagger anyway. He had other alter egos. He claims in his book that the psycho-gangster Chas in *Performance*, played by James Fox, is based on him.

David Bailey recalls in *Stoned* going to a restaurant with Andrew before doing a photo shoot for the Stones. 'Some guy started wolf whistling at us. I think he thought we were a couple of gay guys. Andrew went over and stuck his heel in the guy's foot while he was sitting down. Then he grabbed him by the tie and shoved his face down into the food – real fast. All the guy's mates, the whole table, backed off. Andrew was slight but fast.'

Michael Lindsay-Hogg, the *Ready, Steady, Go!* director, felt the same vibe and observed, 'I wonder to what degree Andrew's gangster pose and his bravado (you fuck with me at your peril) influenced Mick and Keith as they developed their stage characters, which would then morph with their real selves and vice versa . . . Not a little.'

Andrew finally met his hero, Laurence Harvey, who played the sage for his young celebrity fan: 'Your lads are turning from boys into men, they're leaving home and there's nothing you'll be able to do about it. It's the nature of the beast. The artist has to rise and shine and dismiss his maker – it's as true as Adam and Eve.'

Andrew washed his hands and sealed his fate. Uber-manager Allen Klein, who was to have such a devastating effect on The Beatles, was brought in by Andrew to get rid of Eric Easton and extract some more money from the record companies. Klein, known as the 'Robin Hood of Pop', was as good as his nickname and screwed Decca for higher royalties. While he was there, he grabbed the Stones their £2.8 million advance.

It looked like things were on the up for the band, and for Oldham too, but Jagger had other ideas – and they weren't copies of Andrew's any more.

The band encountered only delirium at gigs now and every record was a guaranteed smash, so some of the sparkle left Andrew's role. Jagger and Richards began to dominate the production of the songs and had rounded their own compound personas. Now, they were steering the ship and Andrew was walking the plank. As he hit the water, he clutched only his bottles – the pills and the booze.

Veteran music writer Nik Cohn observed Oldham's rise and fall: 'Andrew was the genuine young meteor in terms of the impact he made and then in how quickly that peak was passed,' he said. 'But there was something genuinely meteoric about him, there was this thing about him, a vividness. Andrew wasn't off or on stage, he was all the time, that is what made him unique.'

Oldham's wife Sheila observed, 'Andrew was cracking up. He had a lot of drugs prescribed for him and I think he chose the wrong doctors, who gave him the wrong drugs, mainly tranquillisers and painkillers. Andrew hurt so much. He was losing control and it frightened him.'

Photographer Gered Mankowitz described the final night: 'To

my surprise, there was an evening where Mick and Michael Cooper, who was becoming increasingly a part of the Stones' camp, came in and told Andrew in the recording studio what they were going to do for the *Satanic Majesties* cover. This was a *coup d'état*. It was the first time Andrew hadn't been involved in an image-making aspect of the Rolling Stones' career. The recording sessions were pretty ghastly – they were falling apart and they were beginning to move into an entirely different world.'

Oldham walked out of the studio and into the vortex. He phoned from the car to offer his farewell to his erstwhile merry prankster friend-turned-nemesis.

'So that's it, then?' said Mick.

'Yep, that's it, Mick.'

'OK, Andrew, goodnight.'

'Goodbye, Mick, have a good life.'

For Andrew and the Stones, things were really over by 1967. Loog Oldham was 23.

The innocent days of pop were over, too. The Stones were busted for drugs at Keith's house, Redlands, and even the best lawyers thought that they might go inside. While on bail, they did a European tour. In terms of seats sold, it was a wild success, but the mood was ugly. At several venues, crowds had been broken up with baton charges and tear gas.

The Beatles had stopped touring altogether. The USA stank of the canker of the Vietnam War. The drugs had taken a grip: they didn't add to the vibe, they were the vibe. There was Charles Manson. It wasn't so much the day the music died as the day it shook off its innocence and reached its majority. The Stones became street-fighting men.

His once impeccable sense of timing had deserted him and Andrew was suddenly out of time. He rose into a rage and then he sank into manic depression, checking into a nursing home in Highbury staffed by sympathetic nuns. It had been his regular detox bolthole.

Sheila Oldham knew how her husband felt more than most: 'I

don't think any one of them ever turned around and said, "Thanks, Andrew, for what you did." It was excruciating for Andrew, the feeling how was he going to go on from that point, because of the drug thing getting in the way and not knowing how to deal with the bust . . . [When Jagger and Richard were arrested at Redlands, Andrew went into a panic, thinking he would be next on the arrest list, and split to America, leaving Allen Klein to clear up the mess.] I think Andrew in some interview said he lost his bottle. He was devastated by the whole thing, and I don't think he's recovered.'

There was still Immediate Records, though (and the reported £1 million he got from Klein for signing away the Stones' management), and for a short while the label may have served to forestall Andrew's eventual descent into smack-drenched oblivion.

'Happy to be a Part of the Industry of Human Happiness' was the slogan of the Immediate label Andrew set up in 1965 with another ex-Beatles publicist, Tony Calder. It was to be the first-ever major British independent label and, for many, it was a Swinging '60s icon in much the same way as Tony Wilson's Factory Records was in the mid-'80s. Immediate cemented Andrew's status as a Great British music business legend. He signed the Small Faces and later Humble Pie, The Nice, P.P. Arnold, Amen Corner and Chris Farlowe. Jimmy Page was resident session player.

The first release, 'Hang on Sloopy' by The McCoys, made it into the top ten. Chris Farlowe's version of 'Out of Time' by the Stones reached the top slot. When Andrew paid Don Arden for the Small Faces, he was rewarded with a small string of hits: 'Here Comes the Nice', 'Itchycoo Park', 'Tin Soldier' and 'The Universal'. The album *Ogdens' Nut Gone Flake* is widely regarded as their finest hour.

Other magic Immediate moments include P.P. Arnold's 'Angel of the Morning' and Fleetwood Mac's 'Man of the World'.

However, Andrew was flaking up and there were money problems. He was acquiring songs from the US that had already been hits and he was paying too much for them. The Small Faces had been allowed virtually unlimited studio time and their recording costs had mounted up. The band was suffering 'musical differences' and broke up in 1968. Steve Marriott formed Humble Pie and Immediate had a hit with 'Natural Born Boogie', but by then the label was going down the pipes. Andrew stayed in contact with Marriott right up to Steve's sad death, despite keyboard player Ian McLagan's antipathy. Band member Ronnie Lane continued to say that Andrew was the best manager they'd ever had.

But the label was in crisis and so was Andrew. If he'd been on full beam, he might have averted disaster, but his lights were dimming and even electro-shock therapy couldn't jump-start his fused, frazzled brain. The plug was eventually pulled in 1970.

Andrew's Immediate Records legacy (along with that of Chris Blackwell's Island Records) provided the inspiration for a whole new swathe of entrepreneurs to come along and have a crack at running their own record label themselves. He'd blazed a trail for the likes of Charisma, Chrysalis and Creation along the way. But for Andrew many acts that would never have got past the A&R wastepaper bin saw the light of day. On a personal level, he'd done it again, achieved massive success in double-quick time only to crash and burn even faster . . . and he was still only 25.

The light that burns twice as bright burns only half as long.

That he went off the rails implies that he was ever really on them. And the pioneering Andrew was to lead the way yet again as he embarked on a downhill race – the archetypal rock-star spiral into drink, addictions and a particular kind of madness that drove him into experimental medical treatments and three years of electro-shock therapy.

He managed to produce an album for Donovan in the early '70s and one for Humble Pie in 1975 before moving to New York. There, he had another crack at band management with an outfit called the Werewolves, but nothing clicked and he was basically living on advances from Allen Klein's office. These were apparently desperate times for Andrew – years and years on the skids, lost in cocaine psychosis, blown up by booze, keeping no one busy but the Manhattan dealers. All that mad energy was funnelled into the relentless pursuit of drugs – finding them, financing them, finishing them off, then finding some more . . . Anyone seeing the grizzled old junkie in those dark days would have been hard pushed to discern within a man who had once been one of pop's brightest Svengalis. Nik Cohn got it in one: 'In career terms, Andrew made a big mistake by not dying.'

He gave it his best shot, though.

Strangely, along the way he recovered consciousness long enough to bang out a book about Abba, with one eye on the cash and the other on a perfect pop product. He wrote it with his old mate Tony Calder, who had by now married Oldham's ex-wife.

But change had to come. He weaned himself off the Colombian marching powder and then went to settle in Colombia, which is a bit like a wino going into the off-licence business. However, his new wife, a Colombian film star, seemed like good medicine for him, and Andrew knows a bit about medicines.

He admits and then denies that he originally went to Colombia to take advantage of bargain-basement cocaine supplies, but now it's Perrier, early nights to bed and stay-clean pills only.

And he has had a good cause to energise himself. Thousands of Bogotá street kids are frequently the victims of vigilante death squads, who regard them as litter and dispatch them with brutal frequency. Along with an ex-BBC correspondent, Andrew has been attempting to halt the slaughter and give the kids a break in life, at not inconsiderable personal risk. He apparently shovels money into Fundación Renacer, the charity on the ground there.

On the way to his clean regime, he has experimented with the whole panoply of therapies and healers, philosophies and gurus, including a spell of Christian Science courtesy of L. Ron Hubbard.

His autobiographies *Stoned* and *2Stoned* have also provided succour. Andrew started *Stoned* in 1995, when he finally decided to clean up and not die a drug-related death. He'd flushed away the cocaine and replaced the booze with bottled water, then opened the laptop and moved his cursor to 'File – New Document . . .' He now describes himself as a survivalist and a writer, and is soon to release a third book entitled *On Hustling*, though at one time its working title was *Pimpresario*. The book apparently covers notable hustlers in history such as Russian ballet promoter Sergei Diaghilev, movie producer Michael Todd, director Otto Preminger, Malcolm McLaren and Bob Dylan's manager, Albert Grossman. If it's anything like the other two, we're in for a treat.

Recently, he took up residence in Vancouver, where he does speaking engagements and DJ's for Sirius Channel 25. 'I'm fulfilling my American fantasy. I'm Johnny Carson,' said the 61 year old. The playlist even includes the Stones. 'Nothing slow,' he said in a recent interview. 'Basically, it's British, it's New York punk, it's thrash, it's Stones, it's R&B and new stuff.'

He recruited Marlon Richards, the son of Rolling Stones guitarist Keith Richards, to interview two subjects: label boss Alan McGee and former Smiths guitarist Johnny Marr. He also visited Charlie Watts and Keith Richards when the band performed in Seattle, but as yet he and Jagger haven't spoken since they parted in 1967.

In 2002, Andrew was in court, asking that the Immediate catalogue be returned to him and demanding that Charly Records and Castle do the decent thing over years of unpaid royalties to him and the label's artists.

He'd made the costly mistake of claiming that he owned certain rights to some of the label's catalogue and that he intended to release some of the material, which presumably meant that he'd got some master tapes stashed somewhere. Again, the forces of the establishment rose to beat on a Stone, even if it was a once-removed Stone. High Court judge Mr Justice Pumfrey said, 'Some play has been made of the fact that from 1967 or so until comparatively recently he was frequently drunk or drugged. Indeed, Mr Oldham attributes any inconsistency between the indisputable record and his recollection to his mental state.'

Whether the learned judge really felt that Oldham was completely out of order or was merely punishing him for having the temerity to go AWOL for 25-odd years is unknown. His day in court cost him £470,000 in legal bills and his assets were frozen while he figured out how to pay.

However, you can't keep a good legend down, and Philip Norman, author of *The Stones* and *Shout!*, rightly reckons that Loog Oldham's legacy endures: 'There's still this edge about the Stones, which is amazing now they're all doddery old freaks – they still manage to be outrageous. The funny thing is they're still reading the script [Andrew] wrote . . . not only are they reading the script he wrote but every group that comes along is reading the same script. Every other group that comes along, at any press conference, sprawling on the couch, being a mixture of charming and rude, that's Andrew's script.'

The Stones, of course, plough on into the uncharted waters of old age rock.

'Nobody told these young bucks at 20 that at over 50 their ambition may become an embarrassing disease,' commented Andrew, who has recently referred to Jagger as 'like a first wife'. When he was asked by an interviewer, 'Are you amazed, surprised, delighted that the Stones have lasted this long?', he beautifully bitched on, 'I wasn't aware that they had lasted this long.'

Classic Andrew.

4
KIT LAMBERT

The Who

Behind every band is some sort of mentor figure, some Svengali. This is the thing that can't be provided without love, care and full-time attention.

– *Pete Townshend*

The words 'tortured genius' might have been devised solely to describe Kit Lambert. His descent into madness and death came at the end of a short and fiery life. He was just 45 years old – the same age at which his father, Constant, had similarly destroyed himself with drink, although Kit made sure by finishing off the job with a cartload of heroin.

Kit's state of mind was made more than apparent when he described spending Christmas Eve in the Speakeasy just prior to his death. He was alternately firing his pistol into the roof and knocking back champagne cocktails while, on his orders, waiters carried interesting, if comatose, revellers to his limousine. The writing was on the wall as surely as there were bullet holes in the ceiling.

His mother knew what was coming when Kit visited her while

she was making mince pies and she watched him wander around the kitchen shivering and talking madly before making a grab for the mincemeat filling and patting it all over his face.

Yet, along his mad way, Lambert turned The Who into one of the biggest bands in the world, was the catalyst to the creation of the rock opera *Tommy* and founded one of the first truly independent record companies – facts that can be easily overshadowed by his lunacy.

Established Who mythology suggests that Keith Moon was the crazy one, and although it was definitely two-way trade, it's very likely that a good deal of the madness came from Kit Lambert. Establishing, however, just how much each got from the other isn't easy.

Kit, in his turn, had had it passed down to him. The brilliance, the gargantuan appetite for brandy, the 'passion for dark and smoky clubs', the 'eventual madness': it all came from his father. So your mum and dad do indeed fuck you up. But Constant Lambert's defence could be Philip Larkin's rejoinder: 'But they were fucked up in their turn.' Certainly, Kit Lambert's life was set on its doomed trajectory by rejection from his father; and back along the generations, so was Constant's.

The Lambert dynasty – grandfather George, an ostentatious, unfulfilled artist; father Constant, a brooding composer and founder of the Sadler's Wells Ballet; and Kit, the last link in the familial chain, a decadent rock and roll manager – are described by Poet Laureate Andrew Motion in his book, *The Lamberts*, as 'a gifted, controversial and self-destructive trio whose extraordinary lives span and define a century of artistic achievement'.

While we haven't been concerned with the lives of the parents and grandparents of any of the other subjects of this book, in the case of Kit it is interesting to look at his predecessors as a way of understanding how he became what he did and because, courtesy of Motion's fascinating account, we can.

In so far as the Lamberts come from anywhere, they stem from Halifax in Yorkshire, but Kit's great-grandfather, a railway engineer, had lived and worked in Baltimore in the USA (he fought in the American Civil War as a cavalry officer) and St Petersburg in Russia. When he died, the family, including George, went to live in a castle in Germany, then moved to Yeovil in Somerset before settling on a sheep station in New South Wales, Australia. Young George, a sickly youth, grew strong, learned horsemanship and started painting pictures.

Later moving to Sydney, he was drawn to the notable Australian artists of the time and, according to Motion, 'grew his hair longer, began smoking cigarettes' and 'took to wearing a cravat and a cloak'. Despite these impediments, he met and married a striking girl called Amy and two days later took her on a ship bound for Britain and the fame and fortune he so desired.

The family lived hand-to-mouth. George joined the Chelsea Arts Club, epicentre of London's bohemian boozy arts community, and would, when able, buy rounds of drinks and regale other drinkers with tales of the outback. He struck an exotic pose with his moustache and cape. Motion's book recounts how he established himself as a 'character': 'On one occasion – to prove his masculinity – he boxed Augustus John in the street outside the Arts Club, and knocked him down; on another, when visiting a riding school to do some studies . . . he mounted, palette in hand, a particularly violent horse and proudly subdued it, smearing paint over its neck in the process; on a third, he stayed up all night to paint a white rat he had bought on Chelsea Bridge, then took it to the Arts Club where it lived as a Club pet.'

The rodent met its maker when an unobservant member sat on it.

So far so agreeably eccentric, but the theory is that George's flamboyance disguised paralysing shyness and a set of jangling nerves. There may also have been some sexual tension since, as time passed, he became less interested in his wife and may have had a long-term relationship with a statuesque model called Thea, who virtually moved into their home.

Yet, while dressing in the manner of a camp theatrical (one

account has him 'in frock coat, gardenia buttonhole, top hat, spats and yellow gloves'), George was always anxious to prove he was man, all man. When the First World War broke out, he tried to join first the British Army, then the Australian, but was rejected from both because he was too old.

In the meantime, his ten-year-old son, Constant, became ill with a potentially fatal strain of septicaemia and had to endure a number of operations. George feigned fatherly concern, but when he was approached to be a war artist for the Australian Army, he leapt at the chance and dashed off for Palestine. The work suited him, and his output was prolific, but keeping the company of Australians ignited a desire to return there. He made plans to go back – plans that didn't include his wife and children. On and off, George was away from his family for the next 13 years and Constant never saw his father again.

A clean break would have been bad enough, but George immediately went into a period of self-recrimination, writing many affectionate letters to his far-off wife and beseeching her for information about his sons. That he was shortly joined in Sydney by Thea surely confirms his selfishness and deceit, but George always claimed it wasn't planned.

Lambert started to make money in Australia, where he was a revered war artist. He had assistants – he even had a minder – and took up determined drinking. On one occasion, he sank a lot of whisky – he said to ward off a bout of malaria – and experienced hallucinations, complaining that there were spiders crawling all over him.

He was also an unbridled show-off. Motion's book tells the story of how George had been riding in the park with a 'pretty society woman' when his horse stumbled and threw him to the ground: 'He quickly remounted, cantered on a few hundred yards, and then deliberately fell off a second time. This second fall, he told his companion, had been to illustrate the correct way to hit the ground; the first fall was the wrong way. Both falls, he insisted, were intentional.'

George kept up the horse riding even when he became ill. Indeed, it was whilst attempting to tether his horse that he collapsed and died, immaculately dressed in his riding outfit face down in a filthy farmyard.

Lambert, the artist, remains relatively unknown in the wider art world but is still celebrated in Australia, where his work is compared with that of Stanley Spencer. What is plain is that the passion he fed into his work, he starved from his family.

It was Constant's misfortune in 1905 to be born a boy when his mother would have preferred a girl. He was named after one of the family's female friends and dressed in feminine clothes, while his golden hair was allowed to grow long. It doesn't take a professional psychologist to figure out how this might have affected him in later life.

At the age of 12, Constant contracted osteomyelitis, for which, over time, he was required to have 18 operations and take plentiful painkillers. He was prescribed morphine and at other times was quietened with a mixture of champagne and burgundy. When he started to drink for non-medicinal reasons as an adult, he'd screw up his face when he took a mouthful of alcohol, as if he associated it with his illnesses. At school, he wore a blue coat with gold buttons and a white cravat, and slicked down his long hair.

An accomplished pianist, Constant went on to study at the Royal College of Music, where his professors included Adrian Boult, Malcolm Sargent and Ralph Vaughan Williams. At the time, he was described by Edwin Lutyens' daughter, Elizabeth, as 'very beautiful, very thin, rather disdainful and arrogant'.

Moving in these exulted circles, with his quick wit and fine looks, Constant was soon attracting a lot of attention and became what Motion calls 'a fast-talking, cigarette-smoking, outspoken, job lot Apollo'.

His compositional talent, coloured as it was with jazz influences, led to a commission from Sergei Diaghilev to write a ballet – *Romeo and Juliet* – for the Ballets Russes. Constant was aged only 21. It was the Roaring '20s and he very much looked part of that decade in a moody photograph of the time, wearing a black shirt and a pale tie.

The sets and costumes for *Romeo and Juliet* were designed by a young British artist, Christopher (Kit) Wood, who was sufficiently talented to engender plaudits from Jean Cocteau and a personal recommendation from Pablo Picasso himself. Wood was a homosexual drug fiend and undoubtedly influenced Constant, who had been until then only a moderate boozer. Wood committed suicide five years on, but the damage was done as far as Lambert II was concerned. He loved drinking because it disguised his shyness and allowed him to engage with other bohemians who inhabited the bars of London's Fitzrovia, but by the late '30s he was consuming pints of beer with whisky chasers at lunchtime, and a bottle of wine and most of a bottle of brandy later in the day.

Constant would take off on drinking and whoring trips to Toulon in France, sometimes taking with him Laureen Sylvestre, a black girl who sold cigarettes in a West Indian Soho jazz bar called The Nest. Despite this, he was pretty obviously a latent homosexual, although he nevertheless came across a fourteen-year-old girl, Flo, in the East End, married her two years later and went to live in a flat loaned to them by the actor Charles Laughton.

Fortuitously, he was offered the job of conductor and musical director of the newly formed Sadler's Wells Ballet, in partnership with Frederick Ashton. This was a golden period for Kit's father, who now had an income and an outlet for his talents. Financial and professional pressures lifted and he revealed a playful nature. A friend recalls an occasion when she was living in the country in a windmill with her husband and received a surprise guest. 'The door handle banged,' she said, 'and although I don't know how he got there at that time of night, I wasn't surprised to hear Constant's voice. He had been to a wedding reception, then taken a negress to a swimming bath and felt a proper conclusion would be to sleep in a windmill.'

Kit was born in 1935 and named Christopher after the doomed artist Christopher Wood. Perhaps the moniker set the seal on him from day one. Constant, in much the same way as his own father, almost immediately lost interest in the family life he said he had so desired. He similarly feigned regret for his coldness towards his wife and child later. He found fault in his young wife – Flo's lack of education had become annoying and she got drunk too easily when they went out together – while the young Kit was too demanding of his time and always interrupting.

In fact, another child had distracted Constant: the 15-year-old Margot Fonteyn, who had just joined the ballet company. The conductor conducted an affair with Fonteyn and rowed with Flo, who threw her wedding ring into a lake. His response, as ever, was to hit the bottle, and then he divorced her. Her circumstances reduced, she frequently farmed Kit out to relatives and friends. In the words of Frederick Ashton, Constant's drink dependency reached such a level that 'If rehearsals were overrunning, he'd rush the music if the pubs were open.'

One pub in particular, the George near Oxford Circus, was frequented by BBC employees. Here Constant would knock around with Dylan Thomas, once dancing round the bar with him. A friend recalls: 'One would see Constant, *The Times* under his arm, standing, one hand on the bar rail, the other on his ivory-handled stick. Often he was obviously fighting out some mental Don Quixote battle with the Philistines . . . At other times, he would be shaking with inner laughter.'

It's said that one morning Kit greeted his father with, 'Hello, pompous,' a comment that threw Constant into a turmoil: it seems that, despite the dandyism and mannerisms of both his father and himself, they both despised pomposity, especially in their work.

Constant's appearance had markedly deteriorated by now; his face was puffed up and his clothes covered in cigarette ash. He'd started falling over in the streets and toppling unconscious from his bar stool. He was obviously profoundly unhappy even before his relationship with Fonteyn broke up, although he returned to form when a new girl appeared.

Isabel Delmer was an exotic figure who had been living in Paris, hanging out with a set that included Alberto Giacometti, Joán Miró and Jacob Epstein. She and Constant set up home together and, temporarily happy, he straightened himself out. Isabel was introduced to Kit, who was still being shoved from mother to grandmother to friends. She recalled that Kit was 'a very strange boy'.

This period of Constant's sobriety was to be but brief. When he was offered a season at the Metropolitan Opera House in New York, he had to promise the chary promoters that he had taken the pledge. But after a triumphant and sober opening night, he hit the sauce in style and one night actually passed out midway through conducting *Hamlet*.

His friends discreetly suggested that now might be the time to drop out of the public gaze, and that maybe he should take up composing in preference to public performance. Allowing himself to be talked into it, he went to Paris to write.

Kit sometimes asked to visit his father, but Constant denied him, saying, 'Our whole ambiance there is far too sophisticated.' Kit had been rejected by the father he revered yet again and it seems he took it very badly.

In turn, the critics rejected Constant's new composition and he once more sought solace in the bottle. At one party, to which he had taken his sometime girlfriend Laureen Sylvestre, he sat stupidly drunk and unable to react when an abusive guest spat in his face for bringing a black girl along.

Constant now struck a sad figure. Bloated with drink, he'd started rambling and losing his memory; he experienced terrible hallucinations under the effects of the DTs and had threatened to jump out of the window. He'd had to be restrained and sedated. Two days before his 46th birthday, he died. He had been suffering from diabetes and his doctors had failed to spot it.

Flo, the wife he'd abandoned, remained bewitched to the end. Thirty years after his death, she said of her husband: 'Every word he said lifted you up.'

When Constant had left Flo, she'd attempted to find work as a model and had also taken up dancing lessons. Both things took her away from her young son, who, neglected by his father and his mother, was raised by his gran and aunts – all women. Later, Kit would say, 'No wonder my life has been a disaster. Look at the cards I was dealt; look at my parents.'

At boarding school, Kit exhibited classic nerd tendencies: he didn't enjoy games; he was clever but not keen on lessons, preferring instead stamp and butterfly collecting. On a rare occasion when Constant invited Kit to a concert, the bored boy was heard to remark prophetically, 'Daddy – I like music that is short and loud and drinks that are long and fizzy.'

At a new school, Lancing College, where Evelyn Waugh had been an old boy, Kit began to emerge from his shell. He enlisted in the choir and started to put his name up for parts in school plays. Ever cash-hungry, he even felt bold enough to lift some money from a fellow pupil but was caught and forced to repay it.

Kit was showing signs of great intelligence, although his work was scrappy. A report says:

He has the prospect of a brilliant career if he will support his ability with the necessary school discipline, and the alternative, if he will not, of leaving before he achieves the disappointment of not getting anywhere near where he ought.

He was, in turn, saddened by his father's disregard but thrilled by his celebrity. Motion states: 'The rootlessness, the huge enthusiasm to initiate projects and the withering boredom which accompanied their completion, and the deliberate abuse of himself and his talent, were to be written even larger in the son than they were in the father.'

Homosexual desires stirred within him, fanned by the universal high regard for old boy Evelyn Waugh's *Brideshead Revisited* that permeated the school. Kit started dreaming of the 'dreaming spires' of Oxford but would be forced to do national service beforehand. In the army, he managed to wangle a spell in Hong Kong, where he befriended another conscript, Robert Fearnley-Whittingstall, father of the TV chef, who was also bound for Trinity College, Oxford. On his return to the UK, he took on part-time jobs somewhat surprisingly as a mechanic and then a milkman before going up to Oxford and reuniting with Fearnley-Whittingstall. On his first night there, he invited everyone he could think of to a drinks party. Fearnley-Whittingstall said, 'He was a great snob and a good user of contacts.'

Another new friend was Daria Chorley, who would play a major part in his life to the end. When she first saw him, he had long, uncombed hair and wore a cravat, and she assumed he was a tutor. She observed, 'He absolutely hero worshipped his father and feared finding himself simply ignored.' In Kit's efforts to get noticed, he started demonstrating that he could drink anyone under the table and messing around with drugs such as mescaline. Although he was small in stature, he had developed a very loud, plummy voice.

Kit showed early signs of promotional genius when he became publicity manager for the theatre club. Motion's book quotes a contemporary, who says of Lambert: 'He had tremendous enthusiasm, but then would sit about doing nothing. Once, for a performance of *The Changeling*, he showed no sign at all of fulfilling his responsibilities until two days before the first night. He then had hundreds of leaflets printed, hired an aeroplane and threw the leaflets out over the town.'

When Daria complimented him on his ingenuity, he responded, 'It's nothing. Once you've arranged the entire seating of Lancing College Chapel to sit next to the boy you fancy, anything is possible.'

Daria, who was married, was possibly the only woman Kit loved and his mother often blamed her son's homosexuality on the fact that Daria wouldn't sleep with him.

By now, he was living out his *Brideshead* fantasy to the hilt. A friend, Philip French, said: 'He was the kind of person I'd never met before. He belonged to a group of people who were openly camp, and was a marvellously funny, bitchy raconteur, forever joking about his sexual proclivities and activities, saying the sort of thing no one said to me at the time, like, "Jeremy's no good at sex." He was quite corrupt, in fact . . . his appearance was that of a young Charles Laughton, with thick lips which he used to curl . . . but his charm and force of personality completely overrode that.'

Kit furthered the decadent life by taking 'cabaret' trips to Berlin and mismanaging money, once taking a cab from Piccadilly to Oxford so as to be back in time for lectures. When the exams came around, he crammed day and night, fuelled by Benzedrine, to compensate for his earlier negligence. He felt money, or the lack of it, was cramping his style. 'The only important thing is to be rich,' he told Daria. 'It doesn't matter if you're handsome, clever and so on. With money, you can do anything.'

Having failed all his exams, Kit blagged his way into a French film school, figuring that the film business was a way of making a fast buck, but he soon tired of it and returned to starve in London. A chance encounter with an old school friend led Kit into an extraordinary and painful episode.

Richard Mason had secured the finance necessary to explore and map the longest undescended river in the world, the Iriri in Brazil. He and a friend from Oxford, John Hemming, were leaving in a few days' time. Upon hearing that Kit had just attended film school, Mason extended an invitation for him to accompany them to record the expedition. On the spur of the moment, and with nothing much else of consequence going on in his life, Kit packed his bags and went along.

After the sea voyage, they and eight others were deposited by plane in a clearing at the top of the river, where the only way out was through 1,500 kilometres of dense jungle. And so the mapping began. Kit helped with cutting and clearing the jungle as well as carrying the heavy bags. Hemming remembers him being very helpful. 'He was really excellent. He worked hard and put in all his energy. Very cheerful. Very good sense of humour.'

After some progress, it was felt that more supplies were necessary and Hemming was sent to Rio de Janeiro to get provisions and charter a plane for the return trip, which he duly did.

Then things started going wrong. The plane stopped off en route and wouldn't restart. The pilot was then ordered to return to base. Hemming had no choice but to return with him. With great difficulty, he found another plane and set off again. Somewhere along the way, they heard that a member of the expedition had been killed. When Hemming eventually tracked the expedition party down, he found Kit emaciated and distraught, 'in a very bad way. He was very pale after five months in the shadow of the forest, he'd lost a lot of weight, and he was very badly bitten by insects.' It was Mason who had been killed: he'd been ambushed by Indians – clubbed and stabbed to death. Kit had found the body, Hemming said, with 'the top of his head taken off'.

Utterly traumatised by the experience and hounded by reporters intent on romanticising the story, Kit returned to Rio and dived into its fleshpots in an effort to blank out the memories. Instead of finding solace, he picked up a virulent anal infection and had to be admitted to hospital on his return to Britain. He was to have nightmares about the expedition (and presumably the medical treatment) for years.

Back to health, Kit used his connections to get work as a director's assistant and for three years worked on films, the most notable of which were *The Guns of Navarone* and *From Russia With Love*. It was while working at Shepperton Studios that he was to meet (and fall in love with) Chris Stamp, the brother of actor Terence and similarly blessed with Terence's good looks.

The Stamp brothers were sons of a Thames tugboat man and hailed from Bow in the East End. It had been Terence who had blazed the trail across town, up west and into the movies, but Chris followed hot on his heels, although he opted to work behind the cameras rather than in front of them.

Kit and Chris really were an odd couple: they were complete opposites, a dynamic which attracted one to the other, although the sexual attraction was one-sided.

An old Who cohort, Irish Jack, described the first time he and his mod mate, Martin Gaish, met Kit and Chris: 'There was something about Lambert that I couldn't put my finger on at the time. He looked timid and had a small physique, like it had never fully grown to its full proportions. He had a scarf furled over his shoulder and wore a fancy double-breasted jacket. I shook his hand and when he spoke he sounded like he was from the BBC. He already looked like an Oxford don, and the accent, ridiculous as it was, suited him down to his expensive-looking shoes.'

They encountered Stamp at the mansion flat he and Kit had just moved into on Eaton Place. 'This tall, good-looking guy closed the door behind him and joined us. He took a light from Lambert's lighter, sat down and began to study Gaish and myself. He looked a real cool geezer, the kind of guy you could never impress with flash carry-on. He was about the same age as Lambert, but he looked younger and thin-boned, with a parting in the middle of his hair. I have to say that I had been very impressed when Lambert told me he [Chris] was an assistant film director, but when he opened his mouth I couldn't believe my ears: he looked aristocratic but spoke with a cockney accent.

'Stamp aired his thoughts as he rose out of the settee and moved to the window, "What we need, Kit, is some kind of club."

'Lambert was clearly thinking the same thing. "Yes, some kind of mod grapevine."

'They were like two college professors discussing philosophy, and chain smoking at the same time. I mean these guys were fucking light years ahead of the likes of Gaish and myself, even though we both considered ourselves well-sussed mods. Stamp continued to look out the window at the traffic below, and spoke over his shoulder, "Some kind of mods' society, that could put the word around."'

But the proto super-group managers hadn't yet turned their thoughts to running bands. Making a movie about the new teenage pop phenomenon seemed to them a more likely way to utilise their talents and make them some cash, as neither had any knowledge of modern music past The Beatles and the Stones. Since no one was going to let them make a movie about either of those two bands, they figured they would have to go out and find an unknown band and make a film about them.

They apportioned London and the regions like a military exercise and trawled the clubs looking for likely candidates. Kit was quite upfront about their tactics, as he relates in Dave Marsh's definitive book of The Who, *Before I Get Old*: 'Rock and roll is like football. No London boy is going to stand for Liverpool or Manchester winning all the time. I felt partly from being in the army that cockneys had the fastest reactions and the best brains. I didn't feel that London boys would allow a lot of northern oiks, like The Beatles or the Merseybeats, to put it across them indefinitely. There had to be out there, lurking in London, the group of the future, which would be spawned simultaneously by the fact that London had some hate of the north.'

When the dynamic duo spotted a line of mod scooters parked outside the Railway Hotel in Harrow, and felt the heat of the pilled-up parka-clad cult ranged in front of a band which argued onstage and stuck a guitar through the roof, something clicked. 'I paid my few shillings and went to the back,' says Kit in Marsh's book. 'On a stage made entirely of beer crates and with a ceiling so low you could stick a guitar through it without even trying, and lit by a single red bulb, were The High Numbers . . . They were ugly in the extreme. Roger, with his teeth crossed at the front, moving from foot to foot like a zombie. John, immobile, looking like a stationary blob. Townshend, like a lanky beanpole. Behind them, Keith Moon, sitting on a bicycle saddle, with his ridiculous eyes in his round moon face, bashing away for dear life, sending them all up and ogling the audience. They were all quarrelling among themselves between numbers. Yet there was an evil excitement about it all and instantly I knew they would become world superstars.'

Stamp's verdict on first seeing the band was more succinct but just as effusive: 'I was knocked out,' he said. 'But the excitement I felt wasn't coming from the group. I couldn't get near enough. It was from people blocking my way.'

Pete Townshend, John Entwistle and Roger Daltrey had met at Acton County grammar school, where Daltrey was involved with a band called the Detours, although it wasn't until they all left that they got together. By then, Entwistle was working in a tax office, drummer Doug Sandom was a bricklayer, Daltrey was a sheet-metal worker and Townshend was at art school, where his contemporaries included Ronnie Wood, Roger Ruskin Spear of the Bonzo Dog Doo Dah Band and Freddie Mercury.

By 1963, playing R&B in local danceterias, they had become more Beatles-influenced and were opening for the likes of The Hollies, Lulu and even the Rolling Stones. Townshend had spotted Keith Richards swinging his arm around when he was playing and immediately co-opted the extravagant gesture for his own repertoire. Influenced as the band was by ace face Peter Meaden, who'd heard of them via his hairdresser, they also co-opted the look of the mods who were springing up around London. Meaden had recently been hanging out with the Stones and their young manager, Andrew Loog Oldham, and was in the frame of mind to find a band of his own to manage. An evangelist for the mod 'cause', he considered purple hearts the perfect fuel to power the movement.

Sandom was swept away in the stampede for stardom, and a new drummer, Keith Moon, was enlisted when a drunk in the audience at one of their gigs shouted out, 'Ere, mate, I've got a friend who can play better than that.' Moon took to the stage for his audition, playing 'Roadrunner', and impressed them all by immediately breaking the drum pedal and the tom-toms. He was in. Leaving his day job presented no problem: he'd had over 20 jobs in the year before he joined up with the Detours.

Moon had joined a war. Townshend and Daltrey were locked in a fierce battle for control of the band – a battle that often turned into fist fights, which Daltrey invariably won.

Almost immediately, Moon started having disagreements with Entwistle.

Entwistle and Moon's rows usually revolved around music, although Keith's predilection for amphetamines often caused problems. Entwistle said, 'Keith must be the hardest drummer in the world to play with, mainly because he tries to hit nearly every drum at once . . . it sounds like an avalanche.'

The band had decided to become The Who and played gigs under this banner before Meaden stepped in and determined they should become The High Numbers, a name shot through with drug reference.

In 1964, the mods were fighting running battles with bikers (rockers) and the police on various seafronts. Meaden was not the only one to see the potential of harnessing the band's fortunes to the mods. 'One of the things which has impressed me most in life was the mod movement in England, which was an incredible youthful thing,' said Townshend. 'It was an army, a powerful aggressive army . . . with transport.'

Meaden drummed up a one-single record deal with Fontana and the band was booked into the studio to lay down four tracks. So keen was he to promote the mod vision that he wrote some of the lyrics himself. On the B-side of the eventual single, 'I'm the Face', Meaden has Daltrey singing about clothes.

A press report in *Boyfriend* magazine, which may well have been written by Meaden himself, stated, 'This disc is already going down well in the centre of London's mod world, the Scene Club.'

Enter Kit Lambert, who met Meaden at the Railway Tavern and said he was looking for a band for a club he ran. Meaden, spying an opportunity, went into a speed-fuelled sales spiel, ruefully saying later, 'I hard-selled myself right out of a band.' Meaden and The High Numbers were about to enter the full-throttle world of Stamp and Lambert. The High Numbers would soon become The Who.

'Kit was an utter maniac who lived off nervous energy and the sound of his own voice, who was so tense it hurt, who hardly ever went to sleep,' wrote Nik Cohn. 'Chris, by contrast, was the voice of sanity, very cool and hard. Together they fitted like Laurel and Hardy.'

It soon became clear that, inventive and energetic as Meaden was, he was a speed freak and would never last the course. He had to go.

Kit telephoned Meaden and uttered the line that would become immortalised in rock-business vernacular as the last words a band member hears on his way out of the door: 'Let's have lunch.'

Meaden recalled in Marsh's book, 'Kit took me to the Number Four restaurant in Frith Street. I had steak and kidney pie or something and Kit said, "How much do you want?" I said, "I don't know how much I want, Kit. I don't know what sort of value you put on it." I was frightened out of my life because I'd made a monster. I knew it was a monster. And he said, "I'll give you £150 for them." I learned later that I was supposed to accept £5,000, but I just said, "Yeah, that's all right. That'll do. Thanks a lot."

'He said, "I can't pay you right away. I'll pay you in lump sums as much as I can." Which was abusing the right of what he should have done. Still, at least he didn't just rip them off me.'

The band members' parents then presented problems – or at least Daltrey's and Townshend's did. Daltrey's mother wanted him to finish his apprenticeship. Cliff Townshend, Pete's father, on the other hand, had been in the music business himself and knew smarmy when he heard it. When he saw the contract that Lambert produced, he spotted a clause referring to a percentage of all personal writing. 'I went and got a pen and drew through that line. And Peter said, "Dad, what are you trying to do? This is good. They're all honest and we're going to do good with these fellows." I said, "Not that, no."'

Cliff undoubtedly saved his earnest son many thousands of pounds with that stroke of the pen, and in the light of some of the ludicrous deals that Townshend and Lambert were involved in later, he ought perhaps to have been called on again to impart some wisdom.

Another potential fly in the ointment was Roger's pregnant

girlfriend. It was felt that wives and girlfriends hindered a band's success in those days and Lambert callously urged Daltrey to dump her.

The initial management deal gave New Action Limited (Stamp's and Lambert's company) 40 per cent of the band's earnings, leaving 60 per cent to be split four ways – bullish without being entirely unfair.

Lambert took to his new job with a military zeal. 'Kit had this Shell map of London on the wall,' said Irish Jack, 'and he had it covered all over with drawing pins and red and blue circles where The Who was going to play in different clubs. The place looked more like Churchill's bloody war room.'

But, as Marsh points out in *Before I Get Old*, the devil was in the detail. 'If there was a decidedly militaristic cast to Lambert's approach, it was a mad hatter's version of military. His attempt to reduce everything to logistical order invariably wound up creating a state of chaos and disarray.'

And it wasn't just plans for the band that could be chaotic. Even personal hygiene seemed to stretch Kit's capabilities, as Irish Jack recalls: 'One day, Kit's shirt began to stink a bit under the armpits. Chris said something about it and Kit spoke a bit of Oxford and took off the shirt, but instead of bunging it in the washing bag like we thought he would, he just rolled it up in a ball and stuck it in the wastepaper basket. Then he went into the bedroom and pulled out this great big Victorian drawer, and there's a whole drawer full of fucking shirts, brand new, every one of them.'

Mike Shaw then came on the scene. One of Stamp's friends from Plaistow, he had been working as a lighting engineer in the theatre. Initially enlisted to work on the band's stage shows, his role soon expanded to that of major-domo. Shaw reinforces the stories of logic disorders in high places in *Before I Get Old*: 'Any money Kit got, he'd rush off to the gambling casino and try to win some money to pay for whatever next week. In the first year, it was the money that Chris sent back from the film he was working on that kept us going. But Kit said the best time to borrow money is when you owe some because they'll lend it to you to get the rest back. That was one of his maxims . . . Kit and Chris would try any scam to get some money.'

The lunatic was now in charge of the asylum. 'As solemn management [the situation has] always been farcical,' wrote Nik Cohn years later. 'Lambert is neurotic. Townshend is neurotic. Keith Moon is neurotic. Almost everyone involved is a maniac; almost everyone is extremely bright, and in four years hardly a week has gone by without some kind of major trauma.'

Wham! manager Simon Napier-Bell observed of Lambert, 'He was an opposite of traditional managers. Most of them said to their musicians, "Dress nicely and behave well, boys." Kit directed them to do the opposite: to shoot their mouths off and look scruffy.'

This was the antithesis of the Brian Epstein diktat, but it was Epstein who Lambert most wanted to emulate. He might even have thought he could surpass the achievements of the Liverpool master-manager, a desire built of his snobbish and lofty disdain of provincials.

Keith Moon thought that the 'cash through chaos' theory later espoused by Malcolm McLaren might well apply in the case of his management team: 'Kit and Chris. They were as incongruous a team as we were. You got Chris on one hand, "Oh well, fuck it, just whack 'im inna head, 'it 'im inna balls an' all." And Kit, "Well, I don't agree, Chris. The thing is the whole thing needs to be thought out in damned fine detail."

'These people were perfect for us because there's me, bouncing about, full of pills, full of everything I could get me hands on. And there's Pete, very serious, never laughed, always cool, a grass head. I was working at about ten times the speed Pete was. And Kit and Chris were like the epitome of what we were.'

One of Lambert's smarter moves was to buy two enormous tape recorders for Pete, who immediately locked himself away and started pouring out material. Mike Shaw observed that, 'It was a great outlet for him, once he got a Revox and started putting some songs down. It all came out.'

Kit Lambert

Dave Marsh says that this was the point when a debt of gratitude was struck between Townshend and Lambert, which gave birth to the unshakeable loyalty Townshend felt for his patron almost to the end. Townshend instinctively played new songs to Kit first. Kit's role as manager changed to that of editor. Townshend moved into Lambert's flat when Chris Stamp was away and Lambert started grooming him for success, although Townshend dodged being groomed for the boudoir.

Onstage, the fury grew. 'Stage fights were fairly common,' said Moon in Marsh's book. 'We just generally didn't get on that well. We used to take it out onstage – we used to avoid each other offstage. The only time we would get together was onstage, so all the pent-up aggression would come out then.'

Townshend used to fancy Daltrey's girlfriends; Roger would insult Townshend; Moon would annoy Entwistle. 'So everyone was furious about something almost all the time,' Marsh comments. 'The result was an absolutely murderous show that scared the competition off.'

Monetary control was nil, however, and New Action's stock as deal-makers was rock bottom. 'From the start,' wrote Nik Cohn, 'Kit and Chris spent like madmen. They had no knowledge of management whatsoever, but they made up for it in sheer style and bravado . . . Within three months, Kit and Chris had gone neck-deep in debt.' And most of those debts were incurred in trying to maintain The Who's instruments since, while Keith Moon was attempting to smash his drums to smithereens every evening, Townshend was quite successfully wrecking expensive guitars.

The band played a series of shows at the legendary Marquee club and those who were there (and many pretend they were) remember them fondly. Irish Jack recalls: 'The place would get stuffy with the stink of sweat and the condensation would run off the walls. But you just didn't care that there weren't no more room for dancing when you looked up and saw the madness in Moon's eyes as he waved his drumsticks about in the air like a lunatic. Daltrey, his golden hair soaked in sweat, bashing the skin out of a new tambourine off the mike stand, his harmonica blazing rhythm and blues down the microphone and out into the system. Entwistle, steady as a rock. How he used to do it, I never knew, with all that tension building up around him. Sometimes I think Entwistle created more bloody tension by remaining calm. He didn't do nothing, but you couldn't take your eyes off him.

'Then that mad geezer Townshend, his right arm swinging like a windmill blade gone daft. That Rickenbacker used to go through the face of the cabinets like a sledgehammer through a sheet of aeroboard. When it was over, you felt empty, spent. Then you noticed that your fucking clothes was wringing wet.'

Who needed sex?

Melody Maker noted, 'The Who, spurred by a most exhilarating drummer and a tireless vocalist, must surely be one of the trend-setting groups of 1965.'

It was time to release a record. One of The Who's favourite bands was The Kinks, and one of Pete's favourite Kinks tracks was 'You Really Got Me', produced by Shel Talmy. Townshend wrote 'I Can't Explain', which, according to John Entwistle, was an answer to 'You Really Got Me', and when they wanted a producer for the new track and someone said they knew Shel Talmy, well, what could be more obvious than to get in touch with the producer whose work they so admired? It was a decision made in haste that they all had cause to regret at leisure.

Talmy loved The Who but instantaneously developed a loathing for Lambert. Kit went on to make a production deal with Talmy about which Townshend commented ruefully, 'Kit made the first deal he'd ever made in show business, a deal which was really pathetic, like one-half per cent or something.'

Dave Marsh points out that the deal wasn't quite that bad but that it was right up there in the top half of the premier league of the rottenest deals ever done. The band would get only 2½ per cent of the retail price. Talmy would lease the tapes to a record company and he would retain the difference between the royalty the record company paid him and what he paid the band.

Kit Lambert

The Who went into the studio to meet a wall of session men, including Jimmy Page, preparing to play on their track. Townshend was able to fend off Page from 'I Can't Explain', but Talmy had written a B-side called 'Bald-Headed Woman', which he foisted on the band, along with Page's guitar-playing.

Decca picked up the record, but it peaked at only number 25 in the charts. However, as Jimi Hendrix would find a year later, the seminal TV pop programme *Ready, Steady, Go!* would provide the perfect outlet for their music in the absence of airplay.

To ensure that the band's performance on the show would be given a rapturous response, Lambert recruited a huge squad of mods from the band's home turf to loudly invade the *Ready, Steady, Go!* studio. Programme producer Vicki Wickham witnessed the invasion. 'On the day of the show, suddenly hundreds of Who fans started appearing and besieging the building,' she said, 'all firmly equipped with Who scarves and pop art jerseys and all looking like leftovers from St Trinian's. Somehow they all squeezed into the studio and the show was a phenomenal success.'

The record went back into the charts at number 23, eventually reaching number 8. Dave Marsh did an analysis of its earnings, which must still make uncomfortable reading for the remaining members of The Who: '"I Can't Explain" sold 104,000 copies. That represented a gross (from retailers) of £35,000. Of this amount, Decca got £16,000 as distributor and taxes took another £5,000. The Who, who were on $2^1/2$ per cent royalty, received just £1,000. And remember, Lambert and Stamp were entitled to the first £400 – 40 per cent – under their management agreement, leaving the band to split the remainder, or about £150 per man.'

However, *Ready, Steady, Go!* continued to work its magic and the gigs started rolling in. But the more gigs they played, the more equipment they smashed up. It was an expensive vicious circle. Lambert was in the invidious position of on the one hand advocating the destruction because it was good for business – a policy he called 'choirboys committing mayhem' – while on the other wishing they'd smash less equipment because that would be good for business as well. New Action management opened more bank accounts with nothing in them and wrote more dud cheques between one account and the other in a desperate effort to stay one jump ahead of their creditors.

The infighting continued with a general anti-Daltrey vibe in the band. When Townshend came up with a new song idea entitled 'Anyway, Anyhow, Anywhere', Daltrey was determined that a song he had to front would have something of him in its lyrics. He and Townshend stayed up all night honing the lyrics and it worked well, yet amazingly the single is the only Who composition credited to the two of them.

'Anyway, Anyhow, Anywhere' peaked at number 10 in the charts and hung around for 12 weeks but still sold fewer copies than its predecessor.

'My Generation' was a back-of-the-envelope idea that Townshend put together in response to Kit's demand that he 'make a statement'. However, it was Chris Stamp who championed the cause of the song. He knew a teen anthem when he heard one, but Daltrey didn't want to record it. He was sick of Townshend's dominance of what he still considered to be 'his' band. The subtext to this was his furious condemnation of drug-taking, which was rife within The Who.

He reluctantly recorded the song after heavy lobbying from Stamp and others, who were convinced it was a big hit, but his frustrations soon boiled to the surface. At a gig in Denmark, he chucked all Keith Moon's pills down the toilet. When Moon protested, Daltrey punched him out. It brought matters to a head. The other three members of the band were sick of Daltrey settling disputes with physical force.

'He was a dynamo,' said Townshend. 'If he punched you, it fucking hurt.' The three decided to start another band, effectively sacking Daltrey, and their managers were content to go along with them.

'We really fancied Pete's voice anyway,' said Stamp to a reporter. 'He didn't have a strong voice, but it was an interesting voice.' *no*

To keep the peace, New Action would form another band around Roger, thus allowing him to fulfil his R&B ambitions. Daltrey, having seen red, finally saw sense. He wasn't writing any of the songs. He could never hope to write songs as good as Townshend's, even if he did. 'I thought if I lost the band, I was dead,' he said. 'If I didn't stick with The Who, I would be a sheet-metal worker for the rest of my life.' Daltrey gave up his aggressive stance and it was the dawn of a new regime. From then on, Townshend had a free rein.

'My Generation' struck a nerve and made it to number 2 in the charts in November 1965, selling 300,000 copies. The message of the record is still pretty dangerous stuff and although Townshend didn't die before he got old, he meant what he said – or he did in 1971, when he commented, 'We did mean it. We didn't care about ourselves or our future. We didn't even really care about each other. We were hoping to screw the system, screw the older generation, screw the hippies, screw the rockers, screw the record business, screw The Beatles and screw ourselves. We've been most successful on the last account . . .

'We didn't really want to end up yabbering in pop papers about our hang-ups, we wanted to die in plane crashes or get torn to pieces by a crowd of screaming girls.'

The first album, also called *My Generation*, was a fraught process. Both the producer Shel Talmy and the engineer Glyn Johns hated Kit, and so Kit spent his time profitably sorting through the considerable pile of potential material with Townshend and rationalising Daltrey's vocals before the band went in with Talmy to get the sound. Standout tracks were the title track and 'A Legal Matter', while the standout performances all belonged to Keith Moon. Sales were low in the UK and non-existent in the USA, but New Action were optimistic. They had heard Townshend's next offering, 'Substitute'.

When Keith Moon first heard the track on the radio, he was convinced that he had been sacked (substituted) from the band because, try as he might, he couldn't remember playing on it. He had to be reassured that it was indeed a Moon performance. It shows the state of the drummer's mind even at this early stage. Who else did he think it could possibly have been? Who else sounded remotely like him?

Stamp and Lambert decided to try to exclude Shel Talmy and wrote him a letter to say that his contract was terminated. Talmy duly issued an injunction and, after much shenanigans, there was a hearing, some mud-slinging and a settlement. This was a truly God-awful result for The Who, as Dave Marsh's careful analysis reveals. 'For the next five years, Talmy would receive an override of 5 per cent on all Who recordings – which included the two biggest recordings of The Who's career, *Tommy* (1969) and *Who's Next* (1971).' Talmy had no involvement in either of them, but made them a fortune.

Into the breach stepped Robert Stigwood, who was prepared to release 'Substitute' on his newly founded Reaction label. The new deal with Reaction/Polydor provided a 10 per cent share less Talmy's cut and management charges. The band was now getting 1.25 per cent per musician.

'While this is better than the .75 per cent each received under the original deal,' Marsh continues, 'it is grossly unjust when compared to Talmy's rake off. The settlement ensured that The Who would never receive anything approaching a fair share of the wealth generated by their recordings. [And the albums that made the most money for The Who are not records that Shel Talmy could conceivably have created.]'

'We don't get deals because we're the best negotiators,' said Chris Stamp. 'We're probably the worst.'

At the same time, the big boys started looking at The Who with renewed interest. Lambert was hoping that he could get into bed (in business terms, of course) with his hero, Brian Epstein. Andrew Loog Oldham fancied his chances of taking over the band himself. He'd told Allen Klein that The Who were going to be big and that they had contractual problems and no money. Klein, who had already inveigled his way into the Rolling Stones' management, saw another opportunity to fulfil his ambition of dominating the British music business and rubbed his hands with glee.

Chris Stamp hired Edward Oldman, an establishment lawyer, and flew out with Pete Townshend to meet Klein on his yacht. Townshend was unimpressed, saying they 'ate his caviar, had a look at the Statue of Liberty from his yacht, shat in his toilet and went back to England'. Klein was out of the picture.

Kit dealt with the unwanted advances from Loog Oldham: 'One day, to my horror, I saw Moon and Townshend stepping out of Andrew's Rolls with Brian Jones, all of them chatting conspiratorially . . . So when the boys got to my flat, I drew my old service revolver, an enormous Colt Special, lined the boys against the wall and asked what's up . . . Andrew with his white Persian cat, tame joint roller and laced-up fly buttons was obviously impressing them, so I sort of cut in, in no uncertain way. Next time I saw the Rolls arrive I jumped in, kicked the cat out of the way and told him hands off or else.'

Negotiations with Decca in the USA and Polydor were slightly more fruitful. New Action extracted about £20,000 from the former and £50,000 from the latter, but the band owed so much that this pot evaporated instantly.

These were pivotal moments for the band. Despite 'Substitute' going to number 1 in the UK, there was no money nor would there be, by the look of it. Their only hope was to gig and gig, and they did just that to stay alive. The problem was that they wanted to live like pop stars. They *were* pop stars, for goodness' sake. Chris Stamp commented, 'No point in having the hit record and not being able to buy the flash car . . . We really all owed fortunes – real fortunes. It was incredibly dicey.'

When The Beach Boys released *Pet Sounds* in 1966, like many others Pete Townshend was tremendously influenced and began to talk about making a 'concept' album. Maybe the spirit of Constant rose within Kit, who became very excited about such a project and threw all his energies into it.

Publicist Keith Altham witnessed the three-year build-up to *Tommy*. 'Kit had this enormous output and exuberance that Pete certainly plugged into,' he said. 'I'm sure he encouraged and excited Pete into a whole lot of things. Pete would come up with the idea and Kit would get enthused and take the thing a step further and say, "Fantastic, let's hire the whole world."'

Lambert had become the de facto producer now, despite the fact that Townshend was in the driving seat. Pete described Kit's musical contributions as 'marvellously preposterous and outrageous' but added that there was a greater overall contribution: 'Kit knew the value of burning studio time. He knew the value of saying, "Right, there's too many takes, they're getting worse; everybody over the pub." Pick everybody up and take them out and perhaps not go back into the studio all night. You'd go home feeling terrible, and you'd think, "Oh, we've had a terrible day and why did Kit take us out," but the next day you go in and do that track straight away because you've built up to it overnight and you get this great recording. He knew about techniques like that; he knew human nature and he knew about The Who.'

To raise some money, Kit did a publishing deal with Essex Music. A rather eccentric clause demanded that each member of the band write two tracks. John Entwistle had the greatest problem complying. 'I still had one more number to write,' he said, 'so I went out and got drunk down the Scotch Club with Bill Wyman and we started talking about spiders and why they frighten people and that gave me an idea for a song.'

'Boris the Spider' was born; it was the quirky, standout track on the otherwise average second album, *A Quick One*, and became the most requested stage song the band ever did.

Whatever its failings, the second album made the number 4 slot in the UK. Encouraged, yet poor, The Who cast their eyes to the USA. It would be an uphill slog in a country where they were barely known, where there were no mods and where their record company seemed to lack any interest in them. Townshend wryly observed: 'America is the beckoning dream . . . The first trip to the States of any major English act is always treated as a group's next big step. They wave happily from the top steps of a VC-10 and set off to make their fortune. A couple of months later, after the most gruelling and exhausting work they have probably ever done, they return triumphantly home and start to tell lies. "It was great!" "We made thousands!" It went terribly and they lost thousands.'

'Substitute' was released, but its lyrics caused controversy and damaged the record's chances of radio play. Chris Stamp had to persuade the management of American Decca to hire some staff who were under 40 to work on the band. None of the big booking agencies were interested in The Who, but Stamp, who was by now acting as the American end of the New Action team, slipped them into the stable of the powerful agent Frank Barsalona, who'd already stated that he wasn't interested. Stamp pulled off this remarkable stunt by signing them to Barsalona's partner when Frank was out of town. On his return, Barsalona remained unimpressed.

The Who flew into NYC in 1967. They'd already abandoned gear-smashing in the UK, but knew they'd have to smash it up all over again to grab the attention of the Americans, so the band were issued with amphetamines on arrival, plus some penicillin to be on the safe side.

The reluctant Barsalona had never seen a band smash their kit up before. He didn't realise it was their act. When he eventually twigged, he was converted and became a total Who fan. Back at the hotel, Moon and Entwistle blew £2,500 on champagne and lobsters then smashed the room up. All the money from the shows was gone. Fortunately, 'Happy Jack' was released in the USA and sold 300,000 copies, reaching number 24 in the charts. The Who were off at last.

Back home, Lambert and Stamp were drawing up the blueprint for Track Records. They needed a sceptical Polydor to back them and they only got the investment when Lambert played them their first signing – Jimi Hendrix. The label had a good run. It's first release was 'Purple Haze' and in its first nine months

Track saw seven records in the UK top ten, with hits from John's Children (Marc Bolan's first band), Crazy World of Arthur Brown, Jimi Hendrix and, of course, The Who. The *Observer* newspaper estimated that Lambert and Stamp were making £3,500 a week from Hendrix's first album, *Are You Experienced*.

Townshend then further confounded the American record company by releasing 'Pictures of Lily', a song about masturbation. It reached number 4 in the UK but only number 51 over there. Then out of the blue came an invite to play at the Monterey Pop Festival alongside Hendrix, Otis Redding, Janis Joplin and many more. The bands were expected to play for free – well, it was the summer of love, the zenith of hippydom – so Kit refused to allow the band to take their own mighty Marshall backline equipment in an effort to save some cash.

An already angry Townshend heard a rumour that Hendrix was intending to wreck his equipment and set fire to his guitar – stunts that Townshend thought were his sole province – so The Who ferociously ripped the stage apart and left under a pall of Moon's smoke bombs. Jimi unashamedly did his smash-it-up pyrotechnic thing and was thus launched in the USA. The Who went on to do two nights at the Fillmore, doing themselves a lot of favours on the way.

When they returned to the US a few months later, it was bizarrely as support to Herman's Hermits – big stars in America but pulling a completely different crowd from that of the rough-and-ready Who. One of Herman's roadies said of The Who's performances, 'A lot of times there was no clapping whatsoever, just dead silence. People in the front rows were just sitting there with their mouths open, stunned.'

'I Can See for Miles', a track that Dave Marsh reckons is 'a masterpiece that stands outside of time, sounding as fresh fifteen years later [*Before I Get Old* was first published in 1983] as it did the first time around', was released within a month of The Who returning from the States. Townshend was annoyed that it only made number 10 in the UK but presumably less annoyed when it made number 9 in the US, where it was considered a breakthrough. A quick promo tour included an appearance on *The Smothers Brothers Comedy Hour*, during which Moon famously blew up his own drum kit and half the set, sending a cymbal scything into his own arm, half-deafening Townshend and leaving guest star Bette Davis fainting into Mickey Rooney's arms.

The Who Sell Out, with its pastiche of pirate radio jingles between the tracks, was a low charter on both sides of the Atlantic yet remains a favourite with those who grew up with the pirate phenomenon.

By now, the band had a lot of material released, but they still weren't quite 'the thing'. The band's frustration was palpable. The USA stayed tantalisingly out of reach and Townshend remarked to *Melody Maker*, 'The English scene for us, unfortunately, doesn't compare with America . . . The States offers us more money, fans and excitement.' Later, he was to say, 'Perhaps we have regarded success in the States as being far more important to us than any other English group.'

On the next tour of the US, Townshend gave a long and detailed interview to the editor of *Rolling Stone* about an idea he had for an album, which he called *Deaf, Dumb and Blind Boy*.

Whilst The Who fiddled about, trying to get the new album together, Kit Lambert produced 'Fire' for Crazy World of Arthur Brown and had a worldwide number 1. He was now brimming with confidence.

Melody Maker's Chris Welch had observed how Lambert would sit in the background in the studio until such time as any of the musicians went in to play. Pete explained to Welch:

> Kit was as much a producer in the writing as he was in the studio. Kit was much more involved in the overall concept of the thing – much more than people imagine. Not all that much, in fact, with the overall sound, although he did produce it and mix it and he did make us work at it. Still, the main thing was that he thought of the idea of rock opera.

> We [Townsend and Lambert] went into it in depth before we
> worked out the plot; we worked out the sociological implications,
> the religious implications, the rock implications . . . When we'd
> done that, we went into the studio, got smashed out of our
> minds and made it.

Unsurprisingly, the recording dragged on for months and months and
Lambert, despairing of his protégé ever finalising a coherent story, sat
down and wrote the script himself. However, he refused to rush the
project into the shops before it was finished – properly finished.

Townshend took a break himself from the recording and
produced 'Something in the Air' for Thunderclap Newman, a new
signing to Track. He had now had a hand in a worldwide hit that
didn't belong to The Who.

'Pinball Wizard' was released in March 1969 in the UK. It made
number 4, while in the US it made only number 19. However,
the radio stations thrashed it to death. Back in Britain, the BBC,
personified by Tony Blackburn, objected to the 'deaf, dumb and
blind boy' lyric, labelling the track 'sick'.

Townshend's thundered response was, 'Sickness is in the mind
of the listener and I don't give a damn what people think.'

The Americans went mad for *Tommy*, hailing it a new art form,
and the band were suddenly being taken very seriously, although
there were ambivalent mutterings from John Entwistle: 'Overnight,
we became snob rock,' he said. 'The band that Jackie Onassis came
to see and all that rubbish.'

She may well have seen the band perform the rock opera at
New York's Metropolitan Opera House. Somehow Kit was able to
convince the highbrows of American opera to invite a snotty British
rock band to perform on its hallowed stage. It was the highlight
of a year-long world tour to promote the album, which rose to
number 4 in the US and stayed in the charts for a year.

Simon Napier-Bell describes how this level of success affected
Lambert in his book, *Black Vinyl White Powder*: 'He became
incapable of properly managing The Who. He hired the *Queen*

Mary for a promotional party and supplied a different drug on every deck. He holidayed for a month in Mexico and forgot the two stretch limos that were on twenty-four-hour call outside his hotel in New York. At Sardi's, he set the lampshades on fire to attract the waiter's attention. He loved to walk into hustler bars with the tip of a thousand dollar bill protruding from his half-zipped flies.'

In 1970, the band reluctantly played Woodstock, a performance Daltrey described as 'the worst gig we ever played' and which the crowd and the press described as a triumph.

They were rich now. Entwistle and Townshend weren't profligate, but Daltrey had a farm and, surprise surprise, Keith Moon went for broke. 'I'd bought four 'ouses, an 'otel, eight cars, a swimming pool, tennis courts, expensive wristwatches . . . I'd spent it all,' as he told *Rolling Stone* magazine's Jeremy Hopkins in 1972.

That year, however, events took a more serious turn for Keith when it was claimed he ran over and killed his chauffeur. He was cleared of any misdoing by the coroner, but the accident threw him into a drunken depression and it haunted him to the end of his days. Indeed, it may have tipped his playful nature into a more manic danger zone.

The band's next release, 'The Seeker' (which wasn't produced by Lambert), sold poorly in the US, but the *Live at Leeds* album reached number 3 in the charts and stayed there for 21 weeks.

When Kit read a review of the album, he was staying with a friend, Nancy Lewis. 'I was having my usual Sunday breakfast,' he said, 'which consisted of an ounce of the very finest cocaine, which was sitting on my left knee, in a barrel, with a spoon dipping ever and anon into the precious crystals . . .'

The reviewer had written, 'I believe it to be the very finest live album to have ever been made.'

Kit continues: 'I sprang into the air, crying, "Eureka!", forgetting, of course, that I had an ounce of precious cocaine on my knee as I did so. It fell down in a thousand tiny snowflakes into the deep pile of the white carpet and vanished without trace. "Nancy, quick," I said. She had to grab me by the ankles and mow the lawn with me feverishly up and down, as I tried to snort the remaining £1,000 worth of coke from out of the carpet.'

Relations between Lambert and the band became strained; Kit was preoccupied with Track Records and was miffed that he hadn't been asked to produce 'The Seeker'. He also felt that Townshend was being obstructive in his plans to make a movie about *Tommy*.

Townshend had become embroiled in his esoteric *Lifehouse* project – a complex music and performance synthesis that even those who were involved in found difficult to understand. The project floundered and so did Townshend, who seemed to be having some sort of mental breakdown.

Lambert and the band tried to salvage some of the material from the project to release as an album but failed, basically because of Townshend's mental state and the antics of a dangerously unpredictable Keith Moon.

But when he was funny, he was very, very funny. One of the best Moon stories is one rarely heard but related in *Rogues, Villains and Eccentrics* by William Donaldson: 'While appearing in the film of the rock opera *Tommy*, Moon gave [Oliver] Reed a tortoise. When drinking, they would encourage the tortoise to cover the ground between them with a bottle of whisky on its back – by this method, since the tortoise moved so slowly, managing to reduce their alcohol consumption by several bottles a night. The tortoise, which travelled with them everywhere, was put to other amusing purposes. Sometimes Moon and Reed took their clothes off in the public rooms of hotels and entertained the other guests by wearing the tortoise as a makeshift codpiece. According to Ken Russell, who directed *Tommy*, it looked, when the tortoise stuck its head out, as if the one who was wearing it had an erection. At other times, they turned the tortoise upside down and used it as an ashtray.'

It took their engineer, Glyn Johns, to pull together the next album, *Who's Next*. The Who were back on track. Many regard *Who's Next* as their finest work, though Lambert had little to do with it, not least because of Johns' animosity towards him. It was the beginning of the end for Kit.

Track was doing well, but Kit was spending the money as fast as it came in on drugs, drink, cars, parties and boys. He literally had his hands in the till: a Track publicist remembers Kit helping himself to £400 in petty cash every weekend.

His taste for pills – downers – led to him starting to miss appointments. He'd fall asleep all the time and was constantly burning holes in his clothes with cigarettes. Chris Stamp had drug problems of his own and the two partners left the business to others to run. 'We were well out of it,' Stamp said. 'We were fucking out to lunch, no doubt about that.' When Roger Daltrey became concerned about missing money, Stamp attempted an explanation: 'Loads of people like Moonie used to grab a big bundle of cash, so did Townshend, so did Entwistle, so did Daltrey, right? None of it had actually gone missing – it just wasn't in the books. You knew there was drugs money and madness money, and that's where it went. And over ten years – TEN YEARS – there were millions of dollars that had gone missing – this was years of madness on the road, smashed cars and paid-off chicks and so on. Anyone in rock and roll knew that.'

Daltrey urged Stamp's friend Bill Curbishley to come in to fill the gap left by Kit, which he did very adequately, thus adding to Kit's alienation.

Daria Chorley, Lambert's friend from university, now comes back into the story. She felt compelled to watch out for Kit, who was in a parlous condition. She recalls him going missing for two days. He was eventually discovered asleep under a rug behind someone's door. 'He was always falling asleep during the day,' she said, 'because he dreaded falling asleep at night and waking up to find nobody there. He was terribly lonely.'

Daria suggested he take a break. He went for a trip to Venice with his old friend Robert Fearnley-Whittingstall and Robert's wife, Jane. Daria then went to Venice with him again. Kit was smitten, saying, 'It's so beautiful, I think I'm going to be sick.' He saw a house called Palazzo Dario, commonly held to be one of the most lovely houses in the city; the name suggested Daria's name and he told her he would buy it. He felt exotic Venice, with its reputation for masked balls and scandal, offered a chance for him to engage with the *haut monde* that his father had known and which had been denied him by virtue of his association with a common rock group. He splurged some of his *Tommy* profits on his palace and took up residency in a posh hotel in town while it was being renovated.

Two days after moving in, he held a housewarming that attracted the cream of Venice society, including Peggy Guggenheim and a former British Ambassador. The locals took to the eccentric Englishman in the big house and started calling him 'Barone'. A delighted Kit felt settled enough to take on a live-in lover and for a period seemed happy; however, the allure of his London rock-and-roll lifestyle became irresistible and he returned to a flat in Kensington, where he lived with two Great Dane dogs. He had many rows with The Who and other Track artists who still wanted to know where all the money had gone and, indignant, would often lock himself away, sulking. His housekeeper complained that the flat stank of dope and dog shit all the time.

There was trouble aplenty to come. Kit infuriated Roger Daltrey by refusing to distribute his solo album and antagonised his erstwhile loyal supporter Pete Townshend by stopping a cheque that Pete needed to build a special studio to record *Quadrophenia*. His boozing – usually brandy, Dad's favourite killer tipple – was increasing, while his consumption of cocaine was unrivalled; he was also clearly addicted to heroin.

Lambert's self-destruct mechanism, coupled with a sense of betrayal, brought out wilder and wilder methods of self-expression, including the notorious shoot-up in the Speakeasy, which he described in a rambling but comical interview just before his death, published in *The Lamberts*: 'The worst thing in the world, I think, is waking up alone on Christmas Day. I used to go to enormous lengths when the money first started to come in not to have to go through this. I bought a pistol and went down to the Speakeasy [one] Christmas Eve. I thought things were pretty dull, so I fired a few rounds into the ceiling and ordered champagne cocktails all round and then ordered another round and fired a few more shots into the ceiling and things started to liven up slightly. Then I got the man on the door to order some hire cars as I began to chat up various people who walked in and I plied them with more and more champagne. I said to each one, "Why don't you go and wait in the car?" I thought one of them is bound to come across. There were about three of them in this car with the driver. Then the head waiter came down and said, "Look, I'm awfully sorry, but we had to carry the last two out and the other guy's snoring loudly and the driver doesn't look too happy either." I said, "Well, order another car." . . . About an hour later, it was the same story as the next three candidates had been carried out of the club and put into the second car. There were now two cars with, so to speak, dead bodies. It was getting awfully near the witching hour, which I absolutely did not want to spend alone, so firing a few more rounds from my pistol into the ceiling, [I ordered] another case of champagne; things were really beginning to hot up now, the place was going thick and fast. Finally, I left with the organist – or was it the bass guitarist? – from the group that was playing in the fourth limousine. He was the last person able to stand. He was very nice. The first and the last time I've ever had an organist (tell me about boys in black leather raincoats and eyes like swimming pools, their wonderful featureless smiling faces, their brainless heads rising from their swanlike necks).'

If there is an edge, Kit was on it.

Townshend was apparently depressed by the wall that had grown between him and his ex-mentor but ploughed on with the *Quadrophenia* album to great effect. When The Who toured the USA to promote its release, they played four gigs at Madison Square Garden and sold 80,000 tickets after a single announcement on the radio. The Who were now fully fledged superstars and, with the demise of The Beatles, the second-biggest band in the world.

In the years before Track Records was wound up in 1976, Daltrey became more insistent in establishing where the money had gone. Townshend at first resisted his efforts to sue Kit and co., but then relented. When the accounts were audited, the hideous truth was out. As Daltrey characteristically put it: 'We'd been screwed up the fucking alley.'

The film of *Tommy*, made by Robert Stigwood, omitted Kit from the credits while including Chris Stamp as executive producer. Kit lashed out. He claimed world copyright to the piece and demanded that Stamp be removed from the board. He claimed that he had also sacked Curbishley, although it seems Curbishley had already resigned.

As a result of all this, the bank accounts of Track Records were frozen and suddenly The Who had no access to money. Once again, they were forced into long spells of touring to keep the show on the road, as it were.

Things started to get pretty ugly as Kit descended into mental anguish and large-scale drug-shovelling. Andrew Motion's book avers that a young Irish rent boy died of a drug overdose in Kit's spare room. Another young man died having an epileptic seizure while staying with Kit. When he was in Venice, a woman friend was given a drug-filled suppository and passed out. When she awoke, she was naked and had rope burns on her ankles and wrists. Beside the bed were photographs of her being abused by other 'guests'.

Townshend reinstated Curbishley, whose diagnosis was 'Kit had gone completely bananas'. Chris Stamp tried to have his erstwhile partner committed.

A concerned Daria visited him in his flat. 'He was living in unbelievable squalor. There had been a fire and he was virtually living under a tarpaulin over the fire damage,' she said. 'He had his two dogs and seven puppies with him and there was dog shit everywhere. You had to hold your nose when you went in. And it was terribly hot – he had to have heaters on all the time because of his druggy state.'

She observed that Kit's hair was falling out and his face was bloated, and that his creditors were closing in. If she didn't act fast, he would be declared bankrupt.

Daria went to the law and arranged for the Court of Protection to take over Kit's finances under her stewardship to pre-empt an application from his bank to seize his assets. Kit, seeing the sense of the plan, went along with Daria and made an effort to pull himself together, checking into a clinic that Keith Richards had recommended to him to try to get himself off the smack.

On his return, he moved in with his mother, but after only a few days he had beaten her up and smashed up the flat. Daria found him a new one and worked out some settlements with his creditors, but Lambert, seeing treachery everywhere, had by now convinced himself that she was working against him and made an application to be released from the court's control, though his doctor advised the court that he wasn't fit to look after his own affairs.

In the summer of 1978, Pete Meaden died of a drug overdose and a month later so did Keith Moon. Kit's mental state worsened. When Daria was forced into selling the Venice house and its contents, he felt absolutely betrayed. His behaviour became more and more erratic. He moved in with a girl he knew slightly and lived on a diet of brandy and painkillers while hanging out in the Coleherne pub in London's Earls Court and the Yours and Mine club in Kensington – both notorious gay hangouts.

Another failed application to be released from the Court of Protection dejected him further. Friends suggest that it was then that Kit decided to die. He went back on heroin with a vengeance, upset his temporary landlady and moved in with another acquaintance, Deirdre Redgrave, the ex-wife of Corin Redgrave, and her children. He told her he wanted to marry her and even told the newspapers of his plans. Deirdre realised that he couldn't stand being a homosexual but had little control over himself. He started bringing rent boys back to her house. She insisted, not unreasonably, that he should only bring men back when the children were at school.

'He would wake up at eight-thirty demanding bacon and eggs,' she said, 'then would get stuck into the brandy and DF118s [strong codeine-based painkillers].' Even in this desperate state, she says, he never lost his sense of humour. 'However down he was, he was always funny . . . He was one of the biggest life forces I ever met.'

Towards the end, he began listening to his father's recorded work and approached various people, including Pete Townshend, about getting some of Constant's unrecorded pieces performed and on tape. He also tried to sort out his strained and complex relationship with his mother, and it was to her house that he went on the evening of Saturday, 25 April 1981. But the opportunity to mend fences had slipped away. He presented a sorry sight and told her that he'd been beaten and mugged in the toilets of the Yours and Mine. She says his face was cut and bruised, and as he told her the story he kept falling off the chair. He asked her for brandy, then had a bath and went to bed. A while later, she was awoken by the sound of him falling down the stairs. He was unconscious and bleeding from his nose and mouth. Lambert had suffered a brain haemorrhage during the fall and was taken to hospital and put on life support. Two days later, the machine was turned off and he died immediately.

His mother, Flo, maintains that Kit was murdered by drug dealers, that the beating he had taken in the club may well have given him the brain haemorrhage, but the police made no investigation. Kit was cremated at Golders Green cemetery. None of The Who attended the funeral.

In 1984, John Lindsay, a journalist who had been a friend to Kit in his final years and who had attempted to get him to write an autobiography, announced he was going to make a dramatic film of Kit's life called *Hope I Die Before I Get Old* with a $7.5 million budget. Hywel Bennett was chosen to play Kit, but it was never made. There have been rumours that Chris Stamp may be attempting to have a film made about Kit.

5

CHAS CHANDLER

Animals, Hendrix

Knowledge speaks, but wisdom listens.
– *Jimi Hendrix*

Amanager hopes for a moment of epiphany, not an ambivalent moment; no shilly-shallying. It's not a case of gazing up at the stage, thinking, 'Yes . . . No . . . Oh God, I don't know . . . well . . . maybe . . . if we throw a bit of money at it, get a hairstylist in, hire a voice coach perhaps, trowel some make-up on him, buy in some songwriters, rent a man-about-town PR, bullshit the record companies, then maybe, just maybe, we stand a chance.'

Instead a manager hopes for a shaft of light to cut through the ceiling and drive into his forehead like Paul on the road to Damascus. He hopes to be saying, 'That's the best fuckin' thing I've ever heard! This guy's a fuckin' genius. We're all gonna be rich, goddamn it. Rich!' (For which read: 'I'm the genius and this lad is gonna make me rich!')

Of course, the guy is rarely a genius. Quite often, in fact, the guy is totally crap and every dollop of slap in the bag won't stop him frightening children, while the first utterance of his tuneless nasality will have the producer diving for his phone and frantically searching under 'S' for session singer.

131

There is no record of Chas Chandler's first thoughts as he watched Jimi (then Jimmy) Hendrix play support to Jimmy James in jazz club Café Au Go Go in New York's Greenwich Village in 1966. What we do know is that the stunning Linda Keith, who was at the time going out with Keith Richards and who was there with him on this same night, thought he was the very thing, just the ticket; Mr Dynamite, in fact. This was confirmed when she noticed how keen Charlie Watts and Bill Wyman were to stick around after the gig and have a jam with this extraordinary, exotic, loose-limbed guitarist with huge graceful hands.

We also know that Linda kept on at Chas Chandler to see Hendrix again. Chas had obviously told her of his plan to leave his day job as bass player with The Animals and become a band manager, and she had the perfect first-class client for him.

By now, Linda had almost adopted Hendrix as her own. She started giving him bits of cash, her records, a brand spanking new Fender Stratocaster, a bed in her hotel suite. In time, she was even dropping him off at gigs in her chauffeur-driven car and having the limo wait while Jimi finished his set so it could take him home again. History doesn't relate Keith Richards's views on all this.

Under her matronly control, however, the waif-like Hendrix was made to eat a decent meal now and again, was given a regular place to sleep and encouraged to wean himself off the crystal meth that he relied on to get through the endurance-test gigs he was doing. She vowed she would get him up there to the top and, with Chas's help, she did.

It was in the cave-like Café Wha? in Greenwich Village that Chas experienced his divine moment. OK, he'd needed a bit of earthly persuasion, but if a quality manager has any gift it is knowing it when he sees it and Chas was definitely top-drawer manager material. When Hendrix started playing 'Hey Joe', all the synapses in Chas's head lit up like a pinball machine. Connections were made, plans crystallised, ambitions soared. 'Jimi wasn't known at all at this time,' he said, 'but I hadn't any doubt in my mind. To me, he was fantastic. I thought there must be a catch somewhere. Why hadn't anyone else discovered him?'

He would take Hendrix back to the UK with him immediately. Britain was Chas's home, his stamping ground. He knew all the movers and shakers, the gig circuits, the agents, the record companies, the form. He also knew that the British, and more specifically, the highly influential tight set of trendsetters that radiated around the Scotch of St James, Blaises, the Upper Cut and the Marquee, would go absolutely crazy for this new sensation. And he was absolutely right. He'd trusted his instincts and taken a wild gamble on a wild man. Chas happily hung up his bass guitar. His days with The Animals, as far as he could see, were over.

Chas was born Bryan Chandler in 1938 in Heaton, Northumberland. It's not recorded if he was a big baby but he became a big man – six foot four inches big. Size had always been an asset for a band manager and Chas is the biggest in the book. But before managing bands, he would be a bass player and before being a bass player, he would work on a lathe in a steam-turbine factory.

Lathe-turning was a skilled trade, but even so, heavy engineering in the North-east in the late '50s was tough work for tough men. There were harsh conditions in the factories and uncompromising management. However, Chandler stood head and shoulders above the other workers in more ways than one, as John Steel, The Animals' drummer explains in Sean Egan's story of the band, *Animal Tracks*: 'Chas was a very strong personality. He was a trade union shop steward in Parsons factory before he finally burnt his boats, so that will give you a little bit of an idea of Chas.'

Strangely, not only has Chandler entered pop mythology but the very lathe he worked on has too. The 'lucky lathe', if it still exists, should be polished up and exhibited in a Newcastle museum because it had two famous Geordies operating it at different times, as AC/DC vocalist Brian Johnson explained in *The Guardian*:

There was a place where I served my apprenticeship in Newcastle. The foreman comes up to us and he's, 'Right, son, you're going on that lathe there,' and I was like, 'That's a bit big for us,' and he was telling me that it was the lucky lathe. He said Chas Chandler worked on that and he didn't know what strings I'd pulled, but I was on it.

Founding vocalist of The Animals Eric Burdon met Chas pretty early on. 'When I was at school in Newcastle, I was attempting to make a flat-board Fender bass guitar in the woodwork shop. It was a disaster. Then I heard that this guy across town – a shipwright – had made a Fender guitar, so I made a trek to the baddest side of town – to Byker – and there was this dude, Chas Chandler. He was a few years older and he was standing at the bar in this workingman's club, smart in his Burton's suit with a pint of golden ale in his fist. I think he already ran the bingo and bus trips at the weekend. The guitar looked fantastic.

'We all looked up to him; we were at art school, Pricey [Alan Price] was doing an apprenticeship in an office. We used to hang around Whitley Bay, leaning against Wurlitzers. Chas was part of one of those gangs. I think it was the Squatters. There was a dangerous edge. I remember a running fight; one of his mates got knifed in the back.'

Drummer John Steel notes in *Animal Tracks* that Chas was a 'big, red-headed, lanky, big-boned bloke. He had a terrible hangover, I remember. He loved going out for several jars of beer and he was very keen on playing darts. He was like these, "One hundred and eighty!" type of people.'

Chas's first band was the Newcastle-based The Kon-tors, who played covers at village halls and social centres. He ran into Eric again when his band stole Eric's keyboard player, Alan Price.

Elements of the two bands and others joined, split, morphed and rejoined until they ultimately came together with the original Animals line-up – Alan Price, Eric Burdon, Chas Chandler, John Steel and Hilton Valentine on guitar – albeit under the name of the Alan Price Rhythm and Blues Combo.

Price was the real musical talent, but Eric Burdon's gutsy bluesy voice ensured he was the man out front and dominant in the band despite his short stature (5 ft 7 in.). Burdon didn't get things all his own way, however: Chas was nearly a foot taller, which guaranteed he was always heard. So, while Eric pulled the band towards rhythm and blues and rock, citing influences such as Jimmy Witherspoon, Ray Charles, Billie Holiday and Chuck Berry, Chas had other ideas. In *Animal Tracks*, Steel comments: '[Chas] was mostly into good quality popular music. Sam Cooke, that sort of thing. He wasn't into jazz. He just recognised good pop music when he heard it. He was absolutely potty about The Beatles. As soon as they appeared on the scene, he was absolutely crazy about them. He knew which direction he was going in.'

And so Chas stamped his considerable presence on The Animals, despite being, by his own admission, a limited bass player. His pop sensibilities, coupled with Burdon's blues, did a lot for the overall dynamic of the band and prevented Burdon dragging the band into a rootsy but non-commercial cul-de-sac.

'All these little things come into the melting pot,' says Steel. 'It wasn't planned. We drifted this way and that way. Chas had his contribution and, with hindsight, it was probably very significant. He was very hip on the kind of pop music that Eric and me could agree with.'

The band was backed by two saxophonists, Jeff Hedley and Nigel Stanger. Many years later, Stanger and Chandler were to reunite in phase five of Chandler's extraordinary career, when they set up the Newcastle Arena together, but more of that later.

Mike Jeffery (also Jeffrey or Jeffries) arrives on the scene at this time and peppers the story of The Animals and Jimi Hendrix in many dramatic ways. Jeffery, an ex-commando, lurked on the same mean northern streets as the other participants. He ran a jazz club above the Gardeners Arms pub in Newcastle. There he strode around in dark glasses and was already enjoying a reputation as a villain.

'We used to beg Mike to manage us,' says Eric. 'He used to tell horrendous stories about being in the dirty tricks department of the

Palestine police force at the time the Israelis were trying to bomb the British out of Palestine. He was treble "O" seven. The stories were so bizarre, but they were real. I saw him stand up to the Krays once – toe to toe. They'd wanted to take over his operation.'

The local students, including Burdon and his pre-Animals mates, helped Jeffery to decorate a new club to be called the Downbeat and they were rewarded with a weekly residency. There were out-of-town gigs as well, though the band wasn't always as welcome as it was on home turf. 'We were run out of Sheffield,' recalls Burdon. 'They hated Geordies there and half the audience chased us all down the street. I remember Chas going, "I've had enough of this." He turned round and cornered a couple of guys and put the Tyneside nut in. We stood behind him, quaking in our boots, while he barrelled in and split someone's nose open.'

As the combo gelled, they spent most of the time playing in Jeffery's venues, so although he was still reluctant to commit to the task of manager, he was their main employer and financed their earliest recording sessions. The gigs got more and more popular. The band realised just how good they'd become when they spotted the Rolling Stones in their audience at the Club-A-Go-Go one night and Brian Jones was dancing all over the floor.

It was time to head south to the capital.

Jeffery set up some kind of reciprocal deal with Giorgio Gomelsky, who managed The Yardbirds, which allowed the band to do gigs around the west of London, at the Ricky Tick and Eel Pie Island, as well as Ronan O'Rahilly's Scene Club in Piccadilly. (O'Rahilly was later to run Radio Caroline.) Then he handed them a management contract to sign and announced that the band was to be called The Animals – and no one clearly remembers why.

Gigs went well and the London set started swinging to this new band from the North-east, as well as to their rather more famous north-western cousins. However, just as things started to look exciting, the band members turned on one another, as band members so often do, whether times are good or bad.

Chandler's lack of affection for basic rhythm and blues became a topic of conversation whenever he was out of the room. The band agreed: someone else was needed who was more sympathetic to the rootsier tastes within The Animals. But who was going to broach the issue with the towering Chas since his quick temper was legendary? (This fear had also been a factor in their decision to get rid of him.)

In *Animal Tracks,* John Steel asserts that Chandler's bass-playing ability wasn't the issue, but Dave Rowberry, who later joined the band, had a fairly low opinion of it: 'He wasn't a musician. I used to get his bass and tune it before the gig and he would come onstage and say, "Dave, give us a G," and I'd try and ignore him, try and pretend I was doing something else 'cos I knew the bass was perfectly in tune. He'd be plucking one string and turning the hammer on another one. By the time the curtain went up, the bass was out of tune.'

Burdon agrees: 'Well, he wasn't Jack Bruce. But when I listen to the old Animals things now, I think part of the beauty is how little the rhythm section mattered – or how much it is buried in the background. It's the way things were mixed back then. John Steel just kept up a steady backbeat. He never speeded up or slowed down. He was just like Charlie Watts.'

Even so, Chas had to go.

'We were all saying, "Who's gonna tell him? He'll kick our heads in,"' continues Eric. 'And like an idiot, I said I'd do it.' He goes on: 'I thought we should ask him to be the manager. He had star talent at the management end of it. We didn't have a manager then. Chas's father was the road manager. He drove this Second World War ambulance. I think Chas was doing a lot of legwork by then anyway. None of us had a telephone and where he was a member of this workingman's club, he had access to a telephone.'

Chas was clearly upset by the band's decision and made a lengthy case for them to reconsider (he was well known for his indefatigable debating skills). Alan Price allowed himself to be swung over by Chas's argument and the band followed suit; the decision was reversed, although Chas's relationship with Eric suffered as a consequence. 'From that time, I was outside Chas's world as far as buddies were concerned,' he says.

Mike Jeffery needed to find his band better gigs now and, like so many aspirant acts of the era, The Animals found themselves in the company of London's top agent, Don Arden, whose tour manager was Peter Grant, later to manage Led Zeppelin. Grant popped down to see the band play and brought with him his occasional business partner, producer supremo Mickie Most.

This chain of events led to the recording of 'House of the Rising Sun', the band's biggest-ever hit and the cause of much dispute between them – although strangely it never got as far as internecine litigation. Could it be these tough Geordies were more stoic than their southern counterparts? Or were they just more naive?

The story goes that the song was plundered from the first Bob Dylan album but that Dylan had plundered it himself. 'House of the Rising Sun' was a traditional song whose authorship was lost somewhere in the misty history of blues and as a consequence all the royalties, including the writer's share payable on the song, should have gone to whomsoever covered it.

Hilton Valentine's distinctive arpeggio guitar figure met approval from most of the band but apparently not from Alan Price, who, John Steel alleges, objected to it and only reluctantly added his organ part at the end – but boy, what an organ part it was.

The story also goes that Mickie Most didn't initially want The Animals to record 'House of the Rising Sun' and that he had only got them to play it in the studio as part of a soundcheck. The recording took ten minutes and at the end of it Most pronounced baldly, 'OK, that's it.'

The band protested. The song clocked in at four minutes and twenty-eight seconds: in an era of three-minute singles, this was considered commercial suicide. John Steel remembers Most saying, 'Bugger it. We'll go with that.' Steel credits Chas Chandler with being the first in the band to see the potential of Most's mould-breaking snap decision: 'It was the first time really we actually started to think that way. This had a lot to do with Chas's way of thinking. His input was more calculated than ours. Eric wanted to be a success more than anything in the world, but he didn't know how to do it. I just went along with anything that sounded good that I could live with quite happily. But Chas actually thought things through.'

There followed a contentious incident, well documented on the Internet and in *Animal Tracks*. It seems Jeffery announced to the band that only one of the band members' names would be allowed to go on the record sleeve, and that as the arrangement had been done by Alan Price, it should be Price's name. It was only a technicality, he said; Alan would receive all the royalties but then promised that the royalties would be distributed by him to the others.

The band just plodded on, only gradually cottoning on to the fact that they weren't getting any royalties from one of the biggest-selling singles in history. Much later, they realised that they never would.

On what seems to be an ongoing dispute over the arrangement of the hit, Hilton Valentine, who is bitter to this day, says in Egan's book, 'He [Price] knows that he didn't arrange it. No matter how much he wants to convince himself that he did, he didn't. It was agreed verbally and understood that the royalties would be shared. That's the thing that he can't deny.'

Eric Burdon is even angrier, asserting that it had been he who had found the track on the Dylan album and claiming that there had been a conspiracy between Jeffery and Price. He adds that those unpaid royalties might have helped stave off the hard times that all of the band – except Chandler, who had gone on to make a lot of money elsewhere – came to experience.

Anyone listening to Dylan's limp acoustic version of that track now might well appreciate the depth of Burdon's anger: Valentine's mood-setting guitar part and Eric Burdon's soaring vocal performance make 'House of the Rising Sun' an epic modern masterpiece, quite apart from Price's powerful contribution.

Burdon says he originally found the song and, if so, he'd definitely demonstrated remarkably keen vision in spotting the potential to improve on Dylan's effort. That alone might warrant an equal share of the cash, one would think. (The story goes that it was The Animals' version of the track that tipped Dylan over the acoustic edge and into his personal electric-ladyland, although others refute that.) Whatever the facts, Alan Price has remained silent about the matter, once saying enigmatically 'success has a thousand fathers and failure is an orphan'.

Ironically, despite the complacency of Mickie Most and Chas Chandler over the affair of the four-minute-twenty-eight-second single, the BBC, true to form, wouldn't play it and it was only down to the band's barn-storming performance of the song on *Ready, Steady, Go!* that it took off. And take off it did. That one performance sold a quarter of a million copies of the single in three days and it shot up the charts.

Next stop: America. Despite the fact the US label did a brutally botched edit of 'House of the Rising Sun' for the benefit of the American radio stations, the song went straight into the top slot and a tour was quickly arranged. Don Arden packaged The Animals in suits à la The Beatles and the second wave of the British invasion was duly launched.

The Animals undertook a scream-packed ten-day succession of concerts at the Paramount Theatre in Times Square. Initially an exhilarating experience, it soon turned into a grim slog by virtue of a gruelling five-gig-a-day schedule. But there were compensations. Where the band had played as support to Little Richard and Chuck Berry back in the UK, here and now in the USA their heroes were supporting them. And there were adoring female fans in New York – loads of them – a phenomenon to which the gruff northerners were unaccustomed, regarded as they were as a boys' act at home.

A postscript to the Alan Price/missing royalties saga came in April 1965 as the band were about to embark on a European tour: Price vanished off the face of the earth. Chandler was living with him at the time and even he had no idea where the wilful keyboardist had gone. Price, from afar, announced that he was leaving the band and cited his dislike of flying as the reason. Twenty years later, Chandler told *Record Collector* magazine a different story, saying that it had been the royalties from 'House of the Rising Sun' that had precipitated the resignation:

> I woke Alan up, went to the shower, had a shower, got out of the shower and Alan had just gone . . . he'd disappeared. And I never saw him again for 18 months. I believe the first cheque had come that day and he just walked out of the door with it.

'I wouldn't say that Pricey walked off with the lion's share so much as the bones, nails, tail, ears and eyes,' roars Burdon. 'And now we didn't have a piano player either.'

A month later, the matter reared its ugly head again. Out of the woodwork came a pair of property speculators who alleged that it was they who had financed The Animals career so far, along with those of The Nashville Teens and Herman's Hermits. They claimed unpaid royalties from 'House of the Rising Sun' and the summons was issued against Jeffery and Mickie Most. The property dealers won their case; now they had made money as well from a track that most of The Animals had not.

Events like this must have sown the seeds in Chas Chandler's mind: if you want to make money, don't play in the band, *own* the band.

Despite a string of classic hits with Mickie Most – 'It's My Life', 'Bring it on Home to Me', 'We've Gotta Get Out of This Place', 'Don't Let Me Be Misunderstood' and, of course, 'House of the Rising Sun' – when his contract with the band expired neither he nor they were keen to renew it. Most's pop sensibilities were too much for the purist Geordie R&B bluesers.

In his *Record Collector* interview, even the pop man Chas had little good to say about him when asked if Most understood them. 'Not a clue,' he retorted. 'If he did understand, he would have stayed with us. He was such a shallow person, really. We didn't [even] want him . . . to be our producer.'

The rot had set in. In 1966, the band's drummer John Steel resigned, fed up with being poor and convinced he and the band were being turned over by Jeffery. The Animals limped on, but Chas Chandler felt Steel's departure was the writing on the wall for him. He told *Record Collector*:

> If anything, the real sound of The Animals was the swing of John's drumming. I think that's what distinguished us from other bands at the time. And when Barry Jenkins came in, we were just another rock band and I lost interest literally overnight.

The drugs didn't help either. 'Acid changed it all. It seemed to make all the people around you suddenly look crazy,' Chas went on. 'I think it was more or less responsible for the demise of the band. It had an effect on all of us. All of a sudden, we were different people.'

Things really began to unravel when the band were recording in the Bahamas. 'We were on a yacht,' recalls Burdon. 'Chas was out swimming and one of the road managers was cutting up pieces of meat and pushing them out of the porthole trying to attract the sharks.'

The decision was made to split and Jeffery negotiated a deal where Eric Burdon would retain the name The Animals and the other members would get a pay-off. They never received it. The decision made, the band went on their final American tour, playing a mismatched support to Herman's Hermits.

'We all acquired a gun each as soon as we got there,' laughs Eric. 'We went up to the woods blazing away and Jeffery was screaming, "Don't point those at each other." We didn't get any trouble with American promoters or local sheriffs screwing us up, though. Jeffery was colonel-in-charge, but he had Peter Grant behind him as tour manager – ten tons of Grant.'

The Animals Mk 1 had made their last bit of cash together, but crucially Chas went to a New York club and saw Jimi Hendrix.

If they'd only had a decent songwriter, or preferably a pair of songwriters, in the band, then the story of The Animals might have been a completely different one and the band's name would have been up there in the pantheon with that of the Stones and The Beatles. The individuals had a crack at writing now and then, but really it just wasn't happening and their efforts seem paltry when shoved up against those of their contemporaries, Jagger and Richards and Lennon and McCartney.

A fundamental difference may have been that Mick and Keith liked each other, as did John and Paul, whereas most of the time there was little love lost between the members of The Animals, let alone rapport or empathy. They remain a third or fourth in the Premiership of the times with an ever-present and slightly wistful 'if only' tag above their name.

The heavyweight blues beauty of Burdon's voice was a big deal, though. When he opened his mouth, it sounded as if he had a seam of Newcastle coal running deep in his soul, for he was the blackest white man to ever stem from these shores and he held the respect and admiration of the greats – Dylan, Lennon, Jagger, the lot.

Hendrix appealed to Chas on many levels. He was a blues man and he was American. Chas knew the Brits would love Hendrix's 'new' blues angle; they would love his Americanism and his youth. They would love his wild hair, clothes and deep languid drawl. But above all he was the sexiest rock/pop/blues star Chas had ever seen and, as it transpires, the sexiest most of us would ever see.

An excited Chas couldn't wait to get Hendrix on the plane, but Jimi had no passport and to get a passport he would need a birth certificate and he didn't have one of those either, so the two of them had to wait agonising weeks for a copy of the certificate to arrive from Seattle.

Unfortunately, the English immigration officers lacked the prescience of Jimi's new manager and only granted the young guitar god a five-day visa. Chas really had to get his finger out to prove to the authorities that this deranged-looking Cherokee Indian/black dude was different from all the existing UK guitarists and to get him signed and making money before Chas's own limited funds ran out. Re-enter the bad guy, Mike Jeffery, who was commissioned to sort things out. Jeffery, rather mysteriously, was able to obtain the requisite paperwork with little difficulty. But once he'd got his feet under the table, he never left the party.

Right on cue, the unsung hero of Hendrix's career, the beautiful Linda Keith, made her reappearance. She had followed the Jimi Hendrix bandwagon back to London and immediately got on the blower to all her ladies-that-gig to put on their best silks and satins and come down, darling, and see this crazy cat just in from NYC.

Jimi was buzzed at being in the UK and promptly went off to look at Buckingham Palace and Piccadilly Circus while Chas was working the phones. Within three weeks, The Jimi Hendrix Experience was born. Chas and Jimi enlisted Noel Redding, a lead guitarist who happily fell to bass as soon as he clocked the blurred fingers of Jimi, and Mitch Mitchell, a brash young drummer who made it clear he was no mere sideman to Hendrix. Mitch had his own statement to make and that was just the right vibe as far as Chandler and Hendrix were concerned.

Three days later, the Jimi Hendrix Experience played a club gig in London. Three days after that, they were in front of 14,500 people at the Olympia stadium in Paris. Days later, they were supporting Eric Clapton and Cream, and mere days after that they were on *Ready, Steady, Go!* performing 'Hey Joe'. How's that for management?

Hendrix was manoeuvred into the epicentre of London's pop scene and hung out with the likes of Andrew Loog Oldham, The Beatles' publicist Derek Taylor, Brian Epstein, the Stones (particularly Brian Jones) and, of course, Marianne Faithfull, who always seemed to be around when the seismic shifts were going down.

Hendrix, naturally, tried it on with her immediately, even though she had only just moved in with Mick Jagger and he had just picked up with Kathy Etchingham. He sat one side of her while Mick sat on the other and reportedly said, 'What are you doing with this jerk? Let's get out of here.' Whether Mick heard or not, he knew what was going on right under his nose and the two biggest womanisers in rock now held a grudge.

Eric Burdon laughs at the thought: 'They both would have fucked anything that moved.'

(Much later, Jagger was to get his oh-so-Mick-type revenge. Devon Wilson was a beautiful junkie/hooker who'd worked her way into Hendrix's bed and then into a job as his personal assistant. She was devoted to him . . . that is, until Jagger came to town. Every time Mick showed up, she'd almost jump on him and would openly flirt with him right in front of an infuriated Hendrix. On one occasion, Jagger had cut his finger and she at first suggested he wash it and then leaned over and sucked the blood off his finger. Hendrix was later to write 'Dolly Dagger' about her – Dagger for Jagger, hence the lyrics. Wilson had been with Hendrix earlier on during the night he died and may have been instrumental in getting him so off his head that he couldn't make it to the toilet to throw up. She herself died a year after Jimi, when she leapt, or was possibly pushed, from an upper-floor window of the Chelsea Hotel in New York.)

Another member of the rock aristocracy, the Who's manager Kit Lambert, saw Hendrix play at the Scotch of St James. Kit was thinking of launching Track Records and fell over a table trying to persuade Chas to put Hendrix on the label. Chas played it cool and took recent recordings of 'Hey Joe' and 'Stone Free' to Decca. The label that had turned down The Beatles demonstrated more breathtaking, if consistent, ineptitude by turning down Hendrix. A more switched-on Polydor signed the track and it was released just before Christmas 1966. Time was tight, though; Chas was running out of cash fast and the single needed a leg up. He decided to throw a launch party at the Bag O'Nails club. All the 'in crowd' would be there, along with promoters and bookers.

The problem was he couldn't afford to pay to put the gig on, so in an act of faith tinged with desperation he pawned his guitar collection.

The sacrifice paid off. 'Hey Joe' went into the charts, the Jimi Hendrix Experience were contracted to tour with the New Animals and the next London gig set up by Lambert at Brian Epstein's Saville Theatre had the Jimi Hendrix Experience supporting The Who. The audience included Jeff Beck, John Lennon, Klaus Voorman, Spencer Davis, Jack Bruce, Paul McCartney, Lulu and Hendrix's personal guardian angel, Linda Keith.

Four weeks after release, 'Hey Joe' climbed to number 6 in the charts and the Great British public came to understand what the cognoscenti had been babbling about for three months. There was a wild new kid in town.

Jimi sat scheming with *NME* writer Keith Altham, Chas and a roadie before a showcase at the Astoria. What could he do next? Guitar-smashing had Townshend's copyright on it really. Even The Move were smashing up TVs on stage.

'Maybe I could smash up an elephant?' ventured Jimi quietly.

'It's a pity you can't set fire to your guitar,' said Altham. 'But a solid body wouldn't burn.'

Chas turned to the roadie. 'Go and buy some lighter fuel. It'll go up like a torch.'

Hendrix set fire to his guitar and 'Purple Haze' went in at number 3 in the charts.

Hendrix loved a jam with anyone, but the one he was really after was Eric Clapton; in fact, he had made it a condition when he and Chas had been talking in New York. 'I'll come to England with you,' he had said, 'but you have to arrange for me to meet Eric Clapton.'

Good as his word, Chas started putting it around town that home-grown blueser Clapton wasn't in the same league as Jimi, then proved it when Hendrix asked Clapton if he could sit in one night. Clapton had heard the word and then he heard the guitar. Blown away, yet exhilarated and not a little worried,

Eric saw that the rules had changed. His pre-eminence wasn't guaranteed; he was going to have to adapt to survive. Rumour has it that, after seeing Jimi play, he was spotted backstage with shaking hands trying to light a cigarette. Pub toilet doors all over the country that had 'Clapton is God' carved into them soon read 'God is dead'.

The *Are You Experienced* album (producer Chas Chandler) had been patched together in studios around London in between the gigs. It went into the charts at number 5.

'Hey Joe' and 'Purple Haze' didn't have much effect on the American record buyers, but the Monterey Festival did. It was an American festival in America and, on the face of it, an American was behind it – John Phillips of the Mamas and the Papas. However, all the buzz was from Britain and the real power behind Monterey lay with a gang of London's rock aristos, which included Paul McCartney, Keith Altham and Andrew Loog Oldham. The organisers knew that only a big British act would pull the crowds, so The Who and Hendrix were booked as headliners – the Jimi Hendrix Experience was widely regarded as a British act – and, alongside The Animals, topped a list featuring Otis Redding, Jefferson Airplane, the Grateful Dead, The Byrds, Janis Joplin, Canned Heat, Buffalo Springfield and Ravi Shankar.

Brian Jones flew all the way to San Francisco just for the privilege of standing at the mike to introduce his friend to 20,000 stoned Californians – the first Americans to witness the stateside birth of the phenomenon. The irony that Hendrix had needed to travel all the way to London in order to triumph in a field in California was inescapable.

Gigs in LA and NYC followed, then Jeffery booked Hendrix on a highly unsuitable yet profitable tour supporting The Monkees – indeed, for a short while Hendrix and Peter Tork became close buddies. Hendrix would sleep at Tork's labyrinthine mansion and cruise around LA in his GTO car until he crashed it at a petrol station. Apparently, when Jeffery telephoned Chas to tell him about the tour, he hung up on him exasperated.

The Jimi Hendrix Experience returned to Europe for a meandering tour of the UK, Holland, Denmark, France and Sweden, where an exhausted Hendrix trashed his hotel room and spent a night in the cells. A few days later in Stockholm, they were refused accommodation at 30 hotels and the wild reputation of the band was assured with the youth of Sweden.

Axis: Bold As Love, the second album, was assembled with the same apparent ease as *Are You Experienced* (you can hear Chas's footsteps used in the studio as a rhythm effect on the track 'If 6 Was 9'). Many would attribute the rawness and spontaneity of the first two albums to the Jimi Hendrix Experience's recording process, which was rapid, to say the least. The band hardly ever rehearsed, either for gigs or for the studio. Hendrix would show Noel Redding the chords and off they'd go, very rarely doing re-takes. Chas liked to record on the run and not get bogged down with confused ideas, but, in truth, the real pre-determinate was the lack of cash. The band often had to move studios because of unpaid bills. So while quick in-and-out recording was financially essential, it also gave us two albums exploding with creativity and power. Necessity was the mother of invention.

One of Chas's biggest achievements was to get Hendrix to sing. The incendiary guitarist was ashamed of his singing abilities and would request that all the studio lights were turned off when he had to do vocal tracks. He'd even tried to get Noel Redding or Mitch Mitchell to take over the lead vocal job. Chas had gently teased the vocals out of him and, for that, all Hendrix fans should be eternally grateful. It now seems absurd to think that anyone else would have done justice to those songs, but it could all have been so very different.

And then it was back to the States, where Jimi did a gig in his old home town Seattle, then Los Angeles, then at a sold-out auditorium in Dallas, where Chas and Jeffery, expecting to collect $7,000, instead picked up $27,000 – big money in 1967.

During this period, the inevitable contract dispute arose. Mike Jeffery and Chandler had set up an offshore company called Yameta and signed Hendrix to it. The other band members were paid only wages. Yameta signed a deal with Warner/Reprise and the two managers rubbed their hands at the thought of sharing 40 per cent of the spoils – a pretty aggressive deal. The Yameta/Warner deal was quite a coup. There was a $40,000 advance. The label contracted to put up $20,000 for promotion and soundtracks for movies were excluded from the deal. Most significantly, all recordings would remain the property of Yameta.

Out of the blue came a claim from a producer, Ed Chalpin, and his company, PPX, which had signed Hendrix on a three-year deal back in 1965 when he was a sideman with Curtis Knight.

Warner tried to stay out of the action but was hauled into it when it was pointed out to them that they had signed their deal with Yameta and not with Hendrix directly. If Yameta lost, then they would lose too.

There was a rapid settlement. PPX would have a share of the existing recorded albums and all the profits from a future album (*Band of Gypsys*). This was quite a result for a company that had done little except own a piece of paper. Chandler and Jeffery were to remain as managers but on a reduced royalty, and Warner won a buyout of the Yameta/Hendrix deal, which cost them $450,000.

Oblivious to the behind-the-scenes skulduggery, a prolific Hendrix was thinking about the third album and he wanted to record it in New York. The British–American divide began to make itself felt. Both Noel Redding and Mitch Mitchell were keen to get back home to Britain and Chas had just become engaged to be married. He had become disillusioned. His partner, Jeffery, seemed to be treating Hendrix as a mere commodity.

The relationship between Jeffery and Jimi had become strained and had affected Chas's own relationship with Hendrix. Recording sessions had become chaotic. Hendrix had booked himself into the Record Plant on a 24-hour-a-day basis and costs were spiralling. When Hendrix was actually recording, the studio would be packed with hangers-on. There were drugs everywhere.

In complete contrast to the recording of the two earlier albums, the tracks meandered and hours were spent on the tiniest details. Mitch and Noel took to sleeping through long periods of the sessions. Chas's input was received less well. He felt excluded, and when Devon Wilson took over as the buffer between Jimi and the real world, then effectively he *was* excluded.

Hendrix would fly to LA on impulse and be seen charging around Hollywood in a Corvette Stingray with a posse of girls. He was drinking a lot as well, partying on the West Coast while the meter was running at $100 an hour for a studio on the East Coast. Eric Burdon recalls, 'We were running buddies, but he was so loaded all the time.'

Chas felt that he had to get Hendrix back to the relative sanity of the UK. That was where he made his finest material; that was where the band was from; that was where Chas could keep him safe. Hendrix just wanted to make the most beautiful album of all time and have some fun; he wouldn't be persuaded. Chas flew home in disgust.

Electric Ladyland was released in late 1968 and 20 naked girls pictured on the sleeve ensured its notoriety. Mitch Mitchell and Noel Redding left the band as the record hit the number 1 slot in the US – they left on a high, but there's no doubt they weren't feeling it. Chas sold his share of the management to Jeffery for $300,000.

Noel obviously felt that something was awry. There never seemed to be any money. Years later, when all the dust had died down, he still felt the same way, and when anyone asked him for advice on contracts and the music business, he would rumble, 'Study law and buy a gun.'

However, Mitch and Noel rejoined Hendrix for some US dates then returned to the UK with Jimi for gigs. They were scheduled to play at the Royal Albert Hall, but the scenes were so chaotic that Chas was called in to help sort things out. He did his best, but sadly for all he would never again exert the same kind of influence over his protégé.

In the following months, the reformed Jimi Hendrix Experience picked up big gig money, running at around $1 million a month, but Hendrix wanted to work with other musicians. Redding and Mitchell again retreated to London to escape the drifting craziness, the drugs and the liggers.

Hendrix dropped the Jimi Hendrix Experience name and with Billy Cox and Buddy Miles formed the Band of Gypsys and started building the Electric Lady Studios in New York. The studio caused huge problems for Mike Jeffery, who was left holding the baby while Hendrix kept all the tape machines of the Record Plant turning on his 24/7 schedule.

It's reported that Hendrix was taking an acid tab every day at this stage and his hair was falling out in clumps. Eric Burdon reckons this is a conservative estimate. 'More like taking acid three times a day,' he says. 'As for his hair, it might have been falling out of his head, but he was probably growing more of it, on his toes and on the back of his hands.'

There were run-ins with mobsters and an incident so bizarre that it just might not have happened. Early one morning, the story goes, Jimi was alone in his apartment in Manhattan and the doorbell rang. He answered the door to four strangers, who bundled him into the back of a car and blindfolded him. He was dragged forcefully but gently into a warehouse and put in a chair. They threatened him with violence, but it never actually came to pass, so he just sat. Eventually, there were other voices. He heard sounds of a struggle and swearing. Then the blindfold was ripped from his face by Mike Jeffery, who, it seems, with his sidekicks, had just rescued Hendrix from some sort of kidnap. Jimi's questions were inconclusively answered. How did they know where he was? What was it all about? Was it a real kidnapping or some sort of set-up? There was so much LSD and paranoia going on in Jimi's brain at the time, had the episode ever really happened at all?

Hendrix ploughed on to his sad conclusion – the definitive rock star death, choking on his own vomit, while drunk, drugged and asleep. A tragic event that nevertheless left him unassailable as the biggest star in the sky. He used to say himself, 'Once you are dead, you are made for life.'

In some ways, he was born in the UK and it was perhaps fitting that he should die here, too. London had proved to be more of a home for him than anywhere else.

All are agreed that – particularly when he was in the USA – Hendrix was surrounded by awful people: junkies, sycophants and leeches who dragged him down and saw him under the earth. Things weren't helped by Mike Jeffery, who would take new batches of drugs round for Jimi to sample.

Jeffery himself died in a plane crash in 1973, on his way to find out who would be inheriting Jimi Hendrix's British musical royalties.

All are also agreed that the only person who might have been able to prevent the tragedy was Chas. Indeed, there is a story that, hours before he died, Hendrix left a plaintive message on Chas's answer phone requesting that Chas come back and manage him. Keith Altham says the story is apocryphal, but undoubtedly, if Chandler had known how serious things had become, he would have stepped in. After all, he had showed time and time again that he cared more for Hendrix than did many of the others around the star.

Chas, quoted in Chris Welch's book *Hendrix: A Biography*, saw a grim inevitability about it all. 'Somehow I wasn't surprised. I don't believe for one minute that he killed himself. That was out of the question. But something had to happen and there was no way of stopping it.'

Eric reckons Hendrix was unmanageable. 'No one could have done it. I was offered part of the management in exchange for giving up using The Animals name. I said, "Manage that guy? It's like saying, 'Here's a bunch of terrorists – manage them. Oh and by the way, they want to keep their Kalashnikovs.'"'

He adds enigmatically, 'Hendrix passed on, Chas passed on. Mike Jeffery outlived most of them.' When pressed, he continues, 'Jeffery was supposed to have died on an aeroplane. That sounds dodgy to me. He was terrified of flying. He may have engineered it so he was never on the flight. I can see him now, lying back in a hammock in the West Indies.'

Chas's contributions to the Jimi Hendrix Experience are considerable. Undoubtedly, bringing Hendrix to the UK made him. He was unknown in New York and might well have remained that way, plugging away in the background for years, or worse, succumbed far earlier to the drink-and-drugs binge that finally got him and which may have cheated us of some more of the best rock music ever made. Finding Mitchell and Noel Redding turned out to be the perfect foil for the guitar genius. Getting Hendrix to write (he only had one song written when he landed at Heathrow; it was Chas who forced him on: 'That's where the money is,' he would say). Producing the huge sound of the two first albums. Getting Hendrix to sing. Powering those early recording sessions along and giving Jimi encouragement when he wanted to experiment and make things weirder. Letting Hendrix raid his science-fiction collection. (Chas loved sci-fi and so did Hendrix – some of those lyrics come straight out of Jimi's London reading sessions, when they lived together in Ringo Starr's old flat; in fact, the lyric from 'Third Stone From the Sun' is based on Chas's copy of *Earth Abides* by George R. Stewart.) Doing his best to try and keep Jimi's head straight when all around were intent on making him lose it. The down-to-earth giant Geordie was the perfect mentor and father figure to the wayward genius.

However, an indomitable Chas didn't sit around moping when he lost Hendrix, he immediately set about finding himself another act to promote, this time under the auspices of the Robert Stigwood Organisation. When the going gets tough, the tough go shopping . . . for bands.

Word trickled through of a raucous new band that made a colossal noise and stamped their feet and hauled the audience up onstage to sing along with them – a good-time band called Ambrose Slade. Chandler went to see them and was customarily quick off the mark. 'I'm signing you now,' he said, adding, 'you're a breath of fresh air.' Chas's imposing frame and reputation left them suitably awestruck.

The band had been gigging for months as the N'Betweens before they alighted on Ambrose Slade – the former having been dropped because of the fear that they might be regarded as bisexual, not perhaps the kind of image the rough-edged Midlanders wanted to portray. One other possible name, which was thankfully rejected, was Knicky Knacky Noo.

The band released an album called *Beginnings* for the Fontana label, but sales were low. Chas wasn't concerned, though. According to Noddy Holder, in his biography *Who's Crazee Now?*, Chas told them, 'You could be the kings of the short pop song.' He co-opted rock publicist Keith Altham to look at image and promotion and, in an uncharacteristic aberration of taste on both their parts, decided the band would look good as skinheads, complete with Fair Isle tank tops and Dr Martens boots. Slade were never the prettiest band and the publicity photos exacerbated that, leaving them looking uncomfortable rather than menacing as Chas had imagined.

However, the *NME* liked them and a photo session and an associated article lent them a bit of notoriety, though it also attracted skinheads to Ambrose Slade gigs. Bassist Jimmy Lea and the exotic 'Superyob' guitarist Dave Hill were particularly unhappy with the 'bovver boy' image and soon their hair was creeping over their collars again.

The 'Ambrose' was dropped and Slade released a new single, 'Shape of Things to Come', on Polydor. Chas felt more comfortable with a label he knew from the Hendrix days. The band that went on to become the virtual *Top of the Pops* house band played their first show with another first-timer, Elton John, who performed 'Lady Samantha'.

Slade recorded their album *Play It Loud* at Olympic Studios, again familiar territory for Chas. Their fast-moving manager had only allowed them three weeks to do it in, so they had to move quickly. Chas was in his element: in the producer's chair once more and recording against the clock.

Noddy notes in his autobiography: 'Chas was our first proper producer. He sat and listened from the control room, then came into the studio to comment on the arrangements. He made us work on the sound until it was just right. He had great ears for spotting a hit.'

Slade could pack venues all over the country and no one could work a crowd like Noddy. They sounded great and they had Jimi Hendrix's producer: the odds were stacked heavily in their favour. But given all that, the album, their second, didn't sell. The band became despondent, but Chas remained unruffled . . . except when anyone suggested he might be wasting his time with Slade. 'That would infuriate Chas. Whenever anyone made a negative remark, he would go mad,' Noddy said. 'He was a big bloke and he could tear your head off. People rarely said bad things about us more than once to Chas, put it that way.'

Chandler demonstrated his considerable commercial acumen once more when he got the band to record 'Get Down and Get With It'. It had long been the biggest gun in their live set; now, all they had to do was to get that energy on plastic – not an easy task, but they managed it. It was recorded in one take in Olympic. All that had to be overdubbed was stomping boots.

John Peel was one of the first DJs to play it. A lot of his contemporaries considered it too rowdy for radio, but gradually the track caught on and the band was on *Top of the Pops* again. 'Get Down and Get With It' rose to number 16 in the charts and Slade were off and running.

The clothes became more colourful than standard skinhead attire. This was 1971. The singles chart had been in a parlous state, with Clive Dunn's 'Grandad' and Benny Hill's 'Ernie (The Fastest Milkman in the West)' blaring from the radio, but in March Marc Bolan released 'Hot Love'. In June, Sweet slipped into spandex catsuits and sang 'Ho-chi-ka-ka-ho Co-Co'. When Slade's 'Get Down and Get With It' came out in the August, incredibly the press managed to weld these three disparate bands into a movement – glam rock was born.

Chas insisted the band write their own material – he'd been this way before. Noddy and Jimmy came up with 'Coz I Luv You' and tentatively played it to Chas on acoustic guitars. Noddy recalled: 'We were a bit apprehensive about his reaction. Chas was always critical. He didn't pussyfoot around. If he thought something was crap, he would sure as hell tell you. We played it, and then mumbled a few words about wanting to put a violin on it to make it more distinctive. Before we'd even finished talking, he said, "I think you've written your first hit record. In fact, I think you've just written your first number 1."'

Two weeks after the single was released, Chas's prediction came true. Slade entered their golden era and became one of the most successful singles bands since The Beatles.

They recorded their third album, *Slade Alive*, in a live setting and it went straight to number 1 in the album charts. It stayed in the UK charts for 18 months and was a monster hit all over the world. Meanwhile, it seemed that T. Rex, Slade and Sweet were taking it in turns to top the singles charts.

Slade started shuttling around the TV stations of Europe with a bunch of other perma-chart residents who all became friends, Abba and Boney M – a curious bunch of compatriots indeed.

Chas was pushing the band hard now; he wanted singles released in quick succession. Another grammatically challenged single, 'Look Wot You Dun', was released three weeks after 'Coz I Luv You' slipped out of the charts. It wasn't as strong, but it kept the band in the spotlight and encouraged sales of the album. Slade kept up this astonishing output for four years with single after single and only three or four months between releases – and they were all hits.

'Take Me Bak 'Ome', released in June 1972, also took the top slot but only after a slow start. Slade appeared at the Lincoln Festival as the only pop band amongst a line-up of hip acts such as The Beach Boys, The Faces and Lindisfarne. They were booed when they walked out on the stage, but the killer combination of Noddy's vocals and crowd skills and Chas's determination that they went on at twilight with all the stage lights suddenly dramatically visible swung the trendy crowd over. (Led Zeppelin had performed the same stunt at the Bath Festival two years earlier.) And Slade played loud – very, very loud.

That year was a wild ride for the band. After 'Take Me Bak 'Ome' came 'Mama Weer All Crazee Now' in September and 'Gudbuy T'Jane' in November. There were many more glam bands now, or at least bands content to shelter under the glittery umbrella – anything, if it meant hits. The chart was thick with sequins: Sweet, Slade, Gary Glitter, Roxy Music, Alice Cooper, Mott the Hoople and the Glam Queen himself, David Bowie.

But if '72 was good for Slade in singles terms, '73 was great, with 'Cum on Feel the Noize' straight in at number 1 in March, 'Skweeze Me Pleeze Me' released in June and 'My Friend Stan' in October. They then climaxed the year with their boozy Christmas hardy-perennial, 'Merry Xmas Everybody'.

Slade were getting number ones all over the world now – all over the world that is, except the USA, the biggest market of all. With the head of steam the band had built up, it seemed obvious that now was the time to take on the leviathan. Chas set the ball rolling. He employed the biggest agents for the biggest venues and bullied promoters into giving Slade support slots with the biggest bands on the road.

And not many were bigger than Humble Pie. This was the stadium rock era and bands like them were playing get-down no-nonsense boogie, wearing jeans and T-shirts in vast auditoriums. Their audience was thousands of totally stoned kids who all looked the same as the band.

Slade arrived in multicoloured clothes with more tightly structured songs – more boozy than dopey. They didn't go off on fifteen-minute guitar trips or drum solos, and the stoners didn't quite get down and get with it. The band also had trouble with the workload – five or six radio interviews every morning and then soundcheck and gig every evening. And, like many bands before them and since, they had underestimated the sheer size of the

USA, with the associated grinding routine of airport, hotel, radio stations, soundcheck, gig and bed – day after day after day. 'Will Slade break America or will America break Slade?' asked Keith Altham in a 1973 *NME* article. Time would tell.

But they breed 'em tough in the Midlands and they had a right hard manager, too, and Slade gamely hurled themselves at the States time after time, but America obdurately resisted their charms.

There was consolation, though. They returned to the UK for the release of 'Merry Xmas Everybody' (which they'd recorded in New York in the middle of a burning summer). Polydor went nuts about the song and pulled out all the stops. It got 500,000 advance orders and another 300,000 re-orders two days after the release. It had sold a million copies by Christmas 1973 and was at that point the fastest-selling UK single of all time. Somewhat typically, the French were a little slower off the mark than most and 'Merry Xmas Everybody' didn't make it to number 1 there until an unseasonal Easter 1974.

The song that Noddy often refers to as his pension was their biggest number 1 ever, but it was to be their last. Slade never reached number 1 again. The next single 'Everyday' was a ballad and only made it to number 3. Slade weren't used to number twos.

But when in doubt branch out, Chas thought, and decided it was time to make a film. The Beatles had made films after all.

Slade in Flame could have turned out like the later Reeves and Mortimer parody of the band but under Chas's deft guiding hand (he persuaded David Puttnam's fledgling Goldcrest group to take on production), it turned out to be a solid, gritty drama about a band's struggle with bent promoters and managers, dodgy concert halls and a wholly corrupt music business. Noddy acted like a natural throughout.

The standout song from the soundtrack album was 'Far Far Away'. 'I started drunkenly singing it to Chas,' says Noddy in his autobiography. 'Straight away, he said, "Go to your room now and write that down. Try and finish it tonight, while you're on a roll." That was typical of Chas. He never switched off.'

'Far Far Away' made number 2.

But the best was behind them by now and Slade was on the slide. Punk was on the way in and the glam rockers were changing or dying. Slade soldiered on. After all, they had more talent than most. There were a few more hits, but the numbers were dwindling and over time the band disappeared from the radio waves altogether. They were even reduced to doing cabaret, sometimes suffering the ignominy of playing the likes of Bailey's in Watford – the week after Little and Large.

They could still pack them in around Europe, however, and through the late '70s it was these tours that sustained them while the punk storm raged back home. Slade looked to Chas for ideas, but it seemed he was as out of time as the rest of them and the best he could think of was to break up the band and send Noddy and Jimmy Lea out to form another one together.

The duo refused to consider this, but when the others learned of Chas's betrayal they downed tools and went home to think things through and lick their wounds. Slade should have been finished then and there, but events precluded that. When Ozzy Osbourne pulled out of the 1980 Reading Festival just two days before it started, the organisers racked their brains trying to think of a suitable replacement band – they needed an act that was loud, fun and famous. Chas received the call and, having first extracted an outrageous fee, somehow managed to mend fences with the estranged Slade members for the one-off. It was a customary riot-house performance from Slade, and after languishing in obscurity for three years, they were back in the music press.

It was all too late for their relationship with Chas, though. He'd been caught trying to do the dirty and Noddy was deputised to go down to London and do the dirty deed right back.

Slade went on to have success at the Monsters of Rock Festival the following year, then, as a parting gift, Chas set the band up with another record deal. They then released their *We'll Bring the House Down* album, which saw them return to form as hard-rocking rowdies. Then, in 1983, American band Quiet Riot recorded 'Cum on Feel the Noize' and the ensuing album sold seven million copies. Suddenly, Slade were in demand stateside six years after they had given up trying. They signed to CBS America and recorded 'Run Runaway', which went into the Billboard Top 10, effectively their first American hit. A tour beckoned; they did one date with Ozzy Osbourne but, despite the success, the momentum was gone. There had been arguments in the studio, Noddy was going through a divorce, Jim had started seeing a psychiatrist, Dave became a Jehovah's Witness and Don had hit the bottle. There were more singles, small hits even, but the decline in relationships and song quality was ongoing. They tried different producers but to no avail. How much they missed Chas's production abilities and his nose for a good tune cannot be underestimated.

There were occasional reunions, and Oasis covered 'Cum on Feel the Noize', but it was over and the band didn't meet again until Chas's funeral in 1996.

In the years prior to his death, Chas had busied himself with recording studios in the North-east and a long-held plan to build a covered stadium in Newcastle. He went into partnership with a one-time saxophonist with The Animals, Nigel Stanger, and then cast around for the money for the project. There is little doubt that without Chas's larger-than-life persona and indefatigable enthusiasm the 11,000-plus Metro Radio Arena would never have been built. It opened with a David Bowie concert and for the first time the residents of Tyneside would have a local venue capable of housing the biggest star bands.

Stanger told mourners at the funeral that Chas had 'revelled in learning all he could about the construction industry', taking on the mighty task with the same vigour with which he had taken on the music industry. And what foolish site foreman would have had the balls to take on the ex-lathe-turner, union negotiator and band manager?

Noddy Holder was asked to say a few words at Chas's funeral. 'I told a mad story about Chas and us in the Miyako Hotel one night in San Francisco,' he said, 'when he'd walked through a paper

Above: Don Arden (sporting the beard) signing The Move (© EMI Archives/Redferns)

Right: Don's 'Beatles' — The Small Faces (© John Roddgers/Redferns)

Left: Brian Epstein with his 'boys' (© Cummings Archives/Redferns)

Below: Beatles *Yellow Submarine* lunch box and Thermos

Top: Andrew Loog Oldham looks over the mix
(© Gered Mankowitz/Redferns)

Above: Chris Stamp watches Kit Lambert hit the bottle — perhaps worrying about the cost of keeping The Who in new equipment (© Jan Olofsson/ Redferns)

Left: Keith destroying a kit (© Graham Lowe/Redferns)

Above: (left) Chas Chandler with The Animals (© David Redfern/ Redferns) and (right) with The Jimi Hendrix Experience (© Gunter Zint/Redferns)

Right: Slade (© RB/Redferns)

Below centre: Simon Napier-Bell (© Fin Costello/Redferns)

Below left: The Yardbirds, featuring their two guitarists, Jeff Beck and Jimmy Page — it could never last (© RB/Redferns)

Below right: Wham! George gay? Never! (© Gered Mankowitz/Redferns)

The Zep Tour bus
(© Bob Gruen)

Right: With Peter Grant, the power behind
Led Zeppelin (© Tom Hanley/Redferns)

Below left: Syd Barrett, bathed in lights
(© Andrew Whittuck/Redferns)

Below right: Action man Steve O'Rourke
(© Dave Dyer)

Above: A combative Johnny Rotten (© Ebet Roberts/Redferns)

Right: Happier days with Malcolm McLaren
(© Ebet Roberts/Redferns)

The Clash — 'the only band that matters'
(© Erica Echenberg/Redferns)

Alan McGee with ex-Dexy Kevin Rowland (© Nicky J. Sims/Redferns)

Liam gives it the finger (© George Chin/Redferns)

The mighty Spice Girls
(Brits photo © Patrick Ford/ Redferns)

Right: Simon Fuller, King of the Svengalis, and Nicki
Chapman, the power behind the throne
(© Dave Benett/Getty Images)

wall. I thought the image Chas left in that wall was rather like the impact he left wherever he went in his life: a big man with a big personality.'

Among those who attended were Keith Altham, the other members of Slade and Jimi Hendrix's father, Al, who had been on his way to meet Chas to discuss the release of some of his son's material that was still in Chas's possession.

6
STEVE O'ROURKE

Pink Floyd

'The racing driver's mind has to have the ability to have amazing anticipation, coordination and reflex. Because of the speed the car goes.'

– Emerson Fittipaldi,
Formula 1 world champion

Pink Floyd were one of those rare things in the pop business – posh. Although there have been a few others: Genesis were (before Phil Collins joined and lowered the tone); Charlie formerly of Busted is; Will Young is; one of Goldie Lookin' Chain is; Posh Spice definitely isn't, although her family had a few quid.

Conceived in the once brilliant then fried brain of the late Syd Barrett, Floyd were unique. They sat on the floor when they played, they knew a lot and they'd experimented with pure LSD (it was an acquaintance of the band, Michael Hollingshead, an Englishman, who had turned Timothy Leary onto the drug). In 1966, they had moved from Cambridge to London and were doing gigs at the 'Spontaneous Underground' nights at the Marquee club and at London Free School in Notting Hill to a ragbag of hippies, black militant activists and shocked locals. Eerie slides were projected onto the band and the walls. Lots of dope was smoked.

IT, the *International Times* hippie radical newspaper, backed by Paul McCartney and distributed to the Aldermaston CND marchers, carrying headlines like 'Fuck for Peace' and 'Pay the Landlord in Marmalade', was launched at a huge party at the London Roundhouse. Pink Floyd were launched at the same party.

There were no attendants, doormen or security at the gig, but they thought it best to have a doctor in attendance. The Soft Machine played support – they utilised an onstage motorbike which had a microphone taped to the engine. At certain points of emphasis, the bike was revved up.

The *IT* report of the party read:

The Pink Floyd, psychedelic pop group, did weird things to the feel of the event with their scary feedback sounds, slide projections playing on their skin (drops of paint ran riot on the slides to produce outer space/prehistoric textures on the skin) spotlights flashing in time with the drums.

Shortly after, the band signed a management deal with Peter Jenner and Andrew King and they set up Blackhill Enterprises as a jointly run company to look after their affairs.

In December 1966, UFO Club opened on Tottenham Court Road, run by legendary acoustic producer Joe Boyd (who produced Floyd's 'Arnold Layne' – a true story about a transvestite who steals women's underwear from washing lines). Its audience at various times included Malcolm X, the black activist, The Beatles sitting on the floor watching Jimi Hendrix jamming with The Soft Machine, Pete Townshend watching the Crazy World of Arthur Brown. Procol Harum played there when 'Whiter Shade of Pale' was released; the Council for Civil Liberties was in constant attendance in case the police should bust it. By all accounts, the local constabulary hated dealing with the hippies and would draw straws to see who would be given the Friday night detail.

Barry Miles, co-founder of *IT*, reported for the *NME*:

> The principal danger was from acid-crazed Hells Angels, anxious to practise love 'n' peace in order to pull hippie nookie, who would insist on French-kissing every policeman they saw.
>
> Eventually, noddin' and gruntin' arrangements were arrived at. The police would stand at the top of the stairs holding a squirming naked hippie at arm's length, eyes revolving like Catherine wheels. 'One of yours?' they would inquire. 'We'll have 'im,' Mick Farren would reply.

This was way outside the loop of 'smart set' clubs like the Speakeasy and the Cromwellian.

When Floyd signed to EMI and recorded in Abbey Road, just down the corridor were The Beatles, who were working on *Sergeant Pepper*. Floyd popped in to see the greatest band in the world at work. McCartney was very respectful, deferential even. Floyd thought they were in the presence of royalty, however.

'Arnold Layne' reached number 20.

Over the next couple of years, Floyd perfected their intense, stoned, sound-and-light total immersion experience. The light show grew in scale and if the management of venues wouldn't shut down their own house lights, to achieve full effect Floyd's roadies would shoot them out with air rifles. Bowie watched them at the Ricky Tick, they played the legendary Eel Pie Island and they were often accompanied by the ultra-radical Hornsey College of Art Light and Sound Workshop, who were with them at the sold-out Brighton Festival. However, when they did venture outside of London, things didn't always go quite so well. Locals in Dunstable poured beer over them and in Norfolk they were pelted by a crowd of gypsies.

The 14-hour Technicolor Dream at Alexandra Palace is now generally mythologised as the epochal moment of the '60s.

Between 7,000 and 10,000 people turned up for the event, many dressed in velvets and bells but most still in shirts and ties, such was the cusp of the moment. Shocked kids stared at one another in the realisation that they weren't the only freaks in the world. This was the night that the London underground went above ground and the ripples made by the event would wash out over the whole world.

Exotic guests included the Tribe of the Sacred Mushroom, David Medalla and the Exploding Galaxy, the Social Deviants, Yoko Ono (who arranged a model to be seated and then encouraged members of the audience to cut off pieces of her clothes with scissors until she sat naked), Suzy Creamcheese, the Utterly Incredible Too Long Ago to Remember Sometimes Shouting at People, Alexis Korner, Champion Jack Dupree, Graham Bond, Ginger Johnson and his African conga drummers, Savoy Brown, The Pretty Things, The Purple Gang, Crazy World of Arthur Brown, The Soft Machine and at the top of the bill were Pink Floyd.

This was the night that STP, the strongest acid ever invented – one tab of which rendered Andrew Loog Oldham sweating and terrified for days; one tab of which Pete Townshend reckoned had destroyed his personality – was introduced to London. Floyd's singer and guitarist Syd Barrett was on acid and so was his manager Peter Jenner . . . all they could get their hands on.

All eyes were on Barrett, the original hippy. He had that look, Jenner reckoned. 'Syd was a handsome boy,' he says. 'He was beautiful . . . he was true flower power. He came out in this outrageous gear . . . and he looked like a beautiful woman, all this Thea Porter [bohemian rich hippy outfitter to The Beatles and the Stones] stuff. He had a lovely girlfriend, Lindsay. She was the spitting image of Syd.'

DJ John Peel later reported on the 'happening'. 'It was like paradise,' he gushed. 'It was wonderful. You spent a lot of time rushing around saying, "Brian Jones is here, Hendrix is here, where, where?" Rushing around to see famous people, you were still that much of a dickhead. But it was just a great event. All these bands came on; a lot of them were awful. There were a few that were really good, but it was the sense of community, of occasion, the sense that anything was possible.'

Floyd came on as the first light of dawn came through the vast cathedral-style windows. Julian Palacios recorded some audience impressions in his book *Lost in the Woods*: 'The dawn arrived in a triumphant pink hue, the light came cascading in from the huge windows and amidst this awesome display of nature Pink Floyd took the stage. They were wearing outfits with flared trousers and satin shirts that I had not seen them wear before. People began to awake and hold hands as the first notes of "Astronomy Domine" reverberated through the massive hall.

'The atmosphere was electric. There was an extraordinary connection between the band and the audience. Then the magic happened. Syd's mirror-disc Telecaster caught the dawn's pink light. Syd noticed this and with drug-filled eyes blazing, he made his guitar talk louder and louder, higher and higher as he reflected the light into the eyes of his audience and christened those of us lucky enough to be there, followers of Pink Floyd for life.'

Peter Jenner continues: 'The band wanted to go onstage just as dawn was breaking, which they did, and it was incredible. The band played at dawn with all the light coming through the glass at the Palace, the high point of the psychedelic era for me. It was a perfect setting, everyone had been waiting for them and everybody was on acid; that event was the peak of acid use in England . . . Everybody was on it: the bands, the organisers, the audience, and I certainly was.'

Palacios picks up the story again: 'Daevid Allen [of Gong] spoke of the uncomfortably eerie vibe as Pink Floyd played: "the glissando guitar stroker [Syd] looked as though he was not there. It wouldn't be long before he wasn't."'

This, of all their gigs, was the launch pad for Floyd. Every mover and (bell) shaker in the scene was either here or just over there. For a brief moment, flower power had flourished in all its beautiful, fragile innocence but with intensely strong chemicals available everywhere. Inevitably, it wouldn't be long before the acid casualties would start falling by the wayside, brain-fried and soon filling out the wards of the mental hospitals. Incredibly, Syd kept his marbles long enough to write the mini epic 'See Emily Play' and the album *The Piper at the Gates of Dawn*. The single went to number 5 and the album reached number 6. Pink Floyd – although your parents had still never heard of them – were now almost mainstream and would never hold the keys to the underground again.

When the third single, 'Apples and Oranges', failed to chart, Syd was asked to react. 'Couldn't care less,' he said. 'All we can do is make records which we like. If the kids don't, then they won't buy it. The kids dig The Beatles and Mick Jagger not so much because of their music but because they always do what they want to do and to hell with everyone else . . . The kids know this.'

He was now chasing acid tabs with acid tabs, though, and such was his reputation that when he went around to visit a 'friend' for a cup of tea, it would be spiked – just because he was Syd. Storm Thorgerson, who designed a lot of the Floyd sleeves, was on hand to observe the transformation. 'Syd was well into his "orbiting" phase by then,' he says. 'He was travelling very fast in his own private sphere . . .'

Barrett had moved into a flat in the Cromwell Road which, Peter Jenner says, 'was run by heavy, loony messianic acid freaks. Syd got acided out. Acid in the coffee every morning, that's what we were told. He had one of our cats and they gave the cat acid.'

Ian Moore, a friend of Syd, participated in the acid madness. 'We got hold of some liquid LSD bottles,' he said, 'laid out hundreds of sugar cubes in rows and put two drops on each. But the stuff was so strong we were absorbing it through our fingers, or more likely by licking it off them. As it took effect, we had no idea which cubes we had done, so many of them probably got double doses while the rest did not have any. Syd had his plum, orange and matchbox and was sitting staring at them during his trip.

Whatever he was into was his whole world – to him the plum was the planet Venus and the orange was Jupiter. Syd was floating in space between them.'

There is a legend that Cleopatra and Mark Antony were into a concept which they called 'the unparalleled life', where they and their friends would try and reach altered states by drinking heavily. Creatives have turned to drink or drugs since the dawn of time. Drug and drink abuse is endemic in the music business even now, in the workouts and water years, and there have been many, many casualties. 'My drink and drug hell' has become a clichéd newspaper headline; however, there are relatively few who get on the train and never get off it. Syd was unfortunately one of those.

Another of his friends, Sam Hutt, recalls one of Barrett's last public performances. 'I went to UFO quite a lot,' he says, 'saw the bands, the very loud music, the oil lights. I remember near the end with Syd, him coming up and somebody had given him a bottle of mandies. Mandies were the big bouncing-around drug, very dodgy indeed, and probably a very good idea that they took them off the market. Syd appeared on stage with this jar of Brylcreem, having crushed the mandies into little pieces, mixing them up with the Brylcreem and putting this mixture of Brylcreem and broken mandy tablets all over his hair so that when he went out onstage the heat of the lights melted the Brylcreem and it all started to drip down his face with these bits of Mandrax.'

Syd's slide into schizophrenia was rapid now. When the band did a tour of the USA, they guested on the *Pat Boone Show* and Syd refused to respond to questions. His increased exploration of 'inner space' left him paranoid and prone to talking in riddles.

The managers tried to haul him back; they referred Syd to the celebrity psychiatrist R.D. Laing, but when he heard a tape of Syd talking, he suggested that a meeting was unnecessary since Barrett was 'incurable'. 'Creatively, he was as dead as Jimi Hendrix,' Jenner said.

The sense of loss is greater because Barrett's recorded output is so small. Dave Gilmour, an old friend of the band who later became their guitarist/singer and went on to produce some of Syd's solo material, reckons that if Syd had not destroyed himself he could have been one of the greats, right up there with Bob Dylan – a songwriter who could have 'beaten Ray Davies at his own game'.

On a practical level, the band now felt it necessary to bring in a guitarist to bolster their performance and to cover for Syd, who would sometimes be out of key or even playing a completely different track from the rest of them. Dave Gilmour was co-opted. When Syd saw Gilmour, he didn't recognise him, although they had known each other for years.

When they recorded again at Abbey Road, Barrett, who could no longer write or even play, sat pathetically with his guitar in the reception area waiting to be asked to contribute. Floyd decided they had no option but to dump him. Roger Waters forced the issue and the band said goodbye to Syd.

The management, while offering no solution to the problem, rashly felt that Pink Floyd without Syd was doomed so held on to him and said their farewells to the band at the same time. Peter Jenner plugged away in hope, but Syd had gone for ever. The last song he ever wrote for the band was called 'Vegetable Man'.

It seemed to all that the creative spirit of Floyd had been ripped out. How could they possibly continue without their shaman, the burnt-out mad genius Barrett? This was no mere pop band in need of a new writer or front man: Floyd were unique, left field, heavy, intellectual, dark, trippy and now rudderless.

Into this maelstrom stepped Steve O'Rourke.

O'Rourke was an accountant who had worked as a salesman for a pet food company (Roger Waters would never let him forget this and in times of conflict was prone to say, 'What do you know, you're just a dog food salesman!'). Apparently, one of the ways he proved the wholesomeness of his product was to pop open a tin of dog food in front of a customer, pull out a spoon and take a mouthful of it.

He'd lost the pet food job when it was discovered he'd been

racing his company car at Brands Hatch at weekends and palming off his rounds to other salesmen so he could run a club called El Toro in the Edgware Road.

Steve found work as an agent and bookkeeper for the Bryan Morrison Agency, which had been getting gigs for Pink Floyd as well as The Incredible String Band, Fairport Convention, The Pretty Things and Tyrannosaurus Rex. At first, he just handled day-to-day bookings for the band, but when the Bryan Morrison Agency was taken over by NEMS, The Beatles' company, he moved with them. He left NEMS in the early '70s to take over the management of the band with his company EMKA, named after his daughter Emma Kate. O'Rourke would remain at the helm for 35 years – surely a record in the wickedly whimsical world of bands and band management.

However, despite what we know now about Floyd, in those early days O'Rourke's career move should be regarded as a considerable leap of faith; for while the band were pretty popular on the gig circuit, they were a difficult band to book because after 'See Emily Play', they resolutely refused to release singles. Furthermore, they carried with them an enormous light show that always proved difficult to accommodate.

Gilmour signed on the line when the band offered him a regular salary of £30 a week (although in reality the wages were a quarter of that) and O'Rourke installed him in a back room under instructions to learn their repertoire. He mastered it in days.

There were tours and recordings and one final attempt at a single with 'Point Me at the Sky'. In sales terms, it hit the deck and Pink Floyd became an album-only band for years afterwards.

Their atmospheric and experimental musical output brought them to the attention of young film-makers. There were two minor efforts with Floyd soundtracks: a 1967 documentary with a walk-on cast of just about every face in Swinging London entitled *Tonite Let's All Make Love in London*, which was followed by *The Committee* with Paul Jones of Manfred Mann in the lead role. Then followed *More* directed by Barbet Schroeder (a protégée of Jean-Luc Godard) and *Zabriskie Point* directed by Antonioni, which had a big budget, very little plot and the memorable climax of a Death Valley cliffside house exploding over and over again to the shrieking section from 'Careful with that Axe, Eugene'.

The highpoint of 1970 for many was the Bath Festival – possibly the best festival ever staged in the UK. It was the weekend that Led Zeppelin's star rose to its zenith and when Pink Floyd headlined on the Saturday, complete with the mass choir from their *Atom Heart Mother* album. Suddenly everything slipped up a gear. Although you would still have had difficulty recognising any of its members on the street, Pink Floyd were a big, big band. Later that summer, they all went to the south of France in four E-type Jaguars and a Lotus Elan.

In 1972, the band allowed their music to be used on the new-wave surfing film *Crystal Voyager*. Its director, George Greenough, had attached small cameras to surfers' bodies and got exciting footage from inside the wave tubes. The band, in turn, used clips from the movie in their stage performances for many years.

Floyd rattled through a 'Greatest Hits' – *Relics*; the album *Meddle*; UK, European, American and Asian tours; and then threw themselves into their magnum opus, *Dark Side of the Moon*. It was to be a patchy recording process, however, as they squeezed in yet more touring, a soundtrack for *Obscured by Clouds* and their own concert film, *Live at Pompeii*.

Despite the settled family lives, houses and E-type Jags, it was only with *Dark Side of the Moon* that the fortunes of Pink Floyd and O'Rourke were assured. When the album was released in 1973, it wasn't so much another shift up a gear as a quantum leap. However, before the floodgates of cash opened, O'Rourke went in to do battle with the American label Capitol. Floyd's contract was at an end and it was their opportunity to drive a hard bargain. O'Rourke turned the screw on Capitol and, uncharacteristically for an American label, hitherto US-centric and scornful of British underground music, their new boss Bhaskar Menon flew to Europe post-haste to plead with the band. O'Rourke relented and gave

Capitol *Dark Side of the Moon*. In light of what was to follow, the Capitol label, indeed the whole EMI group, had a lot to be grateful for. EMI showed its gratitude to Menon by making him its chairman.

The statistics for sales of the record are staggering and worth relating in brief. *Dark Side of the Moon* has sold 35 million copies worldwide and rising. It's estimated that one in four homes in the UK has a copy. With the 13 October 2001 edition of the Billboard chart, *Dark Side of the Moon* celebrated its 1,278th week (25 years) on either the Top 200 Pop Album or Top Pop Catalogue Album chart. No other album has stayed longer on any chart in history.

With the advent of CDs, EMI re-released the album (its catalogue number is EMI 001) and *Dark Side of the Moon* established itself as one of the top-ten biggest-selling records of all time. Despite this, amazingly, it never reached number 1 in the UK and only made the number 1 place for one week in the USA.

The original record was supposed to have been packaged in a box that included bumper stickers, posters and other treats, but Capitol wouldn't cough up for the marketing goodies. The band had to take a royalty reduction just to get a poster included. They shouldn't have been so worried: it still sells a million copies a year. *Dark Side of the Moon* became the de facto record for demonstrating hi-fi equipment and was once voted the most popular record played during live sex shows.

'I thought it was a good record,' deadpanned Roger Waters.

There was a downside, however, and it kind of caused the further break-up of the band. Floyd had taken a small cult following and turned it into a very large cult following, but with the release of 'Money', which became their only true hit single, their audience changed, as did the venues they played. They were now a stadium and festival band – they couldn't have possibly played anywhere else – and their new audiences weren't content to sit cross-legged for three hours listening to long drawn-out tracks. They wanted hit singles.

Roger Waters commented, 'That's why after 1977 I refused to

play stadiums because the larger the audience, the whole thing becomes more about commerce and less about communication, music, human feelings and values.'

The years after *Dark Side of the Moon* saw the band established as one of the biggest, if not *the* biggest band in the world. O'Rourke moved them from Capitol to Columbia, with a massive accompanying transfer fee. He'd also taken the pressure off the band to release albums to order. As drummer Nick Mason states in his book, *Inside Out: A Personal History of Pink Floyd*, 'We were not locked into a contract that demanded we churn out one or two albums a year. In fact we were under no obligation to deliver within any timeframe. I do not remember any huge pressure from EMI to deliver *Dark Side II: The Lunatic Returns*, but this may well be a tribute to Steve O'Rourke's management ability in deflecting brickbats and any other missiles sent out by the record company.'

There followed a fallow period during which a non-musical album of miscellaneous sounds, *Household Objects*, was put together but never released. O'Rourke and the band members, except for Roger, all had children now; there were short tours and individual band members recorded with other artists, one of whom, a schoolgirl from Bexleyheath, had sent Dave Gilmour a demo tape: Kate Bush.

Their 1975 release, *Wish You Were Here*, which was loosely about and dedicated to Syd Barrett and which featured the epic 'Shine on You Crazy Diamond', was an enormous success. *The Wall*, released in 1979, surpassed *Dark Side of the Moon* for US sales, going 23 times platinum and becoming the third-biggest-selling album in US chart history. It also continues to sell a million copies a year. However, despite their massive album sales, the track 'Another Brick in the Wall' would be the band's only number 1 single.

In the face of such success, everything in the garden should have been rosy, but in the music business it never quite works out that way; in fact, everything was far from lovely. The band discovered that the investment company they had been using in an attempt to defray some of the 83 per cent tax-rate burden on their earnings had made some rather strange investments on their behalf. Floyd found that they were involved in carbon-fibre rowing boats, skateboard manufacture, second-hand Rolls-Royce sales and a failed hotel. All was not well.

An investigation revealed that the company, Norton Warburg, had been siphoning funds from the secure side of its business to speculate on risky, if not disastrous, enterprises on the venture capital side of its business, and the funds they were using for this were Pink Floyd's. There was a £2 million black hole. To add insult to injury, the band were then advised that they might have to cough up the tax on the missing money.

And there was more: in the arcane world of tax law, it seemed that their plight exposed them to even further income tax liabilities and they might have had to find anywhere between £5 million and £12 million to get the Inland Revenue off their case. With the end of the financial year looming and ruin staring them in the face, they had little option but to run. Floyd packed their bags and split to France.

Similarly, one of Norton Warburg's directors slipped off to Spain (on his return, he was arrested and served three years in prison).

In the interim, O'Rourke and his advisors, in conjunction with the Revenue, set about reorganising the whole structure of the band's finances and its various companies, including the Britannia Row studio complex that they had built to record *The Wall*. At one time, there were 200 sets of accounts waiting for Inland Revenue approval, such was the extent of their holdings. Of course, it requires many bean-counters to handle 200 sets of accounts, and Floyd were paying for them all. To finance the salvage operation, O'Rourke had to flog off some of the band's publishing rights, which he sold to Chappell's. Previously, the band had held their publishing rights lock, stock and barrel.

Then cracks started appearing in the band. Keyboard player Rick Wright was given his marching orders in the late '70s when he refused to come back from his Greek villa vacation to record keyboard parts for *The Wall*. Steve O'Rourke had been on the *QE2* en route to the USA when he got a phone call from an angry Waters telling him to have Wright sacked before he arrived in Los Angeles to record (Wright was kept on as an employee during *The Wall* stage shows – and ironically was the only band member not to lose money on them).

O'Rourke's negotiating skills were again called upon when the publishing company refused to treat the double album as two records and demanded to pay a lower royalty. The record company then refused to pay for independent promotion of the record. The band in turn refused to let them have the album at all, to which the record company responded that they would take the album by force.

Just another quiet day at the desk in the music business.

Coincidentally, there was a break-in at the studio and in this highly charged, paranoid atmosphere everyone was issued with a password as a security measure. Similar ill-feeling permeated the band. Despite triumphant sell-out gigs – seven nights in LA, five nights in New York, six nights at London's Earls Court, eight nights in Germany and another five nights at Earls Court for the forthcoming film – the band all retired to their own individual dressing-rooms and even held their own mutually exclusive backstage parties.

However, when it came to financing the movie of *The Wall*, O'Rourke apparently assembled a dazzling set of books that enabled him and the film's director, Alan Parker, to extract $10 million from MGM despite a confession from David Begelman, the MGM executive in charge, that he hadn't the slightest idea what the movie was about. O'Rourke was the executive producer. The film starred Bob Geldof as the character Pink, who shaves off his hair and his eyebrows, an act that Syd had performed in real life. Considering the vagaries of the plot, it's a testament to O'Rourke that it got made at all, let alone went on to make money.

When it came to the album to be called *The Final Cut*, Roger Waters went through a period that he surely can't be proud of today.

He urged David Gilmour to come up with some contributory tracks by a certain date. Gilmour didn't respond well to the imposition of a deadline by a fellow band member but duly came up with some material. According to Nick Mason, Waters then ignored a lot of it and ploughed on alone. 'It may well have been paranoia, but it did look as though David was being frozen out,' he says. Mason himself was reminded that he was just the drummer and shouldn't look forward to extra royalties. 'This really did seem like behaviour beginning to border on the megalomaniac,' Mason added. There was a massive row between the two protagonists and Gilmour's name was removed from the credits, although he was still paid. *The Final Cut* became effectively a Waters solo album with Floyd's name on the sleeve – a sleeve designed by Waters. Roger then negotiated an individual management deal with O'Rourke and insisted that O'Rourke keep the substance of their negotiations secret. O'Rourke would have none of it and informed the other band members, leading Waters to accuse him of treachery and insist that O'Rourke be replaced.

Waters himself departed Floyd in 1983. It was an acrimonious split that even O'Rourke was powerless to prevent, the rumblings of which continued for years. As usual, the only winners were the lawyers.

The band broke up for three years, but then Gilmour and Mason reformed Pink Floyd with Rick Wright. When they continued to use the name Pink Floyd, Waters issued proceedings to prevent them. For some time, he hadn't liked the direction in which the band was headed. He thought the Pink Floyd project was at an end and that any continued use of the name was unworthy of the band's original principles. Floyd without him, he felt, should cease to be.

In turn, Gilmour was upset about the lack of credit he was given for *The Wall*. The legal battle raged for over a year but was eventually settled out of court. Waters would continue to receive royalties for *The Wall* and the other recordings to which he had contributed, while Mason and Gilmour would have the right to continue using the band name and to play its material.

It was obviously a difficult time for O'Rourke, who had been forced into taking sides in the issue. He'd seen Blackhill Enterprises back the wrong horse when Syd left the band and he had to be cautious not to fall into that same trap. Waters had shown himself a prodigious talent who was a more than adequate replacement for the madcap Barrett; but on the other hand, the formidable Floyd brand was rolling on despite the fact that, arguably, its two creative engines had departed. Roger had been given to pronouncements like, 'I am one of the best five writers to come out of English music since the war,' which, even though it's conceivably true, must have made dealings with him more than a little fractious from time to time, to say the least. His ex-manager, Peter Jenner, described him as 'this giant ego striding across the landscape'.

Described as a 'backroom boy', Steve O'Rourke only mirrored the attitudes of the band itself, who avoided interviews and the usual publicity hoopla lesser bands were forced into. (On one occasion after a bad review, they sent the journalist a box with a boxing glove on a spring.) And it is amazing that at a time when the band were among the biggest earners in the world, there were few who could name all or any of its members.

O'Rourke just plugged away, using considerable charm coupled with irresistible forcefulness to protect and promote his act (an associate termed him 'a streetfighter, a larger than life character'). On one occasion when he attended a meeting with sponsors in Germany, a colleague noticed that O'Rourke, who had been carrying a heavy overcoat all day, suddenly put it on just before the meeting commenced. The colleague asked him why. O'Rourke replied that it was his 'mean bastard' coat. It bulked him out and meant that he would have to stand all through the meeting, giving him an ominous demeanour. Another showman tactic by a man who, as a salesman, had been prepared to eat dog food.

The continued success of Pink Floyd, although they were never again to reach the heady heights of their golden years, ensured that everyone had enough money, more than enough money; in fact, diarrhoeas of cash. Floyd and their manager had the lot, all the trappings of the super-super rich: farms, mansions all over the world, private planes (O'Rourke had by now picked up a pilot's licence), boats . . . and very, very fast cars.

O'Rourke became a gentleman racer, and Nick Mason and Dave Gilmour shared his passion. In 1979, he finished 12th in the gruelling Le Mans 24-hour race, driving a 190-mph Ferrari 512 BB. He returned to Le Mans in 1980, but one of his tyres burst on the Mulsanne Straight while driving at 200 mph, destroying the rear end of his car. Action man O'Rourke immediately paid cash for the spare tail of a retired sister Ferrari that was sitting in the pit lane and finished the race in his multicoloured patchwork car.

In 1981, his racing team, also named EMKA, competed in the Le Mans Classic again, this time using a BMW M1 Coupe. O'Rourke was a co-driver with Eddie Jordan, who went on to be the boss of Jordan F1. He had to leave the race to fly to London to oversee a Pink Floyd concert but, duty done, he flew back the next morning and jumped straight into the car for another two-hour driving stint.

More racing success followed. For the 1983 Le Mans, he had an EMKA Aston Martin built especially and, with co-driver and TV presenter Tiff Needell, briefly led the race, finishing ahead of factory teams like Jaguar.

In 1991, he and Dave Gilmour ran a car in the somewhat anarchic Mexican sports car road race La Carrera Panamericana. Gilmour was driving when the car went off the road and over a drop. O'Rourke badly broke one of his legs in the accident.

Undeterred, in 1997 he had his most successful result, coming fourth in the Le Mans race, driving a second-hand McLaren F1 GTR. The money he shrewdly saved by not upgrading the car to full race spec, he spent on the after-race party for his teammates.

A heart problem forced O'Rourke to give up racing, but he continued to manage and finance motor-racing teams and drivers – a tall figure in the sport of the ultra-rich.

He died of a stroke in 2003.

As a sideline almost, O'Rourke had managed the career of Chris

Thomas, the producer who had worked on Beatles' sessions in the '60s. Thomas went on to produce the best Roxy Music albums, the Pistols' only album, The Pretenders' sublime first albums and Pulp's *This Is Hardcore* – oh, and he mixed *Dark Side of the Moon*.

The money that O'Rourke helped Pink Floyd to make, despite the Norton Warburg hiccup, is incalculable. When U2, a band that Pink Floyd surely rivalled in terms of sales, were at the height of their fame, the Irish Inland Revenue had to set up a separate department to deal with their affairs. Occasionally, we can catch tantalising glimpses of the sheer opulence. In 2003, Dave Gilmour sold his London house to Earl Spencer, brother of Princess Diana, for a sum the *Sunday Telegraph* estimated at £3.6 million. Then he gave the proceeds away to homeless charity Crisis. 'I don't need the money and I just thought it would be a good thing to do,' the paper quoted him as saying. 'I've had that house for nearly 20 years. It's made a fat profit and I've scarcely used it for the last six or seven years.'

Gilmour, who has a house in West Sussex and another in Greece, said he had grown tired of having so many expensive possessions (presumably, he means things like the 1954 Fender Stratocaster he has at home, serial number 0001). 'You collect Ferraris and then you've got to collect people to look after your Ferraris, and you've got to collect buildings to house the Ferraris,' the *Sunday Telegraph* quoted him as saying. 'Life gets very complicated. And eventually, at least in my case, you think "I don't need this stuff." And suddenly life gets simpler.'

Crisis are spending the money on low-cost housing for down-and-outs and low-earners in the Liverpool Street area of London.

Nick Mason, as drummer and not one of the main songwriters, is presumably worth less than the others. However, he is not to be pitied: his car collection is an indication that the wolf is not at the door. Mason owns 22 classic machines that have been described as 'priceless'. They include a Panhard B1 and the Ferrari 312T3 that Gilles Villeneuve raced in the 1978 Canadian Grand Prix. His latest acquisition is a McLaren F1 GTR.

O'Rourke was no Peter Grant – although he was a big guy, and it would have taken a brave man to stand toe to toe with him. But if we can be whimsical for a moment, instead of seeing him as the captain of a long ship crewed by barbarians, as perhaps Grant could be imagined, O'Rourke might better be pictured standing on the bridge of a rather grandiose oceanliner dressed in crisp whites, eyes crinkled as he gazes at the horizon – and taking tea at four. Mason, in a letter he wrote after O'Rourke's funeral, retains the nautical analogy but only credits his manager with being the ship's Bos'un, 'frequently required to sail the ship through stormy seas whilst all the crew squabbled below decks about how to divide the treasure'.

Steve O'Rourke's style of management is perfectly encapsulated in an episode in which he had to reprimand a promotions man, Glen Colson, for being late. 'I remember I was late in the office one morning,' Colson said, 'and he bought me a watch. It was a kind of message to get in on time, but I noticed the watch had cost him £400.'

It's a shame O'Rourke never got to see the band re-form. He probably adjudged that, considering the egos involved, it would never happen so there was little point in exhausting himself trying to make it come about. But happen it did – although it was down to Bob Geldof to do the arm-twisting and persuade the old stagers to get back together at Hyde Park, performing 'Breathe' as the climax of Live 8. While the youngsters in London had travelled to see Robbie Williams, there is little doubt that worldwide the big draw was Floyd, who, after a long hiatus, are entering their fifth decade as a band reunited. Nick Mason had been instrumental in the reunification, too. Shrewdly, he knew his men, figuring that Gilmour would be the most intransigent. 'You can take a horse to water, but you can't make it drink,' he remarked. 'In David's case, you can't even get him near the water. However, bringing the Waters to David might just work . . .'

7

SIMON NAPIER-BELL

It's tough out there for the manager – in my opinion, it's the worst job in the world.
– Mickie Most

Simon Napier-Bell is gay (he dubs himself a 'classy English poofter'), which is always handy in the pop business. He has a double-barrelled name, definitely another asset, and an A level in music, which is a considerably higher qualification than most managers in this book have achieved. The son of a documentary maker and a poodle clipper, he played the trumpet at school but was turned down by the Royal College of Music and so, in 1956, got a job as a roadie with jazz-band leader Johnny Dankworth.

After travelling through Europe and North America, Simon found work in his father's film business and networked the '60s London gay scene, sharing the top table with luminaries such as Noel Coward, John Gielgud, Larry Parnes and Lionel Bart. He came across Dusty Springfield, who had heard a song at the San Remo Music Festival that needed words, so together they came up with the title 'You Don't Have to Say You Love Me' and during a half-hour session after dinner tossed off most of the lyrics, finishing them on a ten-minute taxi ride to the Ad Lib club. Dusty's version was a big hit and the cash came rolling in. Then they really hit pay dirt when Elvis did a cover of it.

Napier-Bell was then introduced to The Yardbirds by Vicki Wickham, the producer of *Ready, Steady, Go!* and Dusty Springfield's sometime manager. On the rebound from Giorgio Gomelsky, The Yardbirds needed a manager.

Talk about right place at the right time: The Yardbirds were predicted by all to be the next-wave supergroup after the Rolling Stones. It must have been a hugely exciting moment for Napier-Bell, tempered, as it was, by the thought that he knew next to nothing about band management. However, he rapidly resolved that he wasn't going to let a little thing like that get in his way, as he told *Q* magazine's Dave Rimmer:

> I knew nothing whatsoever about the rock business, rock groups, The Yardbirds, The Yardbirds' music – but I knew it would instantly put me at the top of the business, so I said yes. I certainly quickly confirmed that I didn't know anything, but I also learnt very quickly that nobody in that business knew anything.

In early 1966, he was in the hot seat, managing the band and even producing 'Over Under Sideways Down'. He set about raising some badly needed money for The Yardbirds, but admits his main function was trying to keep the lid on the conflicts that frequently arose between the band members and their mercurial guitar player Jeff Beck. However, try as he might, he couldn't prevent bassist Paul Samwell-Smith leaving. They quickly held auditions for a new bassist, but when rhythm guitarist Chris Dreja agreed to take over the job, Napier-Bell found himself in charge of a band that had two superstar guitarists: Jeff Beck and Jimmy Page.

It could never last.

The film director Antonioni came to town in 1966 to make his Swinging London movie *Blow-Up*. He had been planning to use The Who in the film but changed his mind when he failed to reach an agreement with their manager Kit Lambert. Antonioni then turned to The Yardbirds. Napier-Bell readily negotiated a deal for the band to appear in the film playing onstage at the Marquee club, realising the exposure was priceless. The director wanted the band to trash its equipment and Jeff Beck was happy to oblige: he smashed up his guitar and amp, and it felt good.

When The Yardbirds went on a tour of the USA, Beck repeated nightly his joyous acts of destruction and Napier-Bell began rapidly losing money trying to keep the errant player supplied with fresh equipment.

Beck upped and left the band three-quarters of the way through their tour, citing as his reasons for his departure 'inflamed brain, inflamed tonsils and inflamed cock'.

The Beck–Page partnership reached its nadir with a crass reworking of 'Over Under Sideways Down' called 'Great Shakes', which became a milkshake commercial, and its apotheosis with 'Beck's Bolero' – a piece inspired by Ravel's *Bolero*, named after Beck but credited to Page. Beck, of course, claimed he wrote it.

It was too much for an exhausted Napier-Bell. Later that year, he asked Peter Grant to take over the troublesome Yardbirds and in a not insubstantial way changed the course of history by sowing the seeds that would eventually germinate and blossom into Led Zeppelin.

He wasn't sorry to be rid of The Yardbirds and told the press, 'It was just such a fucking pain being responsible for other people's careers.' But it didn't stop him falling into the trap again . . . and again.

When Simon took an excursion to St Tropez and ran into a bass player from a band called The Silence – he and his friend asked Simon to bail them out of prison, where they were being held on a charge of vagrancy – he found himself present at the birth of another legend. The Silence interested him, but they needed a singer and he didn't like their name. Back home, they were persuaded to change it to John's Children. Then, out of the blue, a young man called Marc Bolan turned up, asking Napier-Bell to manage his pop career. He was a singer/guitarist, he claimed.

'All we gotta do is put up posters,' Bolan told him. 'As soon as people see my picture, they're just gonna flip!'

Napier-Bell agreed, afterwards saying, 'I think Marc summed up everything I thought a pop star should be.'

He put one with the other; the band had a new singer, but it was all short-lived. John's Children dissolved. Bolan got into acid and started his acoustic combo Tyrannosaurus Rex. He and Napier-Bell argued about some of the tracks on the album and the fledgling manager bailed out again.

In his book, *Black Vinyl White Powder,* Simon is vague about his movements over the next ten years. There was a lot of travel and some paid production work here and there, and there was also some good old-fashioned pop scamming, where Napier-Bell would extract cash advances from record companies for upcoming singles by bands that didn't really exist. He was living up to his reputation as a 'dapper rogue', as rock writer Barney Hoskyns once dubbed him.

In 1976, Simon was running a punk band called London that featured Culture Club's John Moss in its line-up, and the following year, after placing an advert in *Melody Maker* asking bands to send in tapes, he was managing Japan, the art/glam band that featured Mick Karn on bass and 'the most beautiful man in pop', David Sylvian, on lead vocals.

Breaking Japan proved to be a toughie. Booed off stage in the UK and ignored in the US, the only territory that went for them big-time was . . . Japan! Big in Japan? They were massive. 'They were *mobbed*,' said Napier-Bell to *Mojo* magazine. 'Thirteen-year-old girls mostly, though they kept that audience for five or six years until those girls grew up.' Napier-Bell even undertook Japanese studies in the hope of giving himself some sort of edge in business meetings and an insight into the culture.

However, despite sell-out tours in the land of the rising sun, Japan the band meant little outside of the country, and four albums down the line, the band and Napier-Bell were in serious debt. It was only when the New Romantic scene sashayed into town that Japan, who had never been reluctant to put on a bit of eyeliner (it's rumoured that Sylvian's bleached blond haircut influenced Nick Rhodes from Duran Duran and even Princess Diana), seemed to find a niche, growing up as they had through the punk/post-punk phases.

Finally, in 1981, they scored a top 20 single with 'Quiet Life'. The follow-up, 'Ghosts', went into the top five and the album went gold, but it was too little too late for Japan. When Mick Karn found Sylvian knocking off his girlfriend, the band surrendered and broke up.

Simon lucked into Wham! management – or 'Whamanagement', as he dubs it in his book. It began when Mark Dean, an ambitious 21 year old from Bushey in Herts, set up a record company called Innervision and took on as one of its first acts Wham!, who hailed from the same commuter-belt town. George Michael had been given an ultimatum by his father: either establish yourself in the music business in the next six months or get to work in the family kebab shop. Perhaps understandably, when Dean offered George and Andrew Ridgeley a deal (which was later described by Tony Parsons as 'tighter than a lobster's ass'), the duo, who had no management, ignored their lawyer's advice and scrambled to get their signatures on the dotted line.

Innervision rushed out 'Wham Rap', which sold only a handful of copies, then 'Young Guns', which made it into the top ten, followed by a re-released 'Wham Rap', which this time got to number 8. The follow-up, 'Bad Boys', got to number 2.

In no time at all, Wham! had become a highly successful band, but the fruits of their success seemed to have eluded them. They were still catching the bus to attend interviews and TV appearances, and couldn't afford to buy their own flats. They figured, rather late in the day, that they needed a new deal and for that they'd need a manager.

Jazz Summers, who would later manage Lisa Stansfield and The Verve, wanted to take them on, but he figured he'd need help, so Simon Napier-Bell got the call. They talked up their strategies to George and Andrew, and by the time of 'Club Tropicana', promising to renegotiate the record deal and break Wham! in the USA, the duo had charmed their way into the job.

The deal had to be the first priority, but what to do about it? Innervision had signed a poor deal with a major label. Consequently, the Innervision deal with Wham! had to be proportionately poorer. Innervision was only a tadpole licensed label of the giant CBS. Where Innervision's MD was a vibrant 21 year old, the CBS MD was a grouchy veteran. They were chalk and cheese. CBS wouldn't budge, Innervision couldn't budge – no deal. Furthermore, there was a suspicion that Wham! had impressed CBS so much that they wanted to cut out the middle man (Innervision) and have the shiny new pop stars all for themselves. The battle lines were drawn. CBS refused to cough up the £30,000 needed for the making of the 'Club Tropicana' video and the new managers had to raise the money from the publishers and elsewhere.

While each side started preparing their case for the fight over the new baby, the new baby scored a number 1 album with *Fantastic*. There was a blitz of publicity elicited by the managers and, while Wham! embarked on a national tour, their solicitors issued papers to Innervision alleging that their contracts had been signed under duress and without proper legal consultation – a powerful opening salvo. It was a landmark case for all young bands in a similar position, and the music business generally. CBS responded with an injunction restraining the band from signing with any other label.

Then George muddied the waters by saying that he didn't want to continue with Wham! anyway and wanted to turn solo.

After the tour, and six months of litigation, Innervision was left unable to pay its lawyers and was on the point of folding when Wham! settled and signed to CBS directly for a substantial advance. The inexperienced Innervision got only a small pay-off for its trouble.

Wham! celebrated their new-found freedom (and wealth) by releasing 'Wake Me Up Before You Go Go', which shot straight to number 1. Inevitably, after such success in the UK, came the time for the managers to raise the game and take on the mighty USA. Napier-Bell and Summers perceived that Wham! were perfect for the American teen market and went to the States to talk to the

CBS label bosses there. Initially, the Americans were unimpressed by Wham! *and* their managers, but they were eventually seduced by the suave, double-barrelled English hustler and his energetic partner, and they were rewarded when 'Wake Me Up Before You Go Go' went to number 1 there.

'Careless Whisper' was the follow-up. It was released under the name George Michael in the UK (although Ridgeley has a writing credit) and 'Wham! featuring George Michael' in the US. Whoever did what, the number 1 position on both sides of the Atlantic belonged to Wham!.

Having conquered one giant, Simon focused on another – a market that was so far totally unsullied by Western pop bands: China. Taking on the Far Eastern colossus – potentially the biggest market ever – became a personal crusade for Napier-Bell and over two years he made no less than thirteen visits in an effort to persuade the authorities to let Wham! perform there live.

China is opening up now – there is less regulation and there are many business opportunities for foreign companies – but the situation was very different 20 years ago. The government was still highly suspicious of capitalist forays from the West, particularly from the notoriously decadent music business. This was four years before the Tiananmen Square protests. The authorities didn't want their youth whipped up into a frenzy by micro-short-wearing members of the material world. But Simon's incessant lobbying inched the tortuous process along. He seemed to be getting subtle signs of favour despite the fact the inscrutable Chinese wouldn't quite go the final mile and make an actual commitment to the project – although they had acknowledged that 7 April 1985 was the date when it might happen.

However, even if the theoretical gig did happen, they pointed out, they – the Chinese government – would pay for nothing: the band would have to pay to get themselves and their equipment to the other side of the world; they would have to foot the bill for the hire of the concert hall and for the cost of ticket sales; and if there were any profits, then they would all have to be donated to a Chinese charity. Who in their right mind would consider such a deal? It was an insane proposition.

Back in London, Napier-Bell and Summers reckoned the total bill would exceed half a million dollars, a bill the management could not afford to pay, so it would have to be met by CBS. He notes, in *Black Vinyl White Powder,* the reaction of the label to the proposition: 'If CBS were to consider it, there would have to be a full-length movie of the event. It meant half a dozen cameramen, a major director and three months of editing. And it doubled the cost. Now we needed a million and the gig was in two weeks' time. We had to have the money from CBS in 24 hours. What record company in the world would come up with that amount of tour support for one single gig in a country where they couldn't sell records?'

Incredibly, CBS bit. They got the cash, the gig went ahead at the Workers' Stadium in Beijing and was broadcast all over the world. It was also a PR triumph. The news broadcasts in the USA were wall-to-wall Wham! for a whole week. The band went global. CBS's gamble had paid off. A few months later, however, much to the annoyance of Napier-Bell, George declared himself a solo artist. Simon had envisaged Wham! undertaking a world tour of Rolling Stones proportions: 'The biggest-grossing tour in the history of rock music,' he told *Q* magazine in 1987:

> They could actually have earned $200 million gross – no, more than that, probably $200 million net – between them, in a year's hard work and of course Andrew would have done it. It wasn't just the money. There was something about doing that. Wham! would then have become part of pop history.

But is wasn't to be. Simon was thwarted, as many a manager has been, by his charges – the ship scuttled by its own crew. George somehow managed to cope without Simon. He set his sights on consolidating his success in America and with a string of hits went on to become the biggest-selling British artist in the USA during the '90s.

Perhaps embittered now, Napier-Bell took over the management of old rock leviathan Asia, which featured Steve (Yes) Howe on guitar, but it was a kind of semi-retirement job for him; he was beginning to think that writing books and TV documentaries was more appropriate employment.

In an interview with the *NME*, he offered an interesting insight into management, and four managers in particular and their relationships with their charges:

> Groups did tend to be a reflection of their managers, like The Beatles were really Brian Epstein's brushed-up middle-class gay presentation of some pretty rough boys and Jagger was so fascinated by Oldham's campness that he started adopting his mannerisms. The Who of course were totally an extension of Kit Lambert's manic attitude to life, and The Yardbirds were a reflection of Giorgio Gomelsky's neurotic, mixed-up mind.

He told Sheryl Garratt of *The Observer* that band management will always inevitably end in tears:

> We always get fired, in the end. Artists are great sponges, they soak things up. They learn it, and eventually they look at the manager and say, 'Why should I pay you 20 per cent?' I don't object to that at all. It's like bringing up a child – you put them through school and then suddenly they're an adult.

Going on, he explains that he now senses an era is ended:

> It's less fun now. There's no creative input any more, and you are just a go-between between all the people involved. There isn't any feeling of outrage in the music business and I don't think it will come back, really.

I'm amazed Robbie Williams got through, because he's an

archetypal star. Record companies take the dullest, most obedient people, the people who do what they're told. Where's the fun in managing that? It's just being a secretary, really.

The record companies got another lambasting in Q magazine:

I do find that the music business is probably the most depressingly conservative and obstructive business you could be in. You have this situation where if you think you have something, you have to go and talk to somebody else [an A&R person] who just thinks you haven't. It's as simple as that. He has no objective judgement, and obviously he's not very good at what he does, because if he was he wouldn't be sitting in a record company taking £20,000 a year salary. If the guy who runs A&R at any record company knew what a hit record was, he could make £20,000 a week.

It's true that Napier-Bell didn't hold down any of his managerial positions for long – perhaps he didn't have the hunger to take an act all the way – but to call him a dilettante, an expression he has used about himself, is to underestimate him. It would have taken the powers of Machiavelli and the patience of a saint to keep The Yardbirds together, or to negotiate the Chinese puzzle of a deal for Wham! Malcolm McLaren, for that matter, wasn't a manager for very long either. And surely the role of elder statesman and waspish observer of the pop world and its machinations is a more suitable occupation for a manager of a certain age.

As an amusing aside, the *Daily Mail*, when printing excerpts from Albert Goldman's book on John Lennon, mentioned that Brian Epstein was gay. They published a picture of Simon, saying underneath that he wasn't gay. Napier-Bell contemplated suing the newspaper but was advised by his lawyers that the action would likely fail, as it could be proved that he had slept with women.

Simon now lives in Thailand with his partner.

8

PETER GRANT

Led Zeppelin

Oh, I could deal with them. I'd just hang them out of the first-floor window.
— Peter Grant on The Yardbirds

If you could see the fantasies inside the fevered head of a schoolboy rock fan, chances are they would play like a saga of swaggering Viking gods marauding across the planet, pillaging the townships, helping themselves to the loot and the ladies and leaving behind only scorched earth, broken swords and tears. A Led Zeppelin tour would surely fit the bill on an epic scale – a voyage with Robert Plant as the figurehead, decked in golden curls, screaming out the war cry from the prow; Jimmy Page and John Paul Jones swinging and slashing their axes to left and to right; below decks, sweating galley slaves straining at the oars to John Bonham's pounding bass drumbeat. And on the bridge, his eyes fixed on the horizon, stands the Overlord – ship's captain Peter Grant, his colours nailed to the mast.

Led Zeppelin got nearer to that Valhalla vision than any other band. None of their countless imitators pushed out the longships as far as they did, not by a nautical mile.

Except their longship was an airship.

The band's numerous American tours have become the stuff of legend. Zeppelin packed out huge auditoriums with gargantuan three-hour performances that often saw fans crushed, tear-gassed or cherry-picked from the crowd by roadies – spoils of war to amuse the band members with later.

At a Zeppelin gig, the air hung heavy with joint smoke, danger and just a whiff of witchcraft. Eyes shone brightly with amphetamines; willing victims flocked, sometimes from homes thousands of miles off, to pour out their adorations.

Everything was huge: the PAs and light shows were the biggest and brightest that had ever been made. Standing structures shuddered with the violent shock of the music. The fees the band could demand were unprecedented; every gig was a sell-out and their album sales broke all known records. At one time, in 1975, Led Zeppelin had nine albums in the American charts. Their sixth album, *Physical Graffiti*, had advance orders of $15 million.

How could a band – any band – have conquered the world so fast and so young? Was it true that Led Zeppelin had struck a pact with the Devil and sold their souls like Robert Johnson was supposed to have done?

Stories of offstage debauchery filtered back. How depraved could it all really have been? It was said that Page worshipped Satan and carried whips around in a special case. Were they just macabre curios or did he really use them on unsuspecting young girls crazy enough to go back to his hotel lair, where the lights were permanently shrouded with coloured scarves?

The whispers also said that girls had been sexually assaulted with live fish, that one had been subjected to full sex on a restaurant tabletop in open view of all the customers. Had Plant, the hot blood of triumph coursing through his veins, really stood on the Hyatt House hotel balcony, looked down on the streets of Hollywood and cried, 'I am a golden god'? Other anecdotes about TVs and fridges being lobbed through hotel windows and motorbikes careering down the corridors seemed run of the mill by comparison.

There were also tales of staggering wealth – mansions and farms, private jetliners, limousines – and extreme drug use. A team of dealers permanently on standby kept the mood suitably unhinged – one reputedly walked off with $25,000 in a single transaction. And there was violence, too. No one had yet been killed and eaten, but . . .

When the Zeppelin entourage hit town, it arrived on its own plane, the Starship, a Boeing 720B jetliner, which had been converted into a 40-seat luxury jet with a bar, video screens and its own bedrooms. 'Led Zeppelin' was emblazoned down its fuselage just like the band names were on the side of Ford Transit vans in earlier, humbler times. A Zeppelin medic accompanied them, tooled up for anything from headache cures to stomach-pumping, with a sideline in 'sex-u-up' pills – so the myth goes.

The devoted hordes of the faithful would scream the band into town as the Zeppelinistas swept away from the airports in a column of limousines with police motorcycle outriders. An army of road crew – around 45 of them – would have arrived beforehand in a convoy of juggernauts, having slogged across the States lugging PA systems, lighting towers, smoke and dry-ice machines, backline equipment, drum kits, guitars, mixing desks and explosives.

At their hotel, the band would barge through the lobby like a slow stampede, a gang of rock and roll riff-raff in leather and velvet, carving a swathe through the tutting guests in the wake of the striding bearded colossus at their head, a man surrounded by almost as much myth as the band he represented, the man who made it all possible: Led Zeppelin's manager Peter Grant. Peter the Great.

It was Grant and Page who had pulled Led Zeppelin together from its disparate scraps: John Paul Jones, an old session-playing pal; Robert Plant rescued from a no-hoper Brummy band called Hobbstweedle; John Bonham, an ex-bricklayer who preferred to stay in Tim Rose's backing band until he was talked out of it. It was to be Grant who booked the gigs and financed them. It was Grant who negotiated the revolutionary deals that were to see Zeppelin earning more from gigs than any of their predecessors.

It was Grant who got them the tough deal with Atlantic Records that not only left the record executives weeping but also sent their earnings from records off the graph and the band into tax exile.

It was also Grant and his henchman, Richard Cole, who fiercely protected the band members from the gun-toting crazies and the revenge-filled police chiefs, from the rabid fans and crooked promoters, from the jealous boyfriends and from each other.

Zeppelin wielded phenomenal power over fans, adoring record executives, groupies, dealers and hotel staff alike. Its members were used to getting exactly what they wanted when they wanted it, all eased by a spew of dollars in the face of which most cheerfully succumbed to the caprices of the Zep machine and turned blind eyes to the fallout. But it was the over-arching influence of the giant ex-wrestler Peter Grant and his exercise in what might be called 'full contact management' that imbued in the band that astonishing level of arrogant self-belief – the absolute conviction that they were the greatest rock band ever.

Grant was born in south London in 1935. Details of his childhood are sketchy, but it is thought that his mother was Jewish. He never knew his father. Like others in this book, he performed poorly at school and was cursed with a report saying 'This boy will never make anything of his life.' Peter must have taken some pleasure in this when he was being driven to five-star hotels in six-door limousines, or perhaps as he acquired yet another expensive antique for his moated country house.

Like Don Arden, Grant left school in his early teens. He suffered a job in a sheet-metal factory, waited on tables, ran around town as a messenger boy and worked as a stagehand at the Croydon Empire before being called up to the army. After two years of national service, he was promoted to the rank of corporal and given charge of the soldiers' canteen, where he arranged shows for the troops. He knew by then that entertainment was his thing and after the army he found work first at a holiday camp and then at a hotel in Jersey. Measuring over six feet tall, Grant's next step was to be the key to his future and his fortune.

Acting as the doorman/bouncer in a coffee bar in Soho doesn't, on the face of it, seem like a major career development, but this was no ordinary coffee bar. This was the 2i's Coffee Bar at 59 Old Compton Street and from these humble premises would spring the first British skiffle bands. Lonnie Donegan played there. Adam Faith sang there. Tommy Steele was to be discovered at the 2i's and Harry Webb and the Drifters, soon to be known as Cliff Richard and The Shadows, did some of their earliest gigs there. Above the 2i's door was a neon sign immodestly declaring, 'The World Famous 2i's Coffee Bar, Home of the Stars'. And it was true.

Two Australian wrestlers had taken over the lease in 1956 and after letting a few bands rehearse in the basement they started booking them in. Coffee bars had become popular in the '50s after the first trickles of intrepid British holidaymakers had begun to venture abroad after the war. They returned excited, with stories of delicious food, wine and coffee at a time when Britain still languished under the deprivation of rationing. Coffee bars became associated with a sense of cosmopolitan style and the exotic Continent.

But you couldn't have a coffee bar without a coffee maker. Achille Gaggia filed for a patent for his espresso maker in Milan in 1948 and the machines started appearing in London around 1952. The first bars were opened by enterprising Italians in Soho and were immediately popular with teenagers who didn't want to hang out with old ladies in tearooms but were too young to go to pubs.

The 2i's was one of the early adopters of Gaggia's creation. It boasted an American jukebox as well as one of the chic espresso makers, and downstairs was the tiny basement that came to be decorated with murals by Lionel Bart, then a young silk-screen printer. It was soon brimming night and day with teenagers, including a young Barbara Windsor and an even younger Marc Bolan. Larry Parnes used to trawl the place, spotting young male talent. Gradually, it became a hangout for aspiring pop performers.

The waiter at the 2i's was a youthful Mickie Most, who'd already seen success playing gigs in South Africa and who occasionally doubled as one of the 2i's acts. He and Grant became firm friends. By this stage, Tom Littlewood had taken over the bar and he was paying Grant £1 a night to sell the tickets for the basement gigs. He kept back 10 per cent for 'commission' and paid the bands on the same basis.

The giant Grant's presence in a tiny coffee bar couldn't be ignored and he soon came to the attention of the manager of the cellar, Paul Lincoln, who was a wrestler. Lincoln found Grant some extramural work as 'the Masked Marauder', a 23-stone giant who would take on all-comers, though Peter was less than enamoured with his wrestling stint, once glumly referring to his image as that of 'a bodyguard in a Turkish harem'. But it is clear that the finger-pointing, puffing-out-the-chest tactics that wrestlers employed then and now were to become invaluable to him later on when it came to extracting Led Zeppelin's fees from recalcitrant American promoters.

Somewhat fortunately for Zeppelin, Grant wasn't entirely enthralled by the dubious glamour of all-in wrestling and quit the ring, but it wasn't to be for rock band management – not yet anyway.

First, Peter was going to be an actor. He had some blink-and-you'll-miss-it parts on TV in *The Saint, Crackerjack, The Benny Hill Show* and *Dixon of Dock Green*, and his movie roles were even less auspicious. He was once employed as Anthony Quinn's body double in *The Guns of Navarone* and was a Macedonian guard in *Cleopatra* alongside Richard Burton and Elizabeth Taylor (although this part sadly found its way to the cutting-room floor).

Acting went the way of wrestling and it was Grant's plan to find a more secure earner that sowed the seeds of all that was to come. He bought a van, which he used to take variety acts around the circuit. This was a defining moment. There are those who aver that this was Peter's métier, his real calling – he'd become a roadie and that's, to some extent, what he remained, albeit a Rolls-Royce version. In time, Grant was to become the biggest roadie of the biggest band in the world, but it was as a humble apprentice that he was to cross the path of the Godfather of Rock, Don Arden.

'In 1963, I got my first big break,' he said. 'That's when I started working for Don Arden, from whom I learned a lot. He brought Bo Diddley over to Britain and I was his tour manager.'

Arden saw the obvious advantages of having on the team a fearsome, bearded man with a van who could also handle himself in a tight situation. 'If there was a cheque to be collected,' Don said, 'I had to make him aware that sometimes the promise of a cheque was broken.' Mickie Most added, '[Grant] always made sure a contract was honoured . . . and he had a very good head for figures.'

Peter became tour manager to all of the visiting American stars that Arden was bringing over and carried out the twin function of driver and bagman. As well as Bo Diddley, he began to look after the Everly Brothers, Chuck Berry and the troubled Gene Vincent.

After smashing up his leg in a motorcycle accident, Vincent's boozing increased with the pain, and despite the brilliance of his performances, he was a nasty drunk and getting nastier. He bullied all around him save for his new tour manager, who apparently used to grab Vincent by the throat and push him onstage when necessary. In Chris Welch's book, *Peter Grant: The Man Who Led Zeppelin*, he tells the hilarious story of Vincent arguing with his wife on the tour bus. They had started hitting each other and Grant had to separate them twice. A surly Vincent, who had secreted a bottle of vodka, sulkily swigged most of it back and lurched to his feet, in the process mangling his good leg between the handrail and the seat. Grant came to his aid by bending the bar back like a circus strongman, but the damage was done and Vincent couldn't stand up. Grant was determined the show would go on – not for the sake of the fans but because the contract stated that if the

American rocker didn't appear, then no fee would be paid. The compère stood in front of the drawn curtains and announced, 'Ladies and gentlemen, all the way from America, the king of rock 'n' roll, Mr Gene Vincent!' When the curtains were opened, Vincent was upright, strapped to a microphone stand. He managed to launch into the first song but only got as far as 'Bebop a—' before he fell forward on his face, yelling, 'F-u-c-k!' The star's nose was splattered and he was knocked unconscious, covered in blood.

Two roadies carried Vincent offstage, Welch says, like 'a pig on a spit', but Grant didn't care, he'd nipped in and grabbed the cash already. The star had come out, although it was almost immediately extinguished, but the contract had been fulfilled. Peter was starting to develop the skills that would hold him in such good stead later.

He ran gigs by the notoriously distrustful and parsimonious Chuck Berry. Eric Burdon of The Animals claimed in his book, *I Used to Be An Animal, But I'm All Right Now*, to have once seen Peter and Don on all-fours poking pound notes under Berry's dressing-room door, beseeching him to open up – the star would not go out onstage or even open the door without first being paid.

Burdon later worked with Grant when he took over tour management of The Animals and, as a consequence, Grant was to work once more with Mickie Most, who had by now begun getting production work, including that of The Animals' worldwide hit record 'House of the Rising Sun'. He and Mickie Most were occasional partners now, as Grant took over the tour management for The Nashville Teens. Most produced their hit record 'Tobacco Road'.

Grant figured he was ready for a proper band management position now – that was where the money was – but first he needed an office. Most needed one too, so the fledgling muso entrepreneurs started sharing some space on London's Oxford Street, where they sat facing each other, banging the phones and promoting their records and acts.

After a couple of flops, it was to be a novelty song that gave Grant his first big-hit band. It was also to lead him to Richard

Cole, the man who was to ride shotgun with the big man on his mad bulldozer rock-business rampage.

The New Vaudeville Band were basically a bunch of session men dressed up in candy-striped jackets. They knocked off a catchy song called 'Winchester Cathedral', featuring vocals sung through a megaphone. For some reason, the Americans loved it and the track went to number 1 over there, giving Grant valuable experience of guiding a band through the cabaret clubs of Las Vegas.

Ex-boxer and scaffolder Richard Cole had been a roadie for a series of acts, including The Who, when he found Peter Grant, who needed someone to help him with the New Vaudeville Band.

The two impressed each other, as Cole recollects in his book, *Stairway to Heaven*. Wages were agreed, but the deal was only concluded when Peter wagged his finger at Cole, saying, 'If you ever fucking repeat anything you hear in this office, I'll cut your fucking ears off!' Cole says he replied, 'If you're going to point your fucking finger at me much longer, I'm going to fucking bite it off.' It was a marriage made somewhere, but not in heaven.

The Most–Grant partnership had set up shop at 155 Oxford Street, a building which itself has become a mini-legend. Chris Wright and Terry Ellis were already ensconced there, running Chrysalis Records with their bands Jethro Tull and Ten Years After. The company's booking agency shared the floor. They were joined by Bill Harry, a friend of John Lennon, who had come down from Liverpool to be a music journalist. Harry was to become the publicist for the New Vaudeville Band and later for Led Zeppelin. A creative nucleus had been forged and there was cross-pollination floor to floor.

Peter had become very ambitious – not least because his tiny wife, Gloria, liked nice things. He needed an act that would start big and grow. Mickie Most had just hooked up with The Yardbirds, a band with supergroup potential who couldn't quite get it together. Although it featured Jeff Beck and Jimmy Page in its line-up, it was heading into meltdown. Manager Simon Napier-Bell was about to throw in the towel.

In his book, *Black Vinyl White Powder*, Napier-Bell says that he and Jimmy Page didn't get along. When he told Peter Grant that the band was a 'bloody nuisance', he got the response, 'Oh, I could deal with them. I'd just hang them out of the first-floor window.'

The creed, according to Grant's surrogate father and music-business mentor Don Arden, had now been passed down to the next generation of rock manager: the threat of being hung out of a window by your feet had become the first resort in negotiation tactics.

Peter toured with The Yardbirds. The band's bass player, Chris Dreja, recalled seeing Grant in full flow when they were late for a gig in Canada. 'These two mafioso guys with veins popping in their necks were going to kill us. Peter was sitting in the back of the bus and they pulled guns. They actually pulled a pistol on him. I'll never forget this, but he got up and barrelled them away with his stomach.

'He said, "You're gonna do WOT?" And they were so taken aback that someone had the nerve to do this, they just ended up laughing. It broke the ice, but it was quite something to take a pistol in the stomach.'

He had guts all right. It wasn't the last time he faced down a gunman equipped with nothing but a huge belly.

But even a five-star tour manager like Peter couldn't prevent The Yardbirds giving up the ghost, knackered and riven by two big guitar egos. Said Chris Dreja, 'We were working 500 days a year, and in those days you didn't travel in executive jets. It was a hard slog – we just burnt out, basically. We should have come off the road and thought about doing another album. We were in perpetual motion, and it finished us off in the end. Also, Jimmy [Page] and I were more on the heavier side of music at that time, and I think Keith [Relf, vocalist] and Jim [McCarty, drummer] – understandably for them, perhaps – wanted to go a more mellow route.'

Grant and Page crawled from the wreckage, somehow clutching in their possession the name The Yardbirds. In a remarkable sleight of hand, Grant had convinced the original band members to sign over the name to him and the parvenu Page. They would build their own supergroup from the ground up under the Yardbirds mantle.

This looked like a good proposition. The new band would have a well-known name and some hits in its portfolio; it had a hard-nut manager and so far it possessed one bona fide guitar hero in-the-making. Dreja stuck around for a bit, but John Paul Jones, an old session-playing mate of Jimmy's, was soon drafted in to replace him on bass. What they needed next was a singer and a drummer.

Robert Plant had been bumming around the Midlands with various slim-chance acts. He looked great, he had a hugely powerful voice, he shared Page's fondness for hard blues and he happened to know a phenomenally loud drummer called John Bonham.

What a package: the band signed, sealed and delivered.

Grant and Page were very tight with each other. It was an interesting and complex relationship, which variously saw Page playing master to Grant's servant and Grant in the role of father to Page as son. Whatever the truth may be, at these early stages in 1968 they were the dynamic hub of the new band and, in musical terms, whatever Page wanted, Grant got for him – as Bonham was to find out in rehearsals.

Page had asked him to make his drum parts a bit simpler, but Bonham kept whacking away regardless and Page became quietly annoyed. But Grant didn't do quiet.

'Do you like your job in the band?' he thundered. When Bonham replied in the affirmative, Grant warned, 'Well, do as this man says or fuck off! Behave yourself, Bonham, or you'll disappear . . . through different doors!'

The name The New Yardbirds had done its temporary job – it had attracted press attention and made the task of getting gigs for the new band easier – but ultimately it proved cumbersome. The new band was flexing its muscles and was ready for a fresh start. When The Who's Keith Moon (once considered a potential candidate for the drum stool) joked that the new band would go down like a 'lead balloon' and Who bassist, the late John Entwistle, pointed out it would be more like a 'lead zeppelin', Grant had found the perfect name for his perfect project.

Yet what a different band it might have been. Prior to Robert Plant's recruitment, there had been speculation that perhaps the Small Faces' Steve Marriott might have made a good vocalist for the seminal Zeppelin – until an unattributable message came to Jimmy Page from Marriott's management: 'How would you like to play guitar with broken fingers? You will be, if you don't stay away from Stevie.' Could this have been a warning from the desk of Don Arden direct to the heart of the camp of his protégé Peter Grant? Even Peter didn't have the stomach to tangle with Arden.

Grant took the renamed band on a tour of Scandinavia, where they were well received, then into the studio, where they bashed out the tracks that were to be the first Zeppelin album. It took a mere 30 hours.

In all things musical, Grant habitually took a back seat and was content for the players to play in any way they thought fit. However, when the band sat talking about what they might release as their first single, Grant stepped in and made his considerable presence felt. Zeppelin would not be issuing any singles . . . ever.

He saw that a new band was invariably judged on its first release and if that flopped, then so did the band. The rationale was that if the band didn't release a single, then the single couldn't possibly flop. The record companies naturally regarded this as commercial suicide, but in time they were forced to concede that Grant's strategy, coupled with his view that Zeppelin would do few if any interviews (he felt the band expressed itself most eloquently through its music), was a marketing masterstroke.

Top of the Pops, so long the omnipotent arbiter of what was hot and what was not, had for once been spurned. Zeppelin, by refusing to make singles, had daringly raised two fingers to the BBC. There were few other TV shows that catered for heavy rock bands in those days (*Ready, Steady, Go!* had ceased two years earlier), so, effectively, Zeppelin had snubbed television altogether.

And because the band refused to cosy up to reporters, the newspapers and magazines, starved of copy, were given to writing yards of hyperbole and speculation about the band's activities, private lives and motives. The more unavailable Zeppelin were, the more the punters and the editors slavered after them.

Bill Harry, Zeppelin's British PR, observed Grant's tactics when he attended the band's gig at the Newport Jazz Festival in July 1969. 'My job basically as a PR was to keep the press away. Peter wasn't interested in the band doing interviews. He might let some of the underground magazines talk to them, like *Friendz*. He wasn't even interested in having them on TV. He wanted to make them superstars that nobody could get near, rather like movie stars today. But in those days, pop stars would do anything for publicity. Peter just wasn't interested.'

'Treat them mean and keep them keen' was the order of the day. An air of mystery grew up around Led Zeppelin; they were a myth before they started.

Peter Grant rarely missed a gig, but on 19 December 1968, while Led Zeppelin were playing in Exeter City Hall for £125, Grant was on a plane to New York to see Ahmet Ertegun at Atlantic Records. He would emerge with an advance of $200,000: a figure commonly held to be the biggest advance ever paid to a new band up to that time. Ertegun had already liked the tapes, but, curiously, it might have been the queen of white soul, Dusty Springfield, who helped to swing the deal, since she had worked with Jimmy and John Paul Jones in their session-playing days and recommended them to the Atlantic bosses.

Peter had pulled off a tough negotiation with a respected label. He had a hot band and a hot album in the can. The only way now was up.

A week after the Exeter City Hall gig, Zeppelin were supporting Vanilla Fudge and MC5 in Denver. Over the next three months, they gigged hard and worked the first album into the charts at number 10. The American press started to get excited about this third wave of the British invasion.

And Zeppelin were excited about the USA, too. America was their element. It's unlikely any band has ever assaulted the ears, hearts, minds, crotches and pockets of American youth with quite the vigour that Zeppelin did. They travelled further, gigged longer and partied harder, thus ensuring their status in the history books as the biggest and the best monsters of rock.

The troops in Vietnam rode jeeps into battle playing 'Whole Lotta Love' on their tape players. Back home, Zeppelin fans bought $5 million worth of albums. There were 700,000 advance sales for *Led Zeppelin II*. The album knocked The Beatles' *Abbey Road* from the top slot. The band members and Grant started looking around for country houses.

Girls crawled over one another to get to the young rock gods, drug dealers queued up to show their wares; there were bars to drink dry, there were hotel rooms to wreck, there were limos to abuse. There was a huge bag of cash to help smooth the ruffled feathers of officialdom and, if things got tricky, there was also the band's small personal army of bodyguards and road crew to beat off unwanted attention.

The band's legendary after-show high jinks originated with drummer John Bonham, according to Richard Cole: 'Bonzo used to say to me it was impossible to come back to the hotel after a performance and sip tea or hot chocolate and watch the telly. After flailing at the drums with the force of an atom bomb, Bonzo literally needed hours to calm down and unwind. "I'm too hyper," he would complain, tapping his foot, scratching at his arms. "I gotta let loose and blow off some steam."'

The trail of carnage that was to ensue involved more than just the regulation telly-out-of-the-window caper. There was bed-smashing, wallpaper-stripping, fishing, girls' bottoms, drug abuse, kinky sex and whips. A room was flooded when a (briefly) live dove found itself stuffed up a bath overflow. There was enthusiastic drinking – Cole figured out that in one gargantuan drinking session, the band, himself and Grant drank 120 Slivovitzes and 160 beers in only four hours.

Grant's bagman, Cole, was paying for it all by now: strippers, motorbikes, cars, cocaine. He took to the job of keeping the band amused onstage and off with considerable verve and, like some lunatic court jester, laid on the laughs while unwittingly, of course, helping to set a course which would ultimately see the great Zeppelin finally spin out of control.

Amidst all this muscular hedonism and chaos, a towering Peter Grant, dressed perhaps in a light-blue kimono and a purple gaucho hat with a blue plume, on his fingers a selection of silver rings, some imbedded with turquoise – the very rock of roll – would smile down at his precocious progeny like some benign bearded Buddha.

But it was only to those inside the Zeppelin camp, to those he protected, that he radiated confidence and security. To those who opposed him, or those he considered on the make, he could be a rude, ruthless, intimidating bully. God help you if you attempted to make an illicit recording of any of the band's performances, for example.

At a concert in Vancouver in 1970, Grant spotted a man with a tape recorder. In *Stairway to Heaven*, Cole wrote, 'Peter growled, "He's right out in the open. What a fool." Some members of the crew and I stormed over, grabbed the fellow by the shirt collar, lifted him to his feet and shouted, "You can't do that here, you asshole! If you want a recording, go to the record store and buy one like everybody else!"

'The man was hoisted into the air and dropped in a heap onto the floor. We grabbed the recorder and smashed it against a security barricade, shattering it into a dozen pieces.'

It turned out the man was from the Vancouver City noise department and he was taking decibel levels. Grant coughed up cash in damages. An enraged Bonham then smashed up a hotel room and Grant was forced to cough up again.

Later that year, a band called Flock were to feel the wrath of Grant when they wouldn't vacate the stage at the Bath Festival.

Peter simply led his gang of roadies onto the stage and started unplugging all their gear mid-performance.

'Hey, we haven't finished yet, man,' said a Flock roadie.

'Oh, yes, you fucking have,' yelled Peter.

Stephen Davis says in *Hammer of the Gods* that Richard Cole punched the roadie and that 'Grant threw a few punches as well and quickly got his band onstage via brute force.' He'd done something right: that gig broke them into the big time in the UK. They were now up there with the Stones, The Beatles and The Who.

Peter set up more tours of the States and, attentive as ever to finance, he dreamed up a new deal which many agree fundamentally changed the gig business. The traditional procedure was that the promoter would split the ticket money with the band on a 60/40 per cent basis. In the case of a big Zeppelin gig, which might gross $50,000, the promoter might pick up a cool $20,000 for one night's work. Grant wasn't having it. He told promoters that the split was going to be 90/10 from now on. They were outraged, they threatened, they fumed and they yelled . . . but eventually they gave in. They needed Led Zeppelin more than Zeppelin needed them.

'I remember [Grant] talking to Bill Graham, who had the biggest venues in rock,' said Mickie Most. 'He'd say to him, "It's 90/10 or you don't fucking get Led Zeppelin." I'd be sitting there listening to the conversation and the phone would ring again. I'd hear Bill Graham say, "How about 80/20?"

'"What, are you deaf? It's 90/10." He'd put the phone down. Then Bill would phone back. "OK, you've gotta deal." Then it became normal practice. Everyone now does that. Peter Grant started that.'

In September 1970, Zeppelin did two gigs at New York's Madison Square Garden and grossed more than £100,000 for each. *Led Zeppelin III* had advance orders of 700,000 in the USA and HM Government wanted to bestow on the band the Queen's Award for Industry, something Grant thought too pro-Establishment to accept.

Peter Grant

Peter's profile was now such that there was speculation that he was to take over the management of another, then mega British band: Emerson, Lake and Palmer. *Melody Maker* ran a cartoon of Grant as a huge whale with the two bands, Jonah-like, inside him. A geyser of bank notes gushed from the whale's blowhole. Grant was furious and directed an onslaught against the paper, which nervously printed an apology. But his fury may have had more to do with the depiction of him as a whale than any projected takeover.

Managing Led Zeppelin was extremely demanding and Peter was in a bad way – stressed out, smoking heavily and extremely overweight. He had to book two seats for himself on aeroplanes and often crushed chairs and toilet bowls.

But if he was big, then his band was bigger. Zeppelin shared a label with the Rolling Stones, who were, and still are, frequently called the Greatest Rock and Roll Band in the World. What was little known outside the business was that Led Zeppelin were outselling them by three to one. Zeppelin were the biggest band in the world bar none.

Led Zeppelin were now living by a different set of rules to mere mortals, as Richard Cole eloquently explained. 'Once we started our momentum, the people knew and we didn't give a fuck. The doors had to open now. If they didn't, we'd break them down. We made our own laws.'

When the band arrived to tour Japan, 'Immigrant Song' was number 1 in the charts and the audience response verged on hysteria. At the end of one show, the screams of the audience still ringing in their ears, an elated band, steaming on Japanese whisky, resumed their offstage pranks. One episode of tomfoolery in particular awoke the wrath of Grant. It was supposed to be an ambush on Jimmy Page by the other band members, but it was a badly aimed shot: they chucked a vile mash of cold tea, sake and rice over a sleeping Peter.

The vengeful Grant rose behemoth-like from his bed and boxed John Paul Jones around the ears before punching Robert Plant in the mouth. Richard Cole appeared and Grant made to punch him out, too. Cole ducked and the fist connected with John Bonham. Grant bawled Cole out and sacked him on the spot, wrongly thinking, for once, that he had been the instigator of the attack. An accompanying Japanese minder witnessed three-quarters of the biggest band in the world being beaten up by their own manager and was not unreasonably appalled, thinking that he had just witnessed the band's break-up. He had to be assured that this was just a regular night of fun for Led Zeppelin.

At a gig in Lyon, Peter witnessed rowdy elements of the crowd knocking over elderly ticket staff as they attempted to get in for free. Grant's roadie army was dispatched to deal with it. Bernoît Gautier, the record company representative in France, recalls, 'They weren't afraid to fight. That's how it was with Peter. If something's unfair, he gets furious. I would say that he could be furious enough to actually kill someone because he's strong and he is big. But he's fair and his word meant something.'

At the next gig in Nantes, as he waited to get through a locked gate to the backstage area, Grant's Mercedes was surrounded by fans. Thinking the band in danger, he revved up the car and rammed through the gates, taking off the car's bumpers in the process.

Reliable album sales figures are hard to find, but there is a lot of common agreement that *Led Zeppelin IV* was the fourth-biggest-selling album of all time, behind the Eagles' *Their Greatest Hits 1971–1975* at number 1, Michael Jackson's *Thriller* at number 2 and another British band Pink Floyd's *The Wall* at number 3. *Zeppelin IV* contained 'Stairway to Heaven', an eight-minute epic beloved of students of a certain age everywhere and which most would identify as the definitive Zeppelin track.

These were Zeppelin's peak years. Post-'Stairway to Heaven' sales would gently decline, but from such a high starting point that they were still selling many millions. The *Financial Times* predicted that Zeppelin would make $30 million in 1973. Concert attendances were still breaking all records.

On yet another American tour, the band returned to the Edgewater Inn in Seattle, scene of the well-known Mudshark story (and not necessary to repeat here). All the TV sets were thrown into the sea below. Resignedly, Peter went to reception to pay the bill for damages only to have the desk clerk say that he'd always wanted to throw a TV set out of a window. 'Have one on us,' Grant is said to have growled before handing over an additional $500. The clerk promptly lived his dream and dropped a huge TV from the balcony to a watery grave.

Zeppelin may have earned bundles, but clearly their overheads were massive. Perhaps it was these frightening outgoings that drove Peter to conceive of more and more innovative methods of wringing yet more money out of the system for his merry band of brothers. He figured that the band should have their own label. The Beatles had Apple, the Rolling Stones had Rolling Stones Records, even Elton John had Rocket Records. The name Swan Song was chosen; the new label would distribute Zeppelin material and also other bands they favoured, such as Bad Company, Maggie Bell and The Pretty Things (Grant turned down the job of managing Queen). Offices and staff were taken on.

Grant asked his publicist to arrange the launch at a Manhattan restaurant and put in a request for some swans to be placed in the chic establishment's small pool. It seems swans weren't that easy to get hold of in NYC but the resourceful organiser managed to find some geese. Grant was wrathful. 'Do you think we can't tell the difference between swans and fucking geese?' he raged at the employee. 'We all live on fucking farms, you c***!'

In 1975, Zeppelin played a string of gigs at Earls Court. The 85,000 tickets were sold out in hours. This turned out to be something of a swansong for the band, although they didn't know it at the time. They were forced into tax exile shortly afterwards and would play only two more UK gigs ever. In Rhodes that year, Robert Plant was involved in a car crash. His wife was seriously injured and he was to be wheelchair-bound for months. Tours were cancelled.

After Plant's recovery, the band recorded *Presence*. The album went straight to the top but all was not well in the Zeppelin camp. During the lay-off, the Devil had made work for idle hands – Bonham, Page and Richard Cole were having heroin trouble and Grant's marriage was breaking up.

One day, Cole says, post-separation, Grant's wife had gone, with a male companion, to Peter's moated country house to collect some belongings and Peter had phoned Cole to come down to help deal with the situation. Cole rushed to his master's aid, as he had many times before. 'I went to an upstairs bedroom,' he says, 'collected two guns, put them in the trunk of my car and drove to Peter's house.' In the event, no violence ensued, but there is little doubt that Cole had been ready to use the weapons should his master have called for it.

Guns. Heroin. Things were getting a little out of hand.

Alan Callan, who ran Swan Song and who often travelled with the band, saw Grant in action on many occasions, however he says he never saw Peter use violence – he never had to. When Grant had once gone to hospital because of an arm injury, says Callan, 'The doctor said to him, "Mr Grant, do you use your hand in your work a lot?" "No, but I do a lot of this," he said, and prodded the doctor in the chest. Only Peter would talk to a doctor like that.'

On most occasions, the big man's mere presence was enough to swing an argument, Callan says. 'Peter was able to achieve all kinds of things by employing his remarkable persona and that included that terrible stare of his. If he decided to stand up and move a bit close to you, he could intimidate you with his body language. And yet it seems that everybody who really got close to him or had dealings with him found he had this extraordinary charm. He had such a great sense of humour, absolutely fantastic.'

Grant would often regale dinner guests with tales from the tours. One of his favourites concerned the time he sat on Elvis Presley's father. The band had seen Elvis play in Las Vegas and were invited backstage. 'I suffer from a lot of back trouble,' said Peter. 'I was talking to Ronnie Tutt and his wife. Ronnie was Elvis's drummer. Behind me was a long couch and I said to Ronnie, "I've gotta sit down, 'cos my back's hurting."I sat down and realised I had landed on somebody's legs. I jumped up and looked around and realised it was Vernon Presley in a white suit. I said, "I'm really sorry, Mr Presley, for sitting on you, but I guess if anybody is going to do that in this room, it's gotta be me."'

An embarrassed Grant left, saying to Elvis, 'I've gotta apologise for sitting on your dad.'

'He looked me straight in the eye,' Grant would tell his audience, 'and said, "Stick around, kid, you might get a permanent job."' It may have been this encounter that led Colonel Tom Parker to contact Grant early in 1977 to see if he would manage a tour of Europe by Presley, but Elvis died in August that year, just as negotiations had begun.

Despite the humour, there was a sickness at the heart of Led Zeppelin. The band were getting an increasing number of death threats to the extent that, at one time, they seriously considered wearing bulletproof vests onstage. Grant became increasingly paranoid, a condition exacerbated by his new appetite for cocaine. His wife, Gloria, had left him for one of Grant's own farm workers, saying that Peter loved Jimmy Page more than her. Alan Callan's marriage folded and Richard Cole's marriage was also on the rocks.

Back in the States, the band were still playing to huge audiences, but there was a wind of change back home. The Sex Pistols emerged kicking and spitting onto the scene and they had what they considered to be the 'dinosaurs' of rock in their sights.

There were other troubles, too. Bonham and Cole were in a posh restaurant in the south of France when Bonham produced a gas gun and wouldn't put it away. Cole broke Bonham's nose in an effort to shut him up. Too late, the police arrived and the pair were locked up, but miraculously the gas gun was never found. The remarkably slack police also somehow missed their pockets full of cocaine. Cole and Bonham were released without charge.

When Zeppelin flew to New York for the premiere of their troubled movie *The Song Remains the Same*, Cole threw a switchblade at someone on the plane. Later, he swung a punch at a *Melody Maker* writer and was thrown out of a restaurant. He appeared the following day with marks on his face and the rumour was that Peter had slapped him around as a reward for his errant behaviour.

The 1977 tour was not the triumphal rush of earlier times. Cole said, 'I think that [Grant's separation from his wife] was really the fucking end of everything. It's funny, but I hated that last tour. You could feel it . . . something very bad. It was all the drugs . . . I dunno, but there was something wrong. It wasn't the same.'

The adulation was greater than ever, though, despite Jimmy Page's rather eccentric choice of a storm trooper's uniform for one of the shows. They played a gig in Michigan to 76,000 people and at the end Richard Cole picked up a cheque for $800,000.

Having a private army that lived on lots of drink and drugs was bound to cause big trouble at some point. And that point eventually came during the band's 1977 American tour. Grant had employed actor/hard man John Bindon to help out with Zeppelin security. Bindon was a major player in one of the nastiest and well-documented scenes of violence in the Led Zeppelin story.

Grant's 11-year-old son, Warren, accompanied his father to a gig in Oakland and had been seen attempting to take a souvenir Led Zeppelin sign from a backstage caravan door. The story goes that one of the promoter Bill Graham's guards clipped Warren round the ear and John Bonham, having witnessed the event, kicked the guard in the balls. This wasn't enough for Grant; he wanted retribution.

While Richard Cole kept guard, he and Bindon attacked the guard inside a caravan. The man was badly beaten. The incident was to lead to the arrest of Cole, Bindon, Grant and John Bonham, who were all charged and led away in handcuffs. They were found guilty and all given suspended sentences. It seemed there had been scuffles earlier that day: during the afternoon, Bindon had hit one of Graham's stage crew, causing his head to strike some concrete. Grant had hit another. Incensed, three of the crew issued a civil action for $2 million in damages against the defendants in a case that was to drag on for months.

Then came the news that Robert Plant's son, Karac, had died of a viral infection. Plant flew straight home, the tour was cancelled and the infamously bad-tempered gig was to be their last in the USA.

Bill Graham later wrote in his book, *Bill Graham Presents: My Life Inside Rock and Out,* how much he liked the band but not the machine that surrounded them. 'I didn't like those people,' he said. 'I didn't like their influence on society or their power. Back then Zeppelin were kings of the world . . . They surrounded themselves with physical might and they were ready to kill at the slightest provocation.'

Robert Plant later said of the gig, 'It was an absolute shambles. It was so sad that I would be expected to go on and sing "Stairway to Heaven". People know how I feel about that song. I had to sing it in the shadow of the fact that the artillery that we carried with us was prowling around backstage with a hell of an attitude. It was a coming together of these two dark forces which had nothing to do with the songs that Page and I were trying to churn out.'

John Bindon, whose colourful life included acting stints in *Performance*, *Quadrophenia* and *The Sweeney*, as well as holidays with his girlfriend, model Vicki Hodge, in Mustique, where he claimed to have charmed Princess Margaret, was later to stand trial for murder. The deceased, Johnny Darke, was a well-known gangland figure. It was alleged that Bindon had stabbed him to death in a contract killing. Bindon admitted stabbing Darke but said it was self-defence. He stood trial at the Old Bailey and was acquitted, partly as a result of actor Bob Hoskins' testimony as a character witness.

Strangely, Bindon had once won a Queen's Award for Bravery, having rescued a drowning man from the Thames – though it is alleged that Bindon had boasted that he pushed the man in the water in the first place after the two had had a fight.

His acting days over, Bindon died from Aids alone and broke.

These were troubled times: Grant retired to his estate; the band were off the road; the label needed constant attention; Peter was fighting a custody battle for his children and his doctor ordered him to lose ten stone urgently. *140 lb*

Months later, the band, bloodied but unbowed, were ready to record and gig again, but Peter had begun to use heroin.

Cole worked at the Swan Song offices for a while, but when he wasn't on the road with the band then he was only really interested in drugs. The violence hadn't stopped; he and Bindon had beaten up a dealer. Not amused, Grant gave his henchman a job as tour manager with another band to get him out of the way. He also thought Cole was too involved with heroin. Soon after, a truculent Cole was sacked altogether by his by now enraged boss. Cole went off to Italy to clean up but ended up in prison. A paranoid Cole alleged Grant fitted him up via an ex-CIA friend. He served two months and then was released with no charge.

The band did a short European tour, but two months later John Bonham was found dead – he'd succumbed to the old rock-star death: drinking 40 measures of vodka in 12 hours and choking on his own vomit.

The glorious flight of the Zeppelin was over.

Grant became a recluse, hiding away behind the walls of his castle with one of Cole's ex-girlfriends, and he stayed that way for years. Perhaps the only man who could have brought him out of his seclusion was Jimmy Page, but Page had problems of his own and the incredibly close partnership that had created the band in the first place was no more. In the wilderness years, Page and Grant lost contact.

Sex Pistols manager Malcolm McLaren, who once harboured plans to make a film about Grant, gives a summary: 'Grant needed the camaraderie of hard dangerous men who gave him a sense of power. The harder they were, the tougher he felt, and only then was his desire for control satisfied. It all fell apart when Grant aped the lifestyle of Jimmy Page, who then ostracised his biggest fan.'

Later in life, Grant finally lost the weight that had so plagued him; he kicked the coke and the smack and seemed to reach a more contented state. He'd managed to keep custody of his children, which had provided him with some stability. He maintained his low profile, sold the mansion and opted for an apartment in Eastbourne. He was by now a grandfather. Grant even returned to acting. He had a role as a cardinal in *Carry On Columbus*.

Peter re-established contact with the remaining Zeppelin members and his industry friends and was inducted into the British Music Roll of Honour. He died aged 60 from a heart attack. The guest list at his funeral indicated the level of respect he'd maintained to the last. Jimmy Page, Robert Plant, Paul Rodgers, Simon Kirke, Denny Laine and Jeff Beck all paid tribute to Peter the Great.

9

MALCOLM McLAREN

Sex Pistols

**When the mode of the music changes, the walls
of the city shake.**

– *Plato*

**Rock music remained the only form of culture that
youth – those most receptive to radical ideas, who
hold the most potential for social action – cared
about. For the young, everything flowed through
rock 'n' roll: fashion, slang, sexual attitudes, drug
habits, and poses.**

– *Malcolm McLaren*

You'd think that having built the most notorious band in the
history of rock, he could have done a little more to keep
them together. Most aspiring managers would happily part with
a testicle to be in Malcolm McLaren's position after the success
of the *Never Mind the Bollocks, Here's the Sex Pistols* album and a
hugely controversial American tour that garnered front-page press
all over the world. OK, things weren't perfect: the band hated one
another's guts, and Sid (John Ritchie Beverly) had just scored,
jacked up, died and had to be resuscitated, but, hey, this was the

Sex Pistols – SNAFU. However, from day one, it almost seemed that McLaren was trying to scupper the Pistols' chances – or at least he seemed unable to stop them from doing it themselves.

In the days and decades that have followed the band's demise, McLaren would have us believe that he hit the destruct button intentionally, that it had been all to do with his breathtaking Situationist art take on life – cash from chaos. In reality, it looked to be more to do with attention deficiency, a pathological bent for destruction, and the friction between McLaren and Lydon. Malcolm changed the name and facade of his King's Road shop at least four times; he became bored with Bow Wow Wow just as they looked like making it; and he attempted to destroy Adam and the Ants before they'd even started. He may not have been a Situationist, but he was (is) certainly a revisionist.

There arguably isn't one definitive account of McLaren's words, actions or deeds – certainly not one spoken by him, anyway – and while his memoirs are hugely entertaining, they would seem to depict him as insecure at times and a confident bullshitter at others. Yet Malcolm is one of the greats – a great creator, a great character, a great agitator, a great thorn in the side – with a mind seemingly unencumbered by a sense of logic or reality. And exactly the same could be said of his partner-in-crime Johnny Rotten, born John Lydon.

Somewhat surprisingly, McLaren's real name is McLaren, although he never knew his real father, a member of the Royal Engineers, who, if you listen to Malcolm, doubled as cat burglar. In the event, McLaren senior split when McLaren junior was two. Young Malcolm was brought up by his would-be actress grandmother, Rose Corrie Isaacs, and was known during his nipperhood as Malcolm Edwards – Edwards being the surname of his stepfather. Malcolm professes great love for his gran, who, he boasted, was descended from Portuguese royalty.

McLaren had a torrid time at a number of schools, all of which he loathed, arriving late and truanting, yet he eventually emerged with two O levels. A short spell at a wine merchant's and an even shorter one with a haberdasher followed. A teenage Malcolm started drifting around the West End of London and was drawn to the nexus that was Carnaby Street and the nearby Saint Martins art school. In the evenings, he was in the clubs – one night with the Teddy boys, another with the Beats – trying to find a sect that would have him. It wasn't until he enrolled at Saint Martins that he felt he belonged. 'Having bought a black polo neck and being a poseur on the scene,' he said, 'I was now going to get this initiation. It meant I was more bona fide. Now I was a member of the club.'

However, his mother had different ideas. When she heard he would be drawing pictures of naked models, she had him withdrawn. A furious Malcolm then bungled an audition for RADA before wheedling his way into Harrow art school. His disapproving parents put the spoke in again. Why wouldn't he get a proper job? Malcolm went on the run.

One legend, as told to Craig Bromberg and related in his book, *The Wicked Ways of Malcolm McLaren*, has him fleeing London with a small rucksack and wandering the Kent countryside. He ran into an old black man who was also on the road and the odd couple travelled together, sleeping rough, first to Eastbourne and then on to a monastery. After saying goodbye to his travelling companion, Malcolm says he hitchhiked to St Ives to work with the sculptress Barbara Hepworth and stayed there for a few months before returning to London, now calling himself Malcolm Corrie (his grandmother's middle name), and bristling with the absolute conviction that he was at last an artist. Bromberg also says none of Malcolm's friends can recall his ever having been away.

It wasn't a triumphal return to the big city by a long chalk. The account goes (and some of it could be true) that he slept variously in a graveyard, the back seat of fellow student Gordon Swire's car and a brothel. Swire had a sister called Vivienne, who'd just married Derek Westwood. She worked for a band management company that handled a band called the Detours, who became

The High Numbers, who became The Who. The die was cast, some might say.

When Gordon moved into a big house in Clapham, Malcolm blagged a room while a recently separated Vivienne Westwood, with her three-year-old son, Ben, took another. He insinuated himself into Vivienne's bed over the months. Now, he had a base, a bird and, when she got pregnant, a baby.

This was 1967, Vietnam et al. There was something in the air. Youth was on the move and while some opted to sit quietly, skin up and play *Sergeant Pepper*, the students of London and Paris were limbering up for confrontation. The legend goes that McLaren got himself arrested for burning an American flag in Grosvenor Square.

He attended Croydon College of Art, where classmates included Robin Scott, who went on to write and perform 'Pop Muzik' as M, and Jamie Reid, who designed the *Never Mind the Bollocks* album sleeve and put a safety pin through Her Majesty's lower lip. Agitators all, the trio took part in a six-day 'occupation' of college rooms before Malcolm moved on yet again to another art school, the renowned Goldsmiths College. There he encountered the Situationists, a French-born clique whose anti-art stance took quite a bit of understanding because they prided themselves on having no manifesto. A pseudo-revolutionary 'movement', its activities were mainly restricted to daubing slogans such as 'sous les paves, la plage' (under the paving stones, the beach) on walls.

Johnny Rotten is characteristically dismissive of the Situationists, as he recounts in his book, *Rotten: No Irish, No Blacks, No Dogs*: 'I always thought it was foolishness, art students just being art students ... the trouble was they thought about "organised chaos". They were too structured for my liking, word games and no work. Plus they were French, so fuck them.'

Malcolm's ready revolutionary sidekick and bedmate became the diminutive South African Helen Wallington-Lloyd, later to star in *The Great Rock 'n' Roll Swindle*. Together with Malcolm, she raided the college paint shop and the canteen, 'liberating' tubes of poster colour and sandwiches. Helen had led a sheltered life in South Africa and found Malcolm's antics amusing.

'He was an agitator,' she said in Jon Savage's *England's Dreaming*. 'There were debates at the students' union, and Malcolm used to put things in terms they could relate to because he's not an intellect: he had more of a ducking and diving kind of life. He loved art, but he didn't want to make pictures for people to buy. He wanted to instigate something and be an imp. An itch in somebody's knickers.'

The climax of Malcolm's college career came as he convinced the authorities to let him run a free festival. There were to be discussions with R.D. Laing, Malcolm X and William Burroughs. Bands would include The Pretty Things and King Crimson. Other bands 'awaiting confirmation' were Pink Floyd, the Rolling Stones and John Lennon no less. When none of the bands turned up, there was a mini-riot. The police were called, but when the heat was on, Malcolm was nowhere to be seen. This was a first valuable exercise in chaos creation.

Yet McLaren's head was soon somewhere else. He decided to become a film-maker and had a project about Oxford Street in mind, for which he needed a professional movie camera. The college obliged and Malcolm shot miles of material with the borrowed machine. Somehow, though, the camera was lost.

It was the '70s, a new era, and the name Malcolm Edwards didn't seem to fit the times. Malcolm applied for a passport and gave his surname as McLaren.

Vivienne had long been supporting her two boys and Malcolm by selling handmade mirrored earrings to market stalls and the shops of Portobello Road. The mini-business had developed with Malcolm's help; he'd introduced old radios, pictures and other assorted tat of the period to the range.

Setting up their own retail outlet now seemed like an obvious move. On the lookout for premises, they happened upon 430 King's Road, situated at the wrong end of the fashionable boulevard at a time when its previous management had either lost interest or simply disappeared. Photographs of the period show McLaren in full Ted gear: drape suit, gold waistcoat, brothel creepers, the lot. It was timely. There was a rock revival going on. Charlie Gillet had just started his *Honky Tonk* radio programme and the Rock On record shop opened up on the Portobello Road. McLaren called their shop Let it Rock and the Teds would come in and jostle at the till with the Chelsea shopping set.

When the shop was asked to provide the togs for the rock 'n' roll revival film *That'll Be the Day*, starring David Essex and Ringo Starr, Malcolm scented success and, in expansionist mood, he and Vivienne took a stall at a New York fashion show. There they ran into Sylvain Sylvain and Johnny Thunders of the New York Dolls, themselves wannabe designers, selling homemade this and that. As well as the seminal Dolls, Malcolm claims to have met Andy Warhol and Patti Smith on this trip, and on his return boasted that the striking-looking Vivienne was to have a part in one of Warhol's films.

Soon, however, his fevered mind started to wander elsewhere, as had his eye, and he began spending less time in the shop. Having tired of the Teds, he claimed he was cooking up a new image for 430 King's Road – bikers and biker wear. The new incarnation would be called Too Fast to Live, Too Young to Die, a slogan that American biker gangs had started using after James Dean's death in a car crash. A new range of clothes – oddities like a T-shirt with chicken bones chained onto it in the shape of 'Rock 'n' Roll' – attracted new punters. Iggy Pop dropped by. Jimmy Page and Marianne Faithfull were regulars.

When the New York Dolls came over to play Europe, McLaren hitched along with them as their most devoted fan. Another idea was forming in his head. He reasoned that if rock stars liked wearing his clothes, then he should have his own band wear his clothes. Since he couldn't play a note, he would run a band – or specifically, *this* band. The Dolls' cartoon-like flash and trash held a strong appeal. They became his ideal fantasy. He made clothes for them, hung out backstage with them and went to parties with them. Sylvain Sylvain has said, 'There never was a bigger Dolls groupie than Malcolm McLaren.'

When the Dolls went home, Malcolm became instantly bored despite the success of the shop, which was still attracting rock luminaries as well as assorted rock-fringe personalities like *NME* writer Nick Kent, who was seeing the shop's latest salesperson Chrissie Hynde. Another shop worker was Glen Matlock, who was attending Saint Martins and moonlighting at Too Fast, silk-screening T-shirts. Matlock was aided by Bernie Rhodes, who had previously worked at the famous rich-hippy shop Granny Takes a Trip (where Keith Richards used to buy his stage clothes). Bernie, a blues buff, was also running a Renault repair shop and became thick as thieves with Malcolm in the early Pistols era before ploughing his own furrow when he went off to run The Clash.

The shop was revamped again. The emphasis was now on fetish wear. Vivienne remembers Malcolm calling it 'rubber wear for the office'. There was the famous T-shirt with the two half-naked cowboys standing face to face and penis to penis. Another had Snow White in an altogether unfamiliar pose with the Seven Dwarfs. Adorning the walls were rubber masks, tit clamps, chains, whips and lacy petticoats. Chrissie Hynde was a walking advert for the newly dubbed SEX shop. 'I began wearing all this stuff,' she said, 'like a rubber skirt, fishnet stockings and these high-heeled shoes . . . It was so hip and well thought out.'

The magnetic shop increased its attraction. Two dead-end kids with a certain look in their eyes started hanging around it. Steve Jones and Paul Cook were bona fide street urchins and school rejects, and in Jones's case practically a full-on kleptomaniac. He was also a rampant sex maniac – bright but, by some accounts, with a reading age of about 11. It was Jones who had the idea for a band and started lobbying Malcolm to run it, although in private he was ambivalent about his future manager. 'I thought Malcolm was a bit of a weirdo,' he said, 'a bit of a pervert kind of guy. But he was different. I used to try to nick stuff, though.'

McLaren's interest in the band idea was aroused. He saw

himself as a latter-day Larry Parnes, the late-'50s impresario who'd packaged up a series of swoon figures such as Billy Fury, Vince Eager and the poor doomed Dickie Pride. (Regarded by many as the most talented of the lot, Dickie, while waiting for success to come his way, had become addicted to amphetamines and heroin, which unhinged him. He attended a mental hospital after trying to rip his own face off. He was given a frontal lobotomy and never performed again. He died aged 27.) Rock journalist Nick Kent commented on Malcolm's dreaming: 'He really was in love with the myth of the working-class barely articulate rock star.'

As Jon Savage points out in his authoritative history of the Sex Pistols, 'Steve Jones was a perfect Artful Dodger to McLaren's Fagin.' He was a classic Shepherd's Bush yobbo from a broken home, the son of an ex-boxer and a hairdresser. 'I was brought up near Goldhawk Road,' Jones said, 'down Benbow Road – little streets – West Indian and Irish people. Wild.'

Cook was just as disadvantaged as Jones but steadier, a trait that manifested itself throughout the Pistols' short and brilliant career, and a quality you need as a drummer. The duo were in musical partnership, if music is the word, with another school friend called Wally Nightingale, who was in the band principally because his parents' house was big enough for rehearsals. When the trio, loosely known as the Swankers, needed a bass player, Malcolm was at hand to introduce them to Glen Matlock.

When the band needed equipment, Jones would steal it, and more besides. He is supposed to have burgled Ronnie Wood's house and had a fur coat away. Keith Richards' Cheyne Walk home yielded a colour TV and some clothes. Cook's drumkit came from the BBC. A tuner was swiped from a Roxy Music gig and two guitars arrived from Rod Stewart's mansion in Windsor. Miscellaneous speakers and amps were dragged out of other bands' vans parked up for the night. But the prize haul was an entire PA system and microphones from a David Bowie gig at the Hammersmith Odeon, which they swiped in the dead of night and bundled into a getaway van Jones had stolen earlier in the evening specifically for the purpose. He stole from the stars and kept the lot.

Jones plagued the life out of McLaren to attend rehearsals and he eventually caved in and went along. He didn't like what he saw. He thought Jones was a rubbish singer, Cook was leaden and Wally was out of the game, as far as he could see. He told Jones to take over the guitar-playing, to sack Wally and to look for a singer – advice that, perhaps unfortunately for Wally, turned out to be good.

When McLaren bought the elegantly wasted leather-clad *NME* journalist Nick Kent down to see them, Kent had a bash at playing the guitar. Jones's ambition switch was turned on as he saw his band in a different light; however, Malcolm could still only see a motley bunch of local no-hopers.

He told Vivienne to mind the store and told Bernie Rhodes to mind the Swankers while he went off to New York in search of his playmates, the Dolls – oh, and his (American) ex-shop assistant girlfriend, Addie. So obsessed was he with the Dolls that despite the fact they already had management, he put himself into the role without either contracts or commitment from the band and knowing that, if anything came of his efforts, he would very likely be rowed out of the game. Deluded as this perhaps was, he made plans.

First step: get them into rehab.

Second step: dress them all up. He figured that in fiercely capitalist America, maybe a blatant communist theme would have the pre-requisite shock value, so rag-trade Malcolm saw red, got straight on the phone to Vivienne and demanded she knock up crimson vinyl wet-look jeans and zippered T-shirts for the whole band.

Third step: get some gigs. He booked the band into a tour of Florida clubs – as far away from New York's narcotics convenience stores as he could conceive. The gigs were a disaster.

Unsurprisingly, the costumes were a big mistake, as Sylvain Sylvain pointed out. 'Let's face it,' he said. 'In America, you could be gay, commit incest, do anything, but you cannot be a communist.'

Two of the band bailed out and flew back to New York to score some dope, leaving Malcolm broken-hearted and broke. He had to be driven back (he had no driving licence) the length of the country in a clapped-out station wagon.

Back in the Big Apple, Addie rejected him, Richard Hell turned down his offer to come back to the UK and be the lead singer in this new band he had, and Malcolm's big American adventure was over.

In London, Nick Kent was making plans to dump his writing career, take over the Swankers and turn them into a band in his own leather-clad image. McLaren thought about and then rejected the idea, but galvanised by the takeover bid, he resolved to solve the singer issue. The Bay City Rollers had just exploded into the charts and Malcolm was thinking pop. Perhaps Scotland was the new Liverpool. Perhaps there was someone north of the border who could take the microphone in hand. Bernie and Malcolm drove north on a trawling mission and somehow came across a petrol-pump attendant called Midge Ure. Did Midge want to move to London and sing with this great new band? No, thanks, was the reply. Ure was in the process of signing his own band, Slik, to Bell Records. Would history have swung on a different tack if Midge hadn't rejected Malcolm's advances? Would Rotten have ever done *I'm a Celebrity . . . Get Me Out of Here*? Would Band Aid ever have fed the world? Would the Sex Pistols have had a number 1 with 'Vienna'? Would Sid be dead?

Thwarted, Malcolm retreated to the King's Road shop, alongside a new manageress, the fearsomely beehived Jordan. The new regime propelled the clothes designs to new levels of perversion. One shirt apparently depicted a naked black footballer with huge hanging tackle; another had a 12-year-old boy smoking a cigarette, an image that could have been taken from a paedophile magazine; yet another had a picture of the Cambridge rapist's leather hood with the zipped mouth. Then he *made* a leather hood with a zipped mouth.

The silk-screeners Matlock and Bernie thought that McLaren had gone too far this time. So did the police, apparently, who, legend has it, raided the shop and took a lot of stock away with them.

Back to the band. Malcolm wouldn't take them seriously with Wally in the line-up. He wanted Jones to play guitar . . . this guitar . . . and Malcolm produced Sylvain's white Gibson Les Paul, which he had acquired. Even the acquisitive Jones's eyes widened. His erstwhile loyalties evaporated. Matlock was deputised to sack Wally. The dirty deed was duly done.

Matlock became key to the story soon after the Wally sacking when he spotted a sneering, hunchbacked loudmouth with peroxide hair in the Roebuck pub just up from the shop. Craig Bromberg's book gives an impression of the early John Lydon. 'Everything he says is "fuck you, fuck that, that's just your tough shit". One long hyperventilated howl of hate against any target he can get his tongue around: pop music, people over thirty, politicians, priests – he even hates himself.'

Ideal.

Matlock, having just thrown an old band member out, was now duty-bound to get a new one in and John was persuaded to go back to the shop and meet a sceptical McLaren. Vivienne reckoned she'd already spotted John and his mates but had thought that Sid Vicious was the most interesting of all of them. (Malcolm told contactmusic.com in 2006, 'Vivienne was infatuated with Sid.')

Lydon, wearing his Pink Floyd shirt with 'I hate' scrawled above their name, used an old shower head as a microphone; someone put Alice Cooper's 'I'm Eighteen' on the shop jukebox and John jumped around, yelled a bit, crashed into things and left the judges doubled up with laughter. A star was born.

Malcolm reckons he spotted the punk pioneer in the making there and then. 'I had an eye,' he said. 'I knew he had something, just as I knew Jones had something.'

'Sex were doing something different from everybody else,' said

John, 'and they weren't liked, which was absolutely brilliant. They were totally horrible people. Vivienne was the most awful old bag and that really fascinated me . . .'

The hunched, spitting hooligan act we grew to know and love was formed early on in Lydon's life. He'd contracted meningitis as an eight year old, which had put him in a coma and wiped his memory. He was off school for a year. It left him with bad eyesight, as his mother told Fred Vermorel in his book, *Sex Pistols: The Inside Story*, 'I don't know if you ever notice John – he stares – sort of a stare in his eyes.'

He was anti-Establishment from the off. 'At school, I knew we were being fobbed off,' Lydon recalls. 'I learned hate and resentment there.'

He met Sid at college. Sid had spent his early years in Ibiza, where his mother had been dumped by his father. She'd survived by selling dope to the hippies. When mother and son returned, life continued in the same chaotic hand-to-mouth vein. Mother and son were close – too close probably – and the many rows often left Sid dossing on park benches and contemplating prostitution as a way out of the claustrophobic relationship.

John and Sid, together with another college friend Jah Wobble (real name John Wardle – they were often referred to as the 'three Johns'), started hanging out on the King's Road, dressing madly and spitting at people in flares. 'I used to wrap myself in trash,' Lydon says, 'like Richard the Third, deformed, hilarious, grotesque. Dogs barked at me.'

'He looked really interesting,' said Steve Jones. 'There was something about him that magnetised you to him. He had all the punk stuff on, the safety pins and everything, that was nothing to do with McLaren. He was wild-looking.'

Most of the young punks are between 17 and 19. To be in your 20s is to be old. They've all grown up with a music that they felt alienated from — groups too old to identify with, musicianship too sophisticated to ape, concerts too expensive to attend, and songs that were no reflection of their feelings or problems.

Steve Turner, *The Guardian*

Punk was a peculiarly British phenomenon. OK, the debate rages on – some say that Iggy was the first punk way back in 1968, that the Ramones were ahead of the crowd in 1975 – but much as some (not Johnny) British punks would concede they were influenced by their American cousins, that particular moth-eaten look (the look Richard Hell and the Voidoids claimed was originally theirs) and that thrashing sound (that every man and his dog claimed was theirs) all gelled in the UK in some unique and dynamic package personified by J. Rotten and the Pistols. It has to do with rage. Beating on a brat with a baseball bat is one thing. Declaring yourself an Antichrist is quite another. Despite the speed they took, the Pistols never played fast; you just think they did.

Let's face it, Americans didn't have a monarchy they wanted to tear down, nor did they have a burning urge to spread the tentacles of anarchy; they (the young American whites, at least) had college degrees, jobs to go to – a future. They also had decent teeth. What was missing from American punk bands was the speed stare, the piercing, the chain-whipping, the self-harm scars, the spit and the bum-flapped, cut-up anti-fashion authenticity. In short, the young Americans lacked the fury, or more precisely what the *Daily Mirror* on the morning after the Pistols appeared on Bill Grundy's show headlined 'The Filth and the Fury'.

And where did all that rage come from? Not just from a yawning boredom and lack of opportunity surely, not just a revolt against the music of Yes and Pink Floyd, not just because the discos were all chrome-and-crisps cattle-market crap-holes. One good theory involves nuclear weapons. To be 19 years old in 1975 is to have lived all your life in the shadow of the bomb, to have known nothing except the prospect of imminent annihilation. The punks had lived out their childhood against a background of student barricades, militant unionism and pictures of body bags coming back from

Vietnam. As Charlotte Pressler commented in *England's Dreaming*, 'We had been promised the end of the world as children, and we weren't getting it.'

The UK punk 'movement' lent the American bands a credibility and a relevance that they would never have mustered on their own. And even if it is accepted that they had invented it, in the time honoured fashion of UK/US youth culture osmosis, the Americans bought punk back from Britain in its radicalised reversion. Any debt, real or imagined, the Pistols owed to the Ramones, the Voidoids or the Stooges, they paid back a thousand times over and created a deluge of American thrash and ersatz punk that we have to endure still.

It's quite difficult to give an accurate impression of what life was like in the UK in 1975, especially for a low-achieving London brat. There is a commonly spouted Pistols legend that the charts were clogged up with the dinosaurs of rock and, indeed, a look at the evidence shows Led Zeppelin in a pervasive position in the culture and the charts with *Physical Graffiti*. But Patti Smith's *Horses* was also around, as was Bowie's *Young Americans* and *Bob Marley Live*. These weren't dinosaurs. However, the singles chart was awash with lightweight pap like the Bay City Rollers, Telly Savalas, Mud and Typically Tropical. The only rockers in earshot were ex-rockers – Rod Stewart's 'Sailing' was number 1 for four weeks and Queen's ultimate pomposity 'Bohemian Rhapsody' took up its residency at number 1 for what seemed like a lifetime.

Elsewhere, an ailing Harold Wilson was preparing to pass his crown to an avuncular but undistinguished Jim Callaghan. Maggie Thatcher loomed on the horizon, the IRA were bombing Britain, the Yorkshire Ripper had embarked on his bloody spree and *Dixon of Dock Green* was still on the telly.

In the Sex Pistols documentary, *The Filth and the Fury*, John Lydon spells it out: 'It was cold and miserable. No one had any jobs. There was race hate, social strife, chaos and rioting. People were fed up with the old way, but we felt powerless.'

The only youth movements of any note were the football hooligans, who, far from being a mindless rabble, had strict behavioural codes and cultural references. Lydon's *No Irish, No Blacks, No Dogs* is punctuated by remarks from an Arsenal boot boy known as Rambo: 'Before "Ziggy Stardust", you had *Clockwork Orange*,' he says. 'Everybody used to dress like the *Clockwork Orange* film as well. When *Clockwork Orange* came out, we used to wear white boiler suits. Some wore bowler hats. Practically everybody who supported Arsenal had a white boiler suit. We were already into rows and that, but then the film came out and that became another fashion to follow. When we played Tottenham, everyone supporting Arsenal was *Clockwork Orange*. You'd write things like "Arsenal" or the manager of the team on the boiler suits. We'd wear red scarves in those days. You would carry canes as far as you could get away with it. But umbrellas were the thing. We had the Arsenal lot from Bethnal Green, who also dressed in the boiler suits. All the Borehamwood Arsenal had tattoos. Newcastle fans used to come down all dressed up like Alice Cooper with all the black make-up and the Alice Cooper gear on. Man United fans dressed like Dave Bowie.'

The clothes salesman Malcolm McLaren identified with this tribalism; the misanthropic Rotten did not, even though he did support Arsenal.

The first rehearsal was almost the end of the line for the embryonic Pistols. 'None of them showed up,' says McLaren, 'because they thought Rotten was a c***. Right there, first day. They never liked him. I liked Jones; Jones didn't mind me. I quite liked Cook, but to me he was a bit boring. I brought Matlock into the group as an anchor of normality: he had a certain intelligence that I thought could be used to help Cook and Jones construct songs. Rotten was just an arrogant little shit who thought he knew everything. He hated their music. Cook and Jones were going for the tradition of mutated, irresponsible hardcore raw power: Iggy Pop, New York Dolls, MC5, The Faces. Rotten wanted it like the '60s – Captain Beefheart, all weird.

'We knew he couldn't sing, that he had no sense of rhythm, but he had this charm of a boy in pain. You knew all the girls were going to love him. I thought they could be the Bay City Rollers: that was in my head. I was so out of it. To think he would be the alternative to the Bay City Rollers: dour and tough and the real thing. A genuine teenage group. For me, that was anarchy in the record business: that was enough for me. That was the best selling point: they were like young assassins. It took on a life of its own.'

At some point in 1975, McLaren left Vivienne to move in with Helen Wallington-Lloyd. Helen's flat became Sex Pistols Central. 'John looked amazing in a mohair jumper,' she said, 'like a young Albert Steptoe. Very queenified, always moaning . . . I think with Malcolm they had a sexual thing. It was narcissistic. They looked so much alike. Both Aquarians, the same bone structure. They've got those eyes and they're absolutely fearless of other people's opinions. They're hard. Obviously different things in their backgrounds made them different and also they had the gift of the gab. They'd come up with the most bizarre innovations.'

According to one account, John was secretive and wouldn't even tell the band what his surname was, but when Steve Jones saw him inspecting his graveyard teeth in a mirror, he said, 'Your teeth are rotten, you look Rotten.' The name stuck.

'John's teeth were like fag ends,' Jones observed later.

Their earliest home-grown track was 'Seventeen', which had music by Jones and lyrics by Rotten – that is until the chorus, 'I'm a lazy sod,' which was Jones through and through – although most Pistols tracks were credited to all four members. Then came 'Kill Me Today' and 'Submission' – all rough-and-ready stuff – but gradually McLaren, who as yet had no contract with the band, thinking that this was to his advantage, began to realise that they were starting to sound good. Very good, in fact. Better than the New York Dolls, in fact.

It was down to the Saint Martins student Matlock to get them their first gig proper at his college. The Pistols supported Bazooka Joe, who boasted Adam Ant as a member. In the set was the Shepherd's Bush anthem 'Substitute' and The Small Faces'

'Whatcha Gonna Do About It?', with Rotten's negative version of the lyric, 'I want you to know that I hate you baby, I want you to know I don't care.'

> Punk was a DIY revolution: iconoclastic and depraved, it was, perhaps, the last working class youth movement. In the late 1970s, before the corporate might of MTV and fashion bibles like The Face magazine came to dominate youth culture, punk rejected the economic and moral constraints of British society by creating an anti-world in which worthless objects like safety pins, bin-liners and hastily drawn slogans on clothing defined a new aesthetic. The elevation of everyday 'found' objects to jewellery and desirable clothing challenged the foundations of the economy. The iconography itself signified glorious moral decay. This re-evaluation of aesthetic values coupled with a laissez-faire, pre-AIDS attitude to sex and drugs seriously undermined the status quo at that time. The music was basic, fast and loud.
>
> Nils Stevenson in *Vacant:*
> *A Diary of the Punk Years 1976–79*

The Saint Martins gig was a ferocious racket; someone pulled the plug on them and there was a fight. No one had seen anything like it. A profoundly affected Adam Ant left his band the next day. McLaren, disturbed that a band he'd helped create, in no small part to promote his shop, showed signs of being exciting – successful even – was forced into getting off his backside to get them some gigs.

By the simple expedient of phoning the venues and pretending that the Pistols were the support act, he was able to set up about 15 gigs in and around London.

Ron Watts of the 100 Club recalls, 'They weren't booked or invited, they just arrived and said they were the support band, set up their gear and played.'

There was almost always the same reaction – stunned amazement, hilarity and fighting. Most of the audience were longhairs who thought the band couldn't play – the Pistols all had short hair and mangled clothing at a time when you might be beaten up in the streets just for having a particular hairstyle. As Suggs observed during a BBC interview, 'If you came up from the suburbs and you had blue hair then, wow, man, you were lucky to get out alive.'

A small minority of each crowd understood, though, and one gang of poseurs, which included a pre-Generation X Billy Idol and a pre-Siouxie and the Banshees Siouxie and became known as the Bromley Contingent, totally got it and started traipsing around after the Sex Pistols. Siouxie described the loose group: 'Before it got a label, it was a club for misfits, waifs, male gays, female gays, bisexuals, non-sexuals, everything. No one was criticised for their sexual preferences. The only thing that was looked down on was suburbia.'

The suburban outcasts made a visually striking mob. When put together with Malcolm's King's Road bondage shoppers, they formed a completely unique ripped-up-rainbow following that attracted considerable attention and even violence everywhere they went.

At one of the string of 100 Club gigs, Sid Vicious whipped Nick Kent around the head with a bike chain; at another the whole band had a stand-up row mid-set and Jones smashed up the dressing-room. At a Marquee gig, Rotten threw two chairs into the monitors. In High Wycombe, when supporting Screaming Lord Sutch, Rotten smashed up the mike stand and messed with a kid's hair in the audience. Someone went for John and the Pistols' entourage jumped on him. It was at the 100 Club that Vicious invented the pogo dance. 'I started the pogo because I hated the Bromley Contingent,' he said, 'and I did it because I had a chance to knock them around all over the place.'

When Steve Jones was asked by a music journalist what his influences were, he replied, 'Actually, we're not into music, we're into chaos.'

The fevered press started talking about the Pistols in terms of spearheading a new generation. Caroline Coon wrote in *Melody Maker*, 'John is the elected generalissimo of a new cultural movement.'

Sounds magazine writer Jonh Ingham interviewed the band with Malcolm in a café; things were proceeding in an OK fashion, but then Ingham became bothered that Rotten had so far remained silent. When he finally dared rattle John's cage, he got both barrels. 'I hate shit,' declared Johnny. 'I hate hippies and what they stand for. I hate long hair. I hate pub bands. I want to change it so there are rock bands like us.'

Two days after the piece came out, the band played at London's Nashville and the future of British punk (as well as Adam Ant) turned out to watch them. The crowd included Tony James (Generation X), Mick Jones (The Clash), Vic Godard (the Subway Sect) and Dave Vanian (The Damned). A lacklustre performance was transformed when Vivienne slapped someone across the face. Her boyfriend went for Vivienne and McLaren went for the boyfriend. A delighted Rotten leapt into the mêlée, fists flying. When the dust settled, Vivienne revealed that she'd slapped the girl just because she fancied it and because the band was boring.

McLaren and Bernie Rhodes began to think that if the Pistols were in the vanguard of a punk movement, then they should form some other bands to join it, and so set about putting together the band that became The Clash. Joe Strummer had seen the Pistols when they supported his band, The 101ers. He referred to them as 'light years ahead' of his own band and when Rhodes asked him to join forces with him and Mick Jones and jump ship, Strummer asked how high. Mick Jones tried to recruit Chrissie Hynde to the new band, which was to be called School Girl's Underwear. McLaren tried to entice her to a band based around Dave Vanian and Rat Scabies to be called Masters of the Backside. Another incarnation of the same band briefly had the delightful name Mike Hunt's Honourable Discharge.

Malcolm sent the Pistols off up north in a knackered van on a tour of pub back rooms and dodgy clubs. He took great pains to avoid the rigours of the road himself. The band fended for themselves on the trips, relying to some extent on Jones's shoplifting talents to keep them fed. Most of the gigs were short and sour.

Back in town, McLaren was having trouble finding gigs for his disruptive act, so he persuaded a friend to let him have the Screen on the Green cinema for an all-nighter that featured The Clash, the Buzzcocks, The Stranglers and, top of the bill, the Pistols. This is the gig that every punk-never-wozzer says they were at; however, the word was out around the record industry, so A&R men from EMI and Polydor were definitely in the audience. And they were impressed. McLaren started negotiations there and then.

At a time when the usual advance for a new band was £15,000 tops, Malcolm was brazenly demanding £40,000, causing *NME* editor Neil Spencer to comment that Punk was conceived 'as a ram-raid on corporate pop's bank vaults and a merry piece of snook-cocking'.

McLaren told Simon Garfield, the author of *Money for Nothing*, 'I was never interested in being polite like other managers before me. "You can keep the royalties," I used to say. "Give me the money now." I thought royalties were a very abstract phenomenon to do with creative accounting – like something you might never see. I never believed what they promised, and I always thought they were all crooks – and that's a fact, they are.'

It was time to sign a contract with the band, he thought, and, enlisting as his partner a solicitor, Steven Fisher, he formed the notorious Glitterbest Ltd as the management company. The contract gave McLaren 25 per cent of the band's income. In return, they would get £25 a week each. A scornful, if negligent, Rotten signed it without reading it and told Glen Matlock (who had read it) that if it turned out there was anything wrong with the deal then it would all be Matlock's fault.

Malcolm was playing EMI against Polydor in a big way now,

shuttling between their offices and spinning tall tales to each. In the stand-off, EMI blinked first, raised their bid and signed the band for the requisite £40,000 for two albums over two years, with two one-year options. The contract was drafted and signed all in one day, a deal which apparently remains the fastest the company has ever done and shows their desperation to be associated with the leading band of the punk generation.

The Polydor A&R man Chris Parry apparently sobbed when he heard the news that he had lost the race to sign them. 'It was one of my blackest days,' he said. 'I was very, very upset.'

The trouble started immediately. EMI booked the band into a studio to record the first single, but when Rotten was caught writing slogans on the walls they were ejected and another studio had to be found. Then Malcolm wouldn't accept the suggested producer and demanded that EMI take on Chris Thomas, who, ironically, had produced *Dark Side of the Moon* for Rotten's pet-hate band Pink Floyd, as well as some Roxy Music albums. It turned out to be an inspired choice. Thomas with Bill Price produced the trademark wall of guitars that makes 'Anarchy in the UK' sound as powerful and dangerous today as it did when it was recorded.

Another tour was now necessary to promote the single – a single which up until then seemed obstinately glued to the shelves. Much as Malcolm didn't want to play the rock-and-roll game according to the Establishment rules, there seemed little choice. He burned the midnight oil arranging transport, lights, PAs and hotels, while EMI's Eric Hall sought some TV exposure. Hall sniffed out a vacant slot on Thames Television's *Today* magazine programme that had arisen when Queen pulled out, owing to Freddie having toothache. Somehow, he'd convinced the show's producers that his label's recently signed lout band, accompanied by an entourage of bizarrely dressed fans, would make a perfect replacement for Queen and would be good TV. It wasn't just good TV, it was great TV, as the hapless (and drunk) host, the late Bill Grundy, fell into the trap of urging the Pistols to say foul things on live television. The alley cat Jones rose magnificently to the occasion and in two short phrases propelled his band onto the front pages of the scandal sheets under screaming condemnatory headlines. Priceless. You couldn't buy it.

Steve: You dirty sod. You dirty old man.
Grundy: Well, keep going, chief. Keep going. Go on, you've got another ten seconds. Say something outrageous.
Steve: You dirty bastard.
Grundy: Go on, again.
Steve: You dirty fucker!

It was just the anti-Establishment trigger 'Anarchy in the UK' needed and it at last started selling nationwide.

McLaren, who had resigned himself to the endless slog of gigs and record releases to incrementally raise the profile of his band, had inadvertently hit the jackpot with the first throw of the dice. Craig Bromberg (although muddling his ball-game analogy) sees this as the pivotal moment, a moment when Malcolm started claiming that he'd planned it all. 'McLaren was like a lucky billiards player whose incompetent bluffing had led to a sudden, incredibly lucky scattering of pool balls into their appropriate holes; from now on, he would have to play the rest of the game as if he had been an expert from the start.'

The managers of Britain's provincial gig venues saw things differently, and after the furore over the TV show, the cancellations came in thick and fast; the band ended up playing only three of the proposed nineteen gigs.

EMI saw things differently, too. The ladies that packed the records into their sleeves refused to pack 'Anarchy in the UK' and had to be talked into it by the management. That made a four-page story in the papers. There were serious concerns at the highest level about the potential damage to the sales of a brain scanner EMI were trying to market in the USA because the Pistols were front-page news in the *Los Angeles Times*. Barely two months after the ink was dry on the contract, Sir John Read, the EMI chairman, addressed his shareholders and denounced the bad boys that comprised his company's new signing.

'Tell him to go fuck himself,' responded a distinctly unimpressed John Rotten.

McLaren, finally seeing the commercial upside of the uproar, began sabotaging his own gigs, according to Steve Jones. 'I got the feeling he'd called up the gigs and said it's going to be fucking hell there, and then the guys would get scared and not put us on.'

The Pistols only had to fart to make the front pages now and often they didn't have to do anything at all, the press just made it up. When the band was supposed to have thrown up at a Heathrow check-in desk on their way to Amsterdam, their EMI minder was able to state categorically that they'd never even been to the desk. The *Evening Standard* ran the tall tale anyway, to the further consternation of the EMI brass.

The decision was made: the band had to be dumped. Nick Mobbs, who had signed them, refused to take part in it and handed in his notice in disgust. EMI wanted a quiet termination. McLaren went to the press, bleating about mistreatment. However, EMI, thinking they could spike McLaren's guns, had arranged for him to have a meeting with a young Richard Branson (whom McLaren would from then on refer to as 'Mr Pickle'). Branson, with his unerring eye for sensation, was offering to pick up the contract. Malcolm refused to even meet the head of what he considered to be a hippy company. To him, it was anathema.

EMI handed over £40,000 to get rid of the Sex Pistols and sent out the order that any remaining copies of 'Anarchy in the UK' be melted down.

McLaren's scouring of London for an alternative deal proved arduous and brought to light the amazing schisms that were breaking out in labels like Island, Chrysalis, Warner Brothers, RCA and CBS. While the young A&R managers and other minions were exhilarated by the Pistols and what they seemed to stand for, the older executives, with more to fear and older ears, ran for cover. McLaren bemoaned the fact that the labels were all scared but to some extent the problem may have been that he was now asking for £100,000 for his notorious band.

It wasn't until Malcolm attended Midem, the music business trade show in Cannes, in late January 1977, that he met a simpatico label boss, Derek Green from A&M. 'I played this little cassette and it just blew me away,' said Green. 'They weren't another American rock band that was churning out the same thing. I was thrilled. Thrilled. I couldn't believe what I was hearing. I was terribly excited . . . I knew at that very moment that I wanted the act badly and in this business you rarely do.'

The A&M label (the 'A' of which is the legendary trumpeter Herb Alpert) wasn't scared by the press clamour that surrounded the *enfants terribles* of British rock. They could handle it – they would milk it, they thought. Discussions began which included some of the first mutterings about a Sex Pistols film.

Of McLaren's negotiating skills, Green had this to say: 'He's a guy who just knows how to trick a deal. One minute he'd be charming the pants off me, the next he'd be telling me how Warner Brothers had offered them X money and that I had to beat that to get them. Of course, I had no way of knowing what was the truth.'

Green felt it necessary to go to Los Angeles to confer with Jerry Moss, the 'M' of A&M. The picaresque McLaren followed him, chasing the money. 'Malcolm arrived at the A&M lot,' said Green, 'on a sunny 90-degree Los Angeles day, dressed in an all-black leather outfit with a chain tying his knees together. It had to be one of the funniest things I've ever seen.' In March 1977, in the face of American staffers saying the band was horrible and that Green must be losing his mind, they finalised a deal. The band signed for £75,000 (shortly afterwards, The Clash were to get £100,000 from CBS).

Meantime, Rotten deposed Glen Matlock from the band and pulled in Sid, an old friend and ally from the past who John felt was essential for the Sex Pistols despite his inability to play bass, or anything else. And another thing, Sid came with baggage. He'd met an American groupie from the appropriately named Main Line, Philadelphia, who despite her youth had already attempted suicide twice. Nancy Spungen joined the Pistols' entourage. She'd tried to get John first, but it was hate at first sight for Lydon, who says in *No Irish, No Blacks, No Dogs* that 'Nancy was a horror freak show, just crying out for a slap in the kisser. Many of us, at one time or another, actually physically hit her because she was that pushy. I know I did.'

Steve Jones felt the bad vibe, too. 'There was a dark cloud with this bird. I just fucking hated her.'

It was the Jubilee year in 1977, so McLaren decided that they should start work on a song Rotten had written a few months earlier. Then called 'No Future', it was re-dubbed 'God Save the Queen'. The day after the official signing, the Pistols turned up to perform a mock signing for the benefit of the press in front of Buckingham Palace. It was the start of a long day for the Pistols and possibly the longest day of Derek Green's life. The band leapt from the limousines, signed some scraps of paper, threw some V-signs at the large house behind them and at the cameras in front of them, and then dived off just as the police started paying them a lot of attention.

Reconvening at a nearby hotel for a press conference, the group began drinking heavily and haranguing journalists before embarking to Wessex studios to hear the latest mixes of the single. Here Paul and Sid had a stand-up row, so the drink-fuelled party departed to the A&M offices. There was a mini-battle in the car, as McLaren relates: 'Paul got the worst end of it and suffered a bashed-in nose and Sid's shoes were thrown out of the window, his foot now cut. Rotten's watch that had been bought by his mother for his birthday the previous week was smashed. He was totally furious. Steve, who had tried to stop the fight, being the toughest, was totally pissed and completely hopeless. The fight was about who was the toughest; who was the most Sex Pistol.'

The drunken band marauded around the offices. Vicious managed to break a toilet bowl and a window, and called a female staff member a bitch. According to McLaren, Jones found some attractive staff in a ladies' toilet and 'had a go'. A few days later, as the record was being pressed, Rotten was being fined for possession of amphetamine sulphate. The same evening, Rotten, Jah Wobble and Vicious became involved in a fracas with 'Whispering' Bob Harris, the presenter of *The Old Grey Whistle Test*. Legend even has it that the Pistols allegedly threatened to kill Harris for not playing their records.

The fallout from this event found its way back to Green and added to his mounting fears that he had done something terribly wrong in signing the Sex Pistols. He rang Moss in the US and offered his resignation, saying that he felt the label should keep the band but that he didn't want to work with them any more. His boss made the decision for him. Green would keep his job and the Pistols would lose their label. A relieved Green promptly issued the following statement: 'There is no longer any association between A&M Records and the Sex Pistols. Production of their single "God Save the Queen", which had been tentatively scheduled for release later this month, has been halted.'

McLaren was summoned to the offices and unceremoniously dumped, but left the meeting grasping yet another cheque. The band had lost their second label in less than a week. The order went out that all copies of 'God Save the Queen' were to be destroyed.

Notionally, the band now had £125,000 – not bad for six months' work – but McLaren feared that its members had become pariahs, that they would never get a label to take them on now and neither could they get any gigs. The band prospered, though – their wages were hiked to £40 a week, and although Rotten was already beginning to become curious about where all the money was going and had asked for the accounts, revealing a shrewdness that the others lacked, he was not to get it, or at least not all of what he was due, for a further nine years.

McLaren was hatching plans. He approached Peter Cook about writing a script for a film. Cook mused and then passed. Monty Python's Graham Chapman and *Till Death Us Do Part* writer John Speight knocked out a treatment, but it was rejected by McLaren. (Ironically, *Till Death Us Do Part* wouldn't have been a bad name for a Pistols film.) Also discarded was Richard Branson, who was still sniffing for a deal and phoning McLaren almost daily. This could be interpreted as either a very shrewd or a recklessly foolish move by McLaren, since Virgin was the only label in town prepared to take the bad boys on. 'God Save the Queen' was also a time-sensitive project – the Queen's Jubilee weekend was only weeks away.

Malcolm tried to strike record deals in individual countries now – lots of small deals that would amount to one big deal – but the only one that worked out was with the French label Barclay, who signed the Pistols to a three-album deal for £27,000. So in the end, McLaren had little choice but to sign with Virgin in a complex deal that effectively gave the band £65,000 for an album. That there was a deal at all was a miracle, since McLaren and Branson didn't like each other. Bernie Rhodes encapsulated the antipathy between the two men: 'Just as Lydon looked at McLaren and thought, "I'll have you," so McLaren looked at Branson and thought the same.'

Problems weren't long in coming. There was a row over whether Virgin should have their name on the label – they weren't that keen to volunteer for the inevitable opprobrium that would follow the record's release. Then, déjà vu, the staff at the pressing plant refused to manufacture the single because of its content. When that hiccup was overcome, the printers refused to have anything to do with the sleeve. No sooner was that solved than the TV company refused the proposed advert, while their comrades at the commercial radio stations did likewise. The climax came when the BBC (with the exception of John Peel) refused to play the song on the grounds of 'gross bad taste'.

When three major chains of shops refused to stock the single, it seemed like only a minor snag in comparison to what had gone before. The music press, however, rallied to the cause – they loved the record and the band made the covers of the *NME*, *Record Mirror* and *Melody Maker*. 'God Save the Queen' sold 150,000 copies in the five days before the Jubilee weekend.

With exquisite timing, the impact of the single was like a bomb going off in the Buckingham Palace yard. While the disaffected youth of the UK had discovered a new bunch of heroes, the Establishment had discovered a vile new public enemy.

Matters became worse when McLaren booked a boat to run up and down the Thames with the band playing on it, in a parody of the river trip Her Majesty was due to make. Rotten, disturbed by the liggers staring up at him from the deck, gave a furious performance as the boat approached the Palace of Westminster encircled by police launches. A panicking captain cut the power to the band as the vessel berthed and McLaren ensured the affair went into pop history by standing at the top of the gangplank shouting 'You fucking fascist bastards' at the police. Eleven were arrested, some of whom had to endure a not altogether unsurprising kicking in the back of the police van.

'God Save the Queen' was selling by the boatload now, but Rod Stewart's 'I Don't Want to Talk About It' made number 1 instead, despite the distributor's assurance to McLaren that the Pistols were outselling Stewart two to one. Could someone, somewhere, have rigged the charts? To suggest that somebody on high was putting the kibosh on 'God Save the Queen' is surely a paranoid fantasy, but Labour MP Marcus Lipton said in a *Daily Mirror* article, 'If pop music is going to be used to destroy our established institutions, then it ought to be destroyed first.' The *Sunday Mirror* echoed its sister paper. 'Punish the Punks', it thundered, and the rabble were roused.

A week later, Rotten was attacked by a gang, as he explains in *Rotten: No Irish, No Blacks, No Dogs*: 'I was stabbed right near the studio, while we were recording the *Bollocks* album. This is before the record was even fucking released . . . We went to a pub round the corner – not far from the same old Arsenal area in Highbury where I was brought up. This bunch of bastards just tore into us with Gurkha knives, blades, razors, the lot. I was with the producer Chris Thomas and Bill Price, the engineer. We managed to run into the car park and lock ourselves in Chris's car. This mob smashed the car and windscreen to shit while we were inside it. They broke one of the windows and stuck a blade in. I had on a pair of very thick leather trousers at the time. It went straight down them. If I'd had on anything else, it would probably have ripped my leg out. The blade stuck in my knee. I got a stiletto blade pushed straight into my hand, next to my thumb. It came out the other side by my little finger. That affected the tendons in my left hand. I'll never play guitar again because of that. Boo. Hiss. I can't close a proper left fist. That's a bit hard because I'm left-handed. I thought I was going to die.'

Then Paul Cook took a battering.

Some sections of the public were clearly not amused by young John's taunting record. 'We love our Queen,' they shouted. Steve Jones said of 'God Save the Queen' and the attack, '[Rotten] wasn't saying "Let's kill her" or "Let's fuck her". He was pretty much saying what the truth was. No future.'

Rotten added, 'If they'd have hung us at Traitor's Gate, 56 million would have cheered. We declared war on England without meaning to.'

To top it all, Sid was in hospital with hepatitis after using a dirty needle and no one was visiting him except Nancy.

Yet, during a period when they needed him, Malcolm seemed distracted. His mind was jitterbugging. He and Vivienne changed the shop yet again – new stock, a new look and a new name – Seditionaries.

Rotten was holed up with Sid, Nancy, Jah Wobble and packets and packets of amphetamines, while Jones and Cook moaned about him. McLaren egged them on. Did he resent John's new status as the leader of the punk 'movement'? Did he resent Rotten's talent and feel it was he who should be the star really?

It was at this juncture that he decided to write, produce and direct a film about the Pistols. This would be his vehicle. Maybe he'd found a way to be the star at last. Rotten was welcome to his notoriety and celebrity. It has been speculated that this was effectively when the Pistols broke up – when they divorced one another in their heads. But in the end, Malcolm couldn't do everything regarding the film – he'd need others to write and direct it – but at the same time he couldn't bring himself to surrender control to anyone.

Sandy Lieberson, a big wheel at 20th Century Fox, loved the film idea and helped McLaren to hunt out a director. Brits Ken Loach and Stephen Frears looked at the project, but Loach saw only differences between him and McLaren, while Frears was rejected by the band. Then Russ Meyer's name came up. The controversial sexploitation director of tit flicks such as *Beyond the Valley of the Dolls* and *Faster, Pussycat! Kill! Kill!* seemed ideal for the job. In turn, Meyer, whose career was on the skids, saw the logic of making a movie about this too-hot-to-handle Brit band with that so-great name, the Sex Pistols. Malcolm thought Meyer and the band were made for each other. He dropped everything, including the planning of a Pistols tour of Sweden, and went a-courting in Hollywood. He found a scriptwriter and the two of them locked themselves away for a month, drafting a 600-page treatment. Meyer hated it and threw it in the bin, but he signed up for the project anyway.

Meantime, Virgin had released 'Pretty Vacant', which steamed up the charts. Lydon agreed to make a promotional video – surely their finest, featuring the classic Steve Jones knotted hankie on the head – to Virgin's requirements and also agreed to a Capital Radio interview. However, he baulked at letting the video be shown on *Top of the Pops*, so he urged McLaren to get on the phone from Los Angeles and have it pulled, but (conveniently) the BBC wouldn't return it.

Left to their own devices on a successful and uneventful Scandinavian tour, the two Johns started openly bad-mouthing

McLaren. 'Malcolm I honestly hate,' said Sid to a newspaper man. In return, it seemed that Malcolm was equally hostile towards Sid, whose drug use ironically was perhaps also grist to the mill, and the mill was his movie.

Lydon met up with Meyer and his writer at a lunch and the Americans tried to get their brains around John's street vernacular.

'A tosspot is even lower than a jerk-off,' he explained. 'A weed is a pansy. If you don't know that, it's just an indication of how fuckin' stupid you Americans are.' Meyer couldn't see eye to eye with McLaren either. 'I could never really put him together,' he told *Search and Destroy* magazine, 'and I'm gregarious. I get along with most everybody, except a wife or so.'

McLaren tried to wrest some control of the film from Meyer – on behalf of the band, he said – at a time when it was clear he barely had any influence over the Sex Pistols. Tales of the breakdown in relations seeped back to Fox in the USA. One of the board of directors was Princess Grace of Monaco, no less, and she couldn't see why the company was involved with a horrid punk group. It seems yet another monarch had taken exception to the Sex Pistols. Meyer left London, saying he would sue McLaren (who he had now started teasingly calling 'Hitler'). Fox coughed up £150,000 to make McLaren go away.

Kerching! went the cash register at Pistols HQ.

Virgin, who had been dragging their feet over the release of the *Never Mind the Bollocks* album on the basis that they could make more money by releasing the individual singles from it, were finally persuaded to release it. Branson had been spurred into action by Barclay, who had released the album in France and were threatening to export thousands of copies to the UK. There was an immediate furore over displaying the sleeve with the word 'Bollocks' striped through the middle of it. W.H. Smith, Woolworths and Boots refused to stock it, but it had 150,000 advance orders and went straight in at number 1. One Virgin record shop manager was charged with offences under the 1989 Indecent Advertisement Act for displaying 'Bollocks' posters, and in the customary air of farce that seemed to surround much Sex Pistol activity, when the manager was hauled before the court in Nottingham the celebrated QC and writer John Mortimer found himself arguing in his defence that 'bollocks' was a perfectly ordinary Anglo-Saxon word. He said in his summing-up, 'One wonders why a word which has been dignified by writers from the Middle Ages in the translation of the Bible to Dylan Thomas and George Orwell, and which you may find in the dictionary, should be singled out as criminal because it is on a record sleeve by the Sex Pistols. It was because it was the Sex Pistols and not Donald Duck or Kathleen Ferrier that this prosecution was brought.'

The chairman of the bench was forced to agree that it was purely because it had been the Sex Pistols. 'Much as my colleagues and I wholeheartedly deplore the vulgar exploitation of the worst instincts of human nature,' he said, 'we must reluctantly find you not guilty.'

After a short tour of Holland, a tour of the USA was mooted. The US embassy wouldn't grant visas because of the array of criminal convictions the Pistols had accumulated between them and it was necessary for the American record company to put up a surety of $1 million to get the band on their way. Jamie Reid felt an ill wind: 'Everybody knew that something awful was coming up.'

Malcolm's somewhat perverse hand rested on the selection of the gigs. 'We had a choice,' he said. 'Madison Square Garden, one show, dollar a ticket, coming in by helicopter, or we could do what we wanted to do. And I realised it might be better to play the southern states, do the places where no one goes and continue the story of this group, because to play Madison Square Garden at that time tended to sum it up and make you end up doing all the things you had said you hated. It would be like Led Zeppelin instead of the Sex Pistols. I wanted to continue the adventure, and if you couldn't continue the adventure at Madison

Square Garden, well then, let's get lost in the swamps.'

It was a tour guaranteed to cause the maximum confrontation.

There remained the problem of Sid and Nancy, whose self-destructive drug binges were becoming more and more violent. McLaren half-joked that Sid shouldn't think of taking a long lease on his new flat, although he did realise that the appalling influence Nancy had on Sid was something he should try and do something about. He deputised the band's roadies to kidnap her and try to put her on a plane with a one-way ticket. Sadly for everyone, the plan failed. The other problem was the withering hatred that existed between the band members and McLaren. A non-conducive undercurrent was the story that McLaren was planning to oust Rotten after the tour was over.

The record company took control of the Pistols as soon as they landed. Two ex-Vietnam vets were to escort them everywhere. There was even a rumour that Sid was to be handcuffed if he proved too difficult to handle. In the event, after each gig Jones and Cook went looking for booze and birds. John would talk endlessly to the record company guys and Sid, wearing his 'I'm a Mess' badge, went on the prowl for smack. He was once found by his minders in a local hospital with self-inflicted knife wounds in his arm.

The craziness got worse. There were rumours that the FBI, the CIA and even British intelligence were watching closely for fear of some kind of youth uprising. The band wouldn't talk to journalists unless they were individually paid. At one sold-out gig, there was a mini-riot. In San Antonio, a blood-smeared Vicious, with 'GIMME A FIX' felt-tipped onto his chest, whacked a member of the audience with his bass guitar. The audience responded by hurling a hail of bottles and cans at the band.

As the Adam and the Ants guitarist Marco Pirroni says in Rotten's book, 'Sid was desperate to get into anything that would kill him.'

Cook and Jones picked up heavy colds, decided they'd had enough of the road and left Rotten and Sid to continue by bus while they and McLaren took a plane to San Francisco. When Sid and John arrived to find they had been booked into a shabbier hotel than the others, Rotten, who was himself now suffering from the flu, took exception. They took the stage at the Winterland and Rotten shouted 'Welcome to London' to a massive roar from the audience, as well as a barrage of coins, tins and spit. In its early stages, the set was a stormer, but when it broke down, it broke down for good, with Rotten sitting on his haunches glaring at the crowd while the band endlessly played Iggy Pop's 'No Fun' as badly as it could be played.

'Ever get the feeling you've been cheated?' he asked – his valedictory comment as the Sex Pistols frontman.

In the fallout from this, Jones, Cook and McLaren decided to wrap up the band and go to Brazil. 'I said to John,' relates Jones, '"I don't want to carry on, someone's gonna end up dead." I decided to go with Malcolm, a thing I regret.'

Jones and Cook went to Rio for the birds; McLaren went with scandalous ideas about appointing a new lead singer – Ronnie Biggs. Sid finally got his fix and his heart stopped. He was resuscitated and lived for a few months more. Both he and Rotten were left in America with no money or plane tickets home – an inauspicious end to a band still hailed as the most exciting of the last 30-odd years.

With the Pistols now over, the planning began. McLaren went back to London to arrange contracts for Ronnie Biggs and to pick up his film director mate, Julian Temple, and a film crew for the Brazil adventure. He also planned a film involving girl band The Slits, who he envisaged 'getting fucked from one end of Mexico to the other'. Richard Branson, who had long regarded Rotten as the power in the band and fearing that he was about to lose his investment, saw that now McLaren was no longer a factor, he could make his move. He took John off to Jamaica with Don Letts, the film-maker, under the guise of using Lydon as an A&R man for some reggae acts he intended signing, but in reality using the trip to win him over.

However, the farce continued. McLaren, obsessed with his film project about the Pistols but now lacking its star, sent a cameraman to Jamaica to get footage of John. When his advances were rejected by Rotten, the cameraman clumsily attempted to film the Virgin party's guest of honour in secret from a hiding place in the bushes. When his cover was blown, he wound up being tossed into the pool.

McLaren had a contingency plan: he filmed Biggs singing Sid's 'Belsen Was a Gas', with a promotional clip suitably fitting for the squalid song involving a strutting actor dressed up as arch-Nazi Martin Bormann in full SS uniform.

The American label Warner Brothers saw that they were £200,000 in the hole as a result of McLaren's film deal and that all they had to show for it was a split band and a film with no star. They tried to unruffle Rotten's feathers and effect a reconciliation, but John was furious. Far from wanting any future involvement with McLaren, he called his lawyer to start proceedings for unpaid monies. His lawyer asked McLaren's company Glitterbest for accounts and, in so doing, kicked off an eight-year battle of claim and counter-claim.

Temple and McLaren went to Paris with Sid to get him to sing 'My Way' on film, but Sid wasn't keen. Things came to a head at the hotel when McLaren phoned Sid and called him a 'fucking junkie'.

Temple recalls, 'What must have happened is that Sid gave the phone to Nancy because Malcolm was still there going on when suddenly this panelled door flew open and there was Sid – in his underpants with a swastika on them and his motorcycle boots but nothing else. He grabbed Malcolm out of bed and he said, "You don't fucking talk to me like that," and he shook Malcolm and Malcolm turned white and started to run – with no clothes on – down the floor of the hotel . . . The chambermaids were screaming, "Monsieur! Oh Monsieur!" and finally Malcolm ran into the elevator and Sid got in with him just before the doors closed.

'We all ran down the stairs and when the door opened there was Malcolm kicked all to pieces. That was enough for Malcolm.

He split and went back to England. Sid finally extracted a signed note from Malcolm saying he would no longer be his manager, and then, after we rewrote some of the "My Way" lyrics together . . . he finally broke down and sang the song.'

'My Way' was released as a double A-side Sex Pistols single, with 'Punk Prayer' – another Biggs-fronted track that at one point was going to be called 'Cosh the Driver', a more than unsavoury reference to the Great Train Robbery. Rotten, now calling himself Lydon, wisely wanted nothing to do with it.

McLaren took his commission and whatever else he needed to finance his film project – now called *The Great Rock 'n' Roll Swindle* – and Ronald Biggs saw very little of the money. Had Malcolm robbed one of the Great Train Robbers?

'History is for pissing on,' he once said.

Sid, hideously debilitated by heroin, or the equally addictive treatment for heroin addiction, methadone, filmed a couple more sequences for the movie then went to New York with Nancy. They checked into the Chelsea Hotel and she checked out of life, either by Sid's hand by or her own, or by the hand of a third party. To his credit, McLaren was instantly at hand with $50,000 in bail that he had loaned from Virgin. He rushed around hiring private detectives to look into the murky events of the evening and accused the police of failing to investigate all the details of the case properly. For example, a junkie from the same corridor Sid and Nancy were staying on had vanished the evening Nancy was killed and some money was missing. But in the meantime, Sid was in Bellevue Hospital in the psychiatric section after a suicide attempt.

McLaren's motives were not entirely altruistic, though: a short while later, his shop started selling shirts bearing a picture of Sid with the caption, 'I'm Alive, She's Dead, I'm Yours'.

On top of the $50,000 Branson had supplied for Sid's bail, Virgin gave Glitterbest £150,000 to breathe life into the film project. Branson's hooks were well and truly into McLaren now – something that surely wasn't in Malcolm's anti-record-company manifesto.

Lydon's case was coming to a head in the High Court and Warner Brothers wanted their £200,000 back. Shortly after Nancy's death, they'd dropped the remaining Pistols and sent some money to Lydon to help out with his lawyer's bill. Glitterbest was in big trouble and McLaren entered into secret negotiations to sell up to Virgin.

Lydon's lawyers alleged that just under £1 million was missing from the accounts – money that was used to make a film that Lydon was obliged to appear in despite the fact he found the material 'obscene and offensive', alleging that there were scenes that included 'incest, cocaine taking, necrophilia, group sex, gross violence and sexual perversion'. He wanted contractual freedom and damages, as well as some details of where all the money had gone. Malcolm became preoccupied with Lydon's lawyers, who were now threatening the commencement of criminal charges.

Meanwhile, Sid's horror story continued and then ended. Out from Bellevue, he went out clubbing and stuck a glass in the face of Patti Smith's brother, Todd. Whisked back to jail, he was suddenly, miraculously, out on bail again, entrusted into the care of his delinquent mother, Anne Beverly. On the very evening of his release, she supplied him with the heroin that killed him (she herself died of a heroin overdose in 1996). Speaking about Sid's death, Lydon says in his book, 'There's nothing glorious in dying. Anyone can do it.'

Five days after Sid's fatal overdose, the *Lydon* v. *Glitterbest* court case kicked off. It was then that the big red 'M' wrinkle that appears on McLaren's forehead when he is under duress started flickering into view. When Cook and Jones turned turtle and transferred allegiances to Lydon, the 'M' positively glowed. In the event, the judge sidestepped the substantive issues of the case and, having declared the Sex Pistols partnership at an end, appointed a receiver to look after Glitterbest's financial affairs until another court could pick over the minutiae of it all.

A relieved McLaren scarpered for Paris the following day.

The winners were to some extent Lydon, Cook and Jones; Vicious had sealed his own fate. But the real triumph belonged to Richard Branson, who now had commanding shares in all the existing Sex Pistols material, as well as the newly formed Public Image. He'd also signed Cook and Jones's projected band, the Professionals, and he held rights to the soon-to-be-completed film. He even offered McLaren via telex £20,000 for a first Malcolm McLaren single. It stated, 'Please stop believing this conspiracy theory, there was and is none.' McLaren took that as an admission that Branson was indeed trying to buy him off. When Branson got word of that, he took the gloves off. McLaren had gone too far. At one point, when McLaren was trying to get money from Branson so he could finish the movie and when Branson wouldn't budge, he visited him on his houseboat. McLaren told Virgin News in 2006: 'I decided to visit Branson on his boat, which was parked on the Regent's Canal in London, to demand that he buy me out of the Sex Pistols so that I could finish *The Great Rock 'n' Roll Swindle* . . . I thought Branson had been two-faced in his dealings with me. So, to register my disrespect, I took out my penis and urinated on his office carpet. I'm not sure how he reacted, as I immediately took my leave.'

Virgin was under orders to rush-release the soundtrack from the upcoming movie to counter the threat poised by imports from French company Barclay – a threat that McLaren could doubtlessly trigger. McLaren (justifiably) thought the album was a shambles and demanded it be withdrawn, but Branson ignored his bleating and McLaren was powerless to act further. He hid away in Paris for a year, licking his wounds.

It wasn't until 1986 that the proceedings came to court for the final showdown. Lydon's and McLaren's zany appearances contrasted with the wigged and gowned counsel. Paul Cook turned up and sat quietly at the back of the room. Steve Jones, who was now into heroin himself, wouldn't or couldn't make the journey from Los Angeles.

Over two excruciating days (with costs running at £10,000 a day), the minute details of the relationship twixt McLaren and Lydon were disseminated. Lydon, the doyen of the Pistols project and the one who Jon Savage says 'gave it life', edged ahead in the battle while McLaren, the Svengali, was increasingly exhausted by it. The case could have creaked on for months, but Malcolm surely couldn't have. The final settlement was an almost complete capitulation on his part. The band would be given control of Glitterbest and the associated Matrixbest. The assets would be transferred from the receiver to the band. McLaren's ambition to grab the film along the way wasn't to happen.

Jon Savage pinpoints a phrase used by counsel: 'McLaren put together the violent and aggressive Punk style; it was his original literary work.' So there was a consensus that he could claim, if he wished, to be the progenitor of punk but little else.

In Paris, he hung out with those around the Barclay label and did some African-based musical scores for some risqué movies. The French were very impressed with the rock and roll 'swindler' and he could take tea with the likes of Serge Gainsbourg and the band Telephone, and enthral them all with tales of Sid and Johnny.

He came up with a plan to make a movie about three young English girls in Paris who encounter a French pop manager. Using the tourist attractions of the city as the backdrop, there would be numerous seductions. When Malcolm went back to London to try and raise some money for the project from Arista, they were horrified by the subject matter. Another film tentatively titled *The Mile High Club*, and again starring young girls, met similar resistance. That put movie projects on hold.

He was casting around for something else to do – something he could make some money from – when his eyes fell on a young man who had been lurking around his shop and flirting with Jordan: Stuart Leslie Goddard, who would soon become Adam Ant.

Adam idolised Malcolm; he wanted what McLaren apparently

had – the kind of juice that could power a bunch of ragamuffins to stardom. Malcolm didn't see the same thing in Adam as Jordan had; instead took £1,000 from the aspiring star to act as his star-maker consultant. He gave Adam's band a load of rhythm-based tapes to study and, somewhat miraculously, they got into the groove and started reproducing things in its fashion. The problem was that Adam couldn't do it – or Malcolm didn't think he could – so he drove a wedge into the outfit. Adam had to go. McLaren passed the job on: the band were to dump him, or specifically Dave Barbe, the drummer. 'I was so under the euphoria of [Malcolm's] personality,' said Barbe, 'I would have gone out and fucking shot somebody if he told me.'

At the same time as Adam was in the dumper, Bow Wow Wow were born.

'He's a band breaker,' grumbled Paul Cook of McLaren at some other time and about some other band.

McLaren, the pop genius who had once declared war on the record business through the Sex Pistols, was now sharpening his spears for a second assault. Walkmans were the new technology – the iPods of their day. Home taping was becoming an issue. Ever riding the wave of controversy, and with a new band to hype, albeit singerless, he wrote 'C30, C60, C90, Go' – a song about stealing tunes from the radio.

The problem was that Adam Ant was showing some true grit. In the face of adversity, he'd pulled together some musicians, vowing to beat McLaren to the draw. He had been working on the African beats, as had the new Bow Wows. He could do that. Malcolm, in the meantime, started drilling his troops in the black arts. He thought they should play the roll of homosexual apaches. Oh, and they should sleep with prostitutes. The band's Lee Gorman says in Craig Bromberg's book, '[McLaren] said,"OK, I'm going to make you into a bunch of sexual perverts."'

A chance meeting between one of the band and the 14-year-old Myant Myant Aye Dunn-Lwin, later to be known as Annabella, in a dry cleaners in the West End Lane gave them their missing jigsaw piece. Bow Wow Wow had discovered a singer. But McLaren found the newcomer less malleable than the opportunist musicians with whom he had previously been dealing. She wouldn't leave school as he asked her and her mother was beginning to mistrust him. Malcolm had a remedy, which was classic McLaren, as he told the *Sun* newspaper:

> The girl was driving us all crazy. I wanted to find some way to make her commit herself to the group. I thought it might help if the guys in the band flattered her and tried to fancy her. So I gave one of them some money and ordered him to seduce her. I made him get up early and wait outside her school gates and get her to play truant. He tried everything. He got himself drunk. He got her drunk. He took her to the movies. Annabella was having a lovely time, but still she couldn't decide whether she really wanted to be a singer with the band or become an air stewardess and see the world that way.

The story continues in Craig Bromberg's *The Wicked Way of Malcolm McLaren*:

> Dave Barbe: 'Eventually, he got her back to his place, this shitty room full of stacked sodden newspapers in the corner, a rancid old bed in a squat. He really loved his bird Gabby, Maf did, but he had to do the job. He started kissing her, but she wouldn't do nothing: she was fourteen years old. But finally she decided to have a go at it . . .'
> McLaren: 'Then suddenly she began whistling . . .'
> Barbe: 'The fucking "Marseillaise" . . .'
> McLaren: 'And at that the poor guy just lost his sex drive.'

EMI, once bitten but apparently not twice shy, allowed McLaren to wheedle £50,000 out of them for the Bow Wow Wow single – one single. If it ever needed saying, Malcolm McLaren can talk up a perfect storm. How else would he have got Britain's biggest record company to invest in him twice, especially in a track about home taping?

In the event, the record stiffed. McLaren cried conspiracy, alleging that the British Phonographic Institute had suddenly twigged on the subject matter of the lyrics and had the record killed. Then he fired up the band to take direct action. They obediently went to EMI to wreck an office and terrorise a minion. Instead of being intimidated, EMI obligingly coughed up another £20,000 in return for twelve tracks. They reasoned that since their company made blank cassette tapes as well as pre-recorded ones, they were in a win-win situation.

Next, McLaren arranged a photo shoot for the new record that by virtue of the raunchy subject matter caused not a little concern amongst the Bow Wow Wowers. Even loyal cohorts, like Malcolm's friend and Sex Pistols chronicler Fred Vermorel, thought that Malcolm had pushed the boundaries a tad too far.

'The man's a fucking voyeur,' said Dave Barbe.

He's also a great survivor and somehow managed to crawl from that particular wreckage unscathed. When the album came out, it died, but the band had developed a sound. Malcolm reasoned, however, that it might be necessary to find a new singer. Where have we all heard that one before?

Into the spotlight stepped Boy George, who was yet to set up Culture Club. The gig never worked out and George moved onwards and very definitely upwards, but say what you like about Malcolm, he sure can dig out the talent – even if sometimes he doesn't know quite what to do with it when he's got it.

Bow Wow Wow had gone as far as they were likely to go with EMI and McLaren was back on the phone hustling, but no one wanted to know. Strangely, McLaren's name and any artists associated with him either caused mirth and ridicule around the industry – some companies wouldn't even give him an appointment – or a massive respect. After a series of rejections, Malcolm was reputedly crying with frustration when, *voilà*, he was suddenly able to extract guarantees of $750,000 over three albums from RCA in America.

Bow Wow Wow's debut album with RCA needed a cover with that certain McLaren spice, not to mention some accompanying press furore. Annabella was coerced (with the aid of vodka and against mother's wishes) into stripping off for a depiction of Manet's *Le Déjeuner sur l'herbe*. Sure enough, she was labelled 'that cheap nymphet' by a tabloid and everyone was happy.

See Jungle! See Jungle! Go Join Your Gang Yeah! City All Over, Go Ape Crazy had a borderline kiddie-porn sleeve. There were tours and great publicity and things looked very favourable for Malcolm McLaren and Bow Wow Wow, but those waves of ennui washed over him yet again. He moaned to journalist David Thomas, 'You see, with the Sex Pistols, I was a manager, but also I wasn't a manager, if you see what I mean. But with Bow Wow Wow, I was becoming too much a manager.'

He revealed some remarkable flaws in his song-spotting talent by rejecting a mix of 'Go Wild in the Country', but the company went ahead and released it in spite of him. It went into the charts at number 7. He also rejected the follow-up 'I Want Candy' and it went in at number 9. Dave Barbe said, 'I only wish he'd fucked off earlier . . . He'd never do anything by the front door. It always had to have some weird angle.'

Effectively, McLaren had left, but no contracts were dissolved and he went on receiving royalties for a good while after his departure, a time in which he'd signed himself to Charisma as a solo artist. The band dissolved a couple of years later. Bassist Leigh Gorman went on to write 'Hippy Chick' for the one-hit-wonder band Soho. Drummer Dave Barbarossa had chart success with Republica. Guitarist Matthew Ashman died in 1995. Annabella and Gorman reunited for a tour in the late '90s.

Malcolm McLaren continues to be a force in the music industry and elsewhere. The instinctive opportunist – Nigel Kennedy called him the 'Diaghilev of the borstal boys' because he 'made opportunism into an art form' – and great British eccentric, he has had numerous solo hits, including 'Duck Rock', 'Buffalo Gals', 'Madame Butterfly', 'Double Dutch', 'Waltz Darling' and, most recently, 'About Her', which features on the *Kill Bill 2* soundtrack (in 2005, McLaren was accused of plagiarising a French artist's song, but was cleared of the charges in the November).

Movies still loom large – perhaps largest – in his life; indeed, it could have been said that until recently his career had been a failure, as far as he was concerned, because he'd never made one. Pop music seems to have only ever been a means to an end for him, and the end was films. McLaren is memorable for his pitches, though. Lynda Obst, the one-time head of Geffen films, reckons McLaren's pitch for a film called *Beauty and the Beast* 'was the most memorable pitch of my career. It was a performance of stellar quality that I have since discovered was entirely rehearsed, because he later did the same pitch for David Geffen word for word, beat for beat, step for step.' The movie that somehow mixed the fairy story with the life of Christian Dior was never made.

He spent two years trying to get a film made about Led Zeppelin manager Peter Grant – the manager's manager – but Grant failed to secure permissions for the use of the band's material. The project died when Peter died.

Observer writer Peter Culshaw spent some time with Malcolm early in 2004, when McLaren was talking about his relationship with Steven Spielberg:

[McLaren] was formally employed twice, at CBS and then as a kind of personal ideas man for Steven Spielberg. There was the attempt to turn Stephen Hawking into 'the most brilliant pop star and have him make love to Chrissie Hynde – a CD-Rom that I tried hard to sell as a bridging between art and science'. He developed such projects as *Heavy Metal Surf Nazis* ('*The Magnificent Seven* meets *Lord of The Flies*', featuring a gang led by a surfer who was born in the sea and has a magical surfboard) on a six-figure salary. Of LA, he says: 'At first it seemed a place to reinvent yourself, but finally I have to admit, its malevolence creeps in through the walls at night, and slowly depressed the hell out of me.'

This is in spite of his affair with the model Lauren Hutton, the beauty queen who graced the cover of Vogue 14 times in two years and who, the story goes, seduced Malcolm by surrounding herself in a bed of flowers outside his apartment door. Spielberg let him out of his contract, provided he come back with his best idea in a year's time. The year over, Malcolm waltzes in and does one of his hyper-pitches: 'It's a musical,' he tells Spielberg, 'and it will be Oscar Wilde discovering rock 'n' roll by accident on one of his lecture tours in the Deep South in the 1880s.'

Incredibly, Spielberg got excited about the nonsense, flew out Tom Stoppard to write a script, gave Malcolm $50,000 and then, when Malcom's magic had worn off and he re-examined the project in the cold light of day, pulled the plug.

Culshaw says, 'Spielberg in the end couldn't really make a film about a homosexual discovering rock 'n' roll. And an Irishman to boot.'

Heroic failures, it has to be said. But back to the Pistols.

Malcolm's downfall, his blind spot, was a low boredom threshold and his conviction that Sid was the talent. 'The best songs the Sex Pistols recorded were the ones without John, such as "C'mon Everybody",' he says. 'At least Sid Vicious could actually sing, and he was potentially a much bigger star.' Many would vehemently beg to differ.

In 2001, the inveterate mischief-maker contemplated standing for London Mayor – his policies included scrapping museum charges, making adult education available for £1 a year, setting up brothels opposite the Houses of Parliament, the decriminalisation of cannabis and the selling of alcohol in libraries.

He is undoubtedly proud of his son, Jo Corre, who runs the Agent Provocateur fashion shop, which has used Kylie Minogue in see-through undies as its model. A chip off the old block.

Malcolm McLaren

Ace hype-merchant PR Mark Borkowski recalls McLaren as 'one of three geniuses I've met'. Julie Burchill says, 'We are all children of Thatcher and McLaren.' As for another PM, McLaren dismisses Tony Blair as 'the first karaoke Prime Minister'.

In 2004, John Lydon made some programmes for Channel Five about sharks – a hilarious irony. Malcolm finally got to make a film, *Fast Food Nation*, Eric Schlosser's acclaimed British-produced exposé of the US food industry, starring Ethan Hawke and Bruce Willis. Malcolm was co-producer and it was his idea to make it fictional rather than as a documentary.

May it not be his last.

10

BERNIE RHODES

The Clash

**He thinks like a Tory and talks like a Radical,
and that's so important now-a-days.**
— *Oscar Wilde*

It's amazing how many of London's young punks knew one
another before they settled down into their different slots. Brian
James, who went on to play in The Damned, answered a *Melody
Maker* advert for guitarists for a new band called the London
SS, featuring Mick Jones, soon to play in The Clash. The London
SS also featured Tony James, later of Generation X. Jones and
James shared a passion for the New York Dolls, the MC5 and The
Stooges.

Jones, in turn, had gone along to an audition for a guitarist in a
rehearsal room in Denmark Street. The band? The Sex Pistols, of
course. They quite liked Mick Jones's playing, but they didn't like
his long, tangled hairstyle, so rejected him. Jones in the Pistols?
That would certainly have thrown punk history on its head.

When the as yet unnamed Clash ran auditions between
November 1975 and January 1976, Rat Scabies, who would later
take the drum stool for The Damned, had a go at it, as did Keith
Levine, who made it into The Clash starting line-up before going

262

on to play with John Lydon in Public Image Ltd (by way of The Flowers of Romance, for which Sid Vicious was briefly lead singer). Morrissey applied for the job by post. He was rejected just for being a northerner. Among the many others who auditioned for the job were Visage's Rusty Egan, Culture Club's Jon Moss and Mark Laff, who went to Generation X.

Non-musician Paul Simonon turned up at one of the sessions to give a mate of his some moral support. Jones wasn't interested in the mate at all; he'd spotted Simonon, and Simonon had the look. He persuaded him to have a go at playing and Paul, who at some time was referred to as 'the coolest man to ever strap on a bass', gave it his best shot. The two ended up living together in a flat, where Sid Vicious was a regular visitor.

The tangled web expands.

And, of course, Bernie Rhodes was Malcolm McLaren's all-round collaborator, printing his T-shirts (with Glen Matlock) as well as acting as caretaker manager of the Swankers (the Pistols pre-Johnny) whenever Malcolm was out of town. At one time, there was even talk of the two managers of the two most prominent punk bands doing a personnel swap – Glen Matlock for Paul Simonon. So the Pistols line-up might have been Paul Cook, Steve Jones, Mick Jones and Paul Simonon, with Johnny on vocals, or Richard Hell . . . or Nick Kent . . . or Midge Ure, for Christ's sake. God knows who would have ended up in The Clash if any of that had happened, or if Morrissey had been a Londoner.

After the Pistols broke up, Steve Jones was approached to replace a sacked Mick Jones in The Clash. A Jones for a Jones.

What an incestuous little world.

According to one account, Bernie met Malcolm during the 1968 Paris student riots. In another, they meet at the slightly less romantic Stamford Hill bowling alley, although, given their talents for self-mythologising, it could have been neither or both.

If ever a band was prefab, it was The Clash. It must have taken more auditions to form the band than it did Steps and S Club put together. Mick Jones and Tony James had bumped into Bernie Rhodes at a Deaf School gig. Jones thought Rhodes was a keyboard player. Rhodes replied that he wasn't, then pointed out that Jones was wearing one of his T-shirts and countered by asking if Jones was in a band. Jones replied that he was forming a band called the London SS. Rhodes, apparently on the recoil from some spat with McLaren, was on the prowl for talent of his own and within minutes was telling Jones and James that he was their new manager. Oh, and by the way, they would no longer be called the London SS. After Mick protested, Bernie, a Jew, brought them round a whole load of Nazi badges and patches and asked which of them they wanted to wear onstage. Mick blanched and agreed a name change might possibly be in order. (Rhodes refused to let Siouxie and the Banshees use The Clash's PA at the fabled 100 Club Punk Rock Festival because she was wearing a swastika on her arm. 'I felt she was mucking about with a loaded gun,' he said to journalist Caroline Coon, 'and we didn't want to have anything to do with it.')

Joe Strummer, who was lead singer with The 101ers, had seen Mick Jones and Paul Simonon in the dole queue in Lisson Grove, Marylebone. They stood out. When the two of them stared back at him, he thought he was in for a fight, but they were just sizing him up. The next time he saw them was when he turned up to audition for their new band after being press-ganged into it by Bernie.

Joe had a Telecaster guitar that he had financed by marrying a South African woman who needed a passport. He played it with swift chops like Dr Feelgood's Wilko Johnson, while his left leg pumped up and down, and he did a nice line in looking a bit deranged. As soon as Bernie, Mick and Paul saw Joe's shtick, they knew they'd found their man. It was mutual. 'As soon as I saw these guys,' says Joe, 'I knew that was what a group, in my eyes, was supposed to look like. So I didn't really hesitate when they asked me to join.'

He'd already decided to break up The 101ers after witnessing the Pistols for the first time. 'As soon as I saw them,' he said, 'I knew that rhythm and blues was dead, that the future was here somehow. Every other group was riffing their way through the Black Sabbath catalogue. But hearing the Pistols, I knew. I just knew. It was something you just knew without bothering to think about.'

In his book, *Passion is a Fashion: The Real Story of the Clash*, Pat Gilbert says, 'Rhodes's selection process was intuitive but utterly ruthless. It was like *Pop Idol* in extremis. He was as hard, if not harder, than the toughest judge on those TV talent shows (and wittier and more intelligent). He and Mick had hand-picked the band from dozens of candidates over a period of nearly nine months. It had been built to exacting specifications, and its international success in the years to come suggests his and Mick's choices were mostly good ones. (Naturally, Rhodes considered Mick as just another musician who passed his auditions; Jones, perhaps naively, saw their relationship as a partnership.)'

In the grand scheme of rock and roll, Gilbert reckons Bernie Rhodes is underrated as a band manager. He thinks that this stems from Bernie's combative style and his pathological aversion to giving interviews and having his photo taken. He makes further claims, saying that, as well as forming and guiding The Clash, Rhodes was responsible for 'nurturing the careers of three of the finest English groups to emerge in the wake of punk: Dexys Midnight Runners, The Specials and Subway Sect'.

Bernie's other claims are that he came up with the idea for Public Enemy and the iMac computer. Oh, and he reckoned he used to advise The Who. Mmmm.

Some of it may be true – the English groups bit, perhaps. Although all of it could possibly be kosher since, as Gilbert asserts: 'In the early 1980s, Rhodes certainly did associate with hip-hop-visionary Russell Simmons, and Apple's Steve Wozniak and Steve Jobs.' However, there is another claim Rhodes is prone to making: that he brought John Lydon into the Sex Pistols. He says it was he who discovered Rotten down the King's Road rather than any of the other claimants to that particular story – although it's quite feasible he was drinking with Glen Matlock on that fateful night . . . In any event, it's pretty clear that The Clash were a band made in Bernie's own image – symbolically speaking, that is, since Bernie is a very small man and The Clash were a very big band.

Its hand-picked members gelled, drilled themselves into a coherent unit and were indoctrinated by Bernie's quasi-radical aphorisms: 'Knives In W1!' 'Sten Guns in Knightsbridge!' 'Creative Violence!' Where did the slogans come from? Did he learn them at the knee of McLaren as he daubed them onto the SEX shop's shirts, or did he develop his agitprop style all on his own?

Wherever, it was Bernie who pulled The Clash together, who instilled in them their work ethic and their professional outlook. He subsidised them with the money he made from the T-shirts and his other business, mending Renault motor cars (his own Renault had the registration number CLA5H). He found them a permanent place to rehearse and he gave them a philosophy: 'Write about an issue, an issue, don't write about love, write about what's affecting you, what's important.'

Mick Jones (who lived in a council tower block) and Joe thought through the issues – the Cold War, unemployment, boredom, the rise of the National Front, police hassle, race discrimination – and the angry words and razor-chop chords spewed forth.

Tony Parsons, possibly the band's most superlative-laden fan, said of The Clash's songs, 'Tower blocks, urban alienation, disaffected youth – that all came from somewhere real.'

Robert Elms recently said of those late-'70s days, when talking to Vic Godard, 'The thing was London was broken.'

Gradually, The Clash became the political wing of the punk movement, fuelled by the same anger as the Pistols (and quite a lot of the same speed) but with a sort of ragbag manifesto to go with it. The Clash berated politicians and pop stars alike. They rambled on to journalists about dole queues, lack of places to go for young people and dull radio stations. They preached, 'Get up, stand up, stand up for your rights! Man the barricades and we'll make a better world. Throw stones at policemen and there is hope.' Conversely, the Pistols (or Johnny) saw no future at all and expressed this through howling nihilistic rage: 'Get pissed! Destroy!'

The Clash piggybacked the Anarchy tour with the Pistols. It took place in the days after the Bill Grundy interview and was a baptism of fire for all. They recorded together for the first time in late 1976, just demos; the semi-legendary pop-nut Guy Stevens produced.

Stevens, who had been in the business since the early '60s, had been a DJ at the Scene club, playing Elmore James's 'Dust My Broom' and Inez & Charlie Foxx doing 'Mockingbird'. Island Records' Chris Blackwell had given Stevens a job and his own label, Sue Records. The label was one of the first to import early R&B tracks and repackage them for the UK. In the following years, his extraordinary career would see him bringing together Procol Harum to record 'Whiter Shade of Pale' (the band was named after Stevens's cat), forming and naming Mott the Hoople, and providing the Rolling Stones with *Sticky Fingers* when they needed a name for their new album.

Stevens had a brief sojourn courtesy of Her Majesty in Wormwood Scrubs for drugs offences, then became an alcoholic. At the time he was recruited by Bernie Rhodes, he was to be seen propping up the bar in the Ship, the nearest pub to the Marquee when it was on Wardour Street and a regular muso haunt. He survived on the £100 a week that Warner Brothers were paying him to stay away from their studio sessions.

In the event, the band were unhappy with the production job Stevens did (although he would triumphantly reappear in the Clash story later on), but the tapes came in handy to play to record companies.

Chris Parry from Polydor (who later went on to found the London rock station XFM) was still smarting from his experiences with Malcolm McLaren – Parry had thought he had a deal with the Sex Pistols in the bag when McLaren rejected his advances and went to EMI – so he thought he would have the next best thing,

The Clash, as a consolation prize, and all for £40,000. Bernie had been playing him off against CBS, however, and went with them. Twice now Parry had been thwarted in his efforts to grab for his label one of the new generation of bands (he did eventually get to sign The Jam, so the story had a happy ending).

The Clash received £100,000 as an advance. It was a deal that dwarfed that of the Pistols – but it was a deal that, when put under the microscope, committed The Clash to making ten albums for the American giant. The more the CBS contract was unpicked, the more it looked like a stinker rather than a saviour. The band were obliged to pay for their own touring and recording costs, which included supporting their road crew. Also Bernie's 20 per cent was to be deducted from the advance – which was already beginning to look less than impressive.

Even so, the punk cognoscenti regarded the signing as a betrayal of its ideals – a sell-out. 'Punk died the day The Clash signed to CBS,' said Mark Perry from Alternative TV in his punk mag *Sniffin' Glue*.

Rhodes was oblivious to the criticism and the effect that signing with a major might have had on the band's do-it-yourself devotees. The advance was, after all, a record amount for one of the new breed of bands. And fulfilling a ten-album deal would only prove to be a problem if punk and The Clash still existed a few years down the line, and few (except perhaps CBS's contract-drafting lawyers, who were obliged to play safe) thought the punk phenomenon might last longer than the end of next week. Bernie redeemed himself by setting up a publishing company for the band that, in effect, meant they retained control over their copyrights. Whether this was a sign of shrewdness on his part or just a matter of good luck, it proved to be a moneyspinner.

Thrown straight into the studio, over three weekends, The Clash struggled to put their first album together. They knew little of the recording process but pretended they did. There was infighting and a lack of trust in the engineer but out of this dissonance came an appropriately raw album that boasted 'Police and Thieves' as the standout track. 'We just banged it out,' said Joe.

'White Riot' was released as a single with a cover designed by the band's number one fan, Sebastian Conran, son of Terence; it got to number 38 in the charts. The album went to number 12.

The American record company loathed the album and refused to release it. They then sat stupidly by and watched it become the biggest-selling American (record) import of all time. A significant number of the American public obviously loved The Clash.

The band played their first bill-topping dates under the banner of the White Riot tour. The Buzzcocks, Subway Sect and The Slits played support. It climaxed at the London Rainbow and the crowd smashed the place up.

While the band were out of town, CBS released 'Remote Control' as a single – without asking the band's permission. Enraged at their record company's high-handedness, Strummer and Jones sat down and wrote 'Complete Control, the lyrics of which reprimand the label.

The band then embarked on the Get Out of Control tour. There was a lot of crowd violence – and spitting. Joe in particular was the target and during gigs would be drenched in it. He later contracted hepatitis B as a consequence of swallowing some of his fans' malodorous contributions.

Remote Control. Complete Control. Get out of Control. Control, or rather the lack of it, was a prevailing theme. In *Westway to the World*, a film documentary of the band, Mick Jones can be heard saying ruefully, 'Complete control was one of Bernie's favourite phrases.'

There followed an episode that reduced Bernie's stock in the eyes of The Clash. One night, drummer Topper Headon and Paul Simonon had climbed up onto the roof of their rehearsal room with a couple of airguns and began taking pot shots at some pigeons. They were spotted and reported to the police by British Rail workers who thought that the pranksters might be terrorists shooting up the nearby passing trains. The police turned out in force and the two Clash members ended up in the local nick for the night.

The following day, they were placed on remand at Brixton prison pending bail being posted. Bernie was tardy about paying up. It's said he thought the experience might do the band a bit of good; teach them a lesson. It was left to Simonon's girlfriend, Caroline Coon, to stump up the money and spring the duo. Simonon responded to Bernie's lack of action by painting on the studio wall a mural of a flock of pigeons relieving themselves onto a naked Bernie below.

Whatever the band thought of CBS, the label thought well of the band. After all, they'd charted with their first album. Now, CBS wanted more. Sandy Pearlman, who had produced for Blue Oyster Cult, was drafted in. Pearlman turned up at a gig to see his new band in action and was promptly punched out by one of the band's entourage backstage after attempting to get access to the dressing-room, yet he somehow remained gung-ho about the project. He was given a brief to develop the sound from chopping, thin and trebly agit-punk to churning, muscular *rark 'n' roll*. CBS thought that The Clash were really a rock band, whatever the band themselves reckoned they were. It's said that, in unguarded moments, the band would admit to wanting to be as big as the Rolling Stones.

Things became worse betwixt manager and band when Bernie sold the publishing rights for the upcoming album *Give 'Em Enough Rope* (which would become known as Give 'Em Enough Dope by the band) but continued to keep the band on wages of only £25 a week. He made disapproving noises about Jones's cocaine use. Then, when the Pistols disbanded, Bernie spotted an opportunity to stir things up in the band (was this a tactic he'd learned from his mentor, Malcolm McLaren – keep the band off balance and keep Complete Control?). Suddenly, Steve Jones started turning up at their gigs and playing encores with the band at the end of the evening. An already paranoid Mick Jones became increasingly so; he felt that some kind of Jones v. Jones takeover bid was going on.

Mick Jones calmed down when he and Joe went out to the

States to mix the album. Sandy Pearlman thought it was the only way to get it finished as the internecine wranglings went on. He told *Trouser Press* magazine in 1979, 'Bernard would come in and they'd argue for five hours and then no one would be able to play.' They chose to ignore the niggling feeling that it was somehow hypocritical to be mixing tracks about life in Camden Town ('All the Young Punks') when they were being paid expenses to be in a studio looking out over a Manhattan skyline, and buckled down to work.

Bernie was miffed by their absence. He thought the band were indulgent, and he felt sidelined and booked them into London gigs in an abortive effort to get them back. When the band reassembled, they had issues. Who was saying what about whom? Where was all the money? In the furore, Bernie, who valued control so much, completely lost it: he was dismissed and Caroline Coon was worked into the job.

Bernie responded by petitioning the High Court to freeze the band's assets. In turn, the band claimed that he had breached his responsibilities as manager.

Pat Gilbert asked an unrepentant Rhodes why he thought the band had given him the heave-ho. 'All those stories that I took from them,' Rhodes said. 'I took nothing, they took from me. I've made my own money. The Clash were offered money by the record company to get rid of me. They were bribed. Because I was too dangerous. They're wimps.'

Bernie might have been forgiven for indulging in the last laugh when *Give 'Em Enough Rope* was eventually released. Although it made a creditable number 2 in the UK charts, an album that had been crafted for an American market didn't even scrape into the Billboard Top 100 in the US. Perhaps the band were getting their comeuppance from the American public, eventually irked by the alienating 'I'm So Bored with the USA' track they'd put on the first album.

That Christmas, The Clash, who had a high-charting album, were penniless: Bernie had had all the bank accounts frozen.

Rhodes didn't hang around waiting for The Clash to beg him to come back. He saw Dexys Midnight Runners backing The Specials in 1979 and set up the appropriately named Oddball label to release their first single 'Dance Stance'. He then managed to get them signed to EMI, where they had an immediate hit with 'Geno'.

The Clash toured the States and when they returned had resolved to sack Caroline Coon from the manager's job. They started writing the tracks that would become the *London Calling* album. They needed it to be good; they were in the red after the failure of *Give 'Em Enough Rope* and it was touch-and-go if CBS were going to pick up the option for a new album. The band ended up begging for the deal to continue – a deal that they had previously considered onerous.

Bernie's influence lingered on. Guy Stevens, who had produced their first recordings and whose name had originally been suggested by Rhodes, was hauled away from the bar of the Ship for a second time and put behind the mixing desk.

Strummer told music writer Charles Shaar Murray of his expedition to find the addled genius. 'I found a row of blokes sitting slumped over the bar staring in their beer,' he said. 'I spotted him because of his woolly hat. I went up to him and tapped him on the shoulder, he looked round and it was like son-finding-father in one of those corny films.'

Naturally, CBS were reserved to the point of panic at the thought of a full-on alcoholic heading up a make-or-break recording for the band, but The Clash prevailed after contracting Bill Price (who produced the Pistols' *Never Mind the Bollocks* album with Chris Thomas) to sit beside Guy.

It proved to be an inspired partnership. Mad enthusiasm from Stevens drove the band into faster and better performances. He'd launch himself across the room, yelling encouragement, and throw chairs around. Bill Price grins as he remembers the experience when interviewed on the *Westway* film: '[Stevens] used to get so excited I'd have to hold him down with one hand and do the manual mix with the other.' Price told Pat Gilbert, 'His idea was to create the right atmosphere and emotion in the studio when the performances took place. The idea was that the highly excited atmosphere would produce highly excitable music.'

Paul Simonon recalls, 'We'd look across the control room and there were two grown men fighting.'

Stevens' odd behaviour reached its bizarre climax when CBS boss Maurice Oberstein called by the studio to hear some mixes. The band had recorded enough material for a double album, but Oberstein wouldn't pay for a double. When he tried to leave the studio car park, Stevens lay in front of his Rolls-Royce shouting that unless they got the double album Oberstein would have to kill him.

Realising that they needed someone to deal with day-to-day management, especially as they wanted to tour in the USA, The Clash contracted Blackhill Enterprises – the outfit that had run Pink Floyd and later managed Ian Dury and the Blockheads. It was when Blackhill took a look at the books that the parlous state of the band's finances came to light. Although the argy-bargy with Bernie had been resolved, they established that The Clash were £50,000 in the red and that the CBS contract was an albatross around the band's neck. Instead of the five more albums the band thought they had to record, the small print seemed to say they had a thirteen-album deal. The Clash would be working with CBS for another fifteen years at that rate. And the royalties were pathetic, running at only 4 per cent in some territories, when 12–15 per cent was more common for an act of their stature. The band's blunt refusal to play major venues or do *Top of the Pops* contributed hugely to their virtual insolvency.

On the ensuing American tour, Topper Headon overdosed on heroin and started turning blue. He had to be kept awake. 'I was out of control,' he said in *Westway to the World*. 'I remember being sick on Buddy Holly's grave. That didn't go down very well. I was into Keith Moon – live fast die young.' He had certainly been living fast, but so far he had somehow managed to avoid the dying bit.

London Calling came out in late 1979 and was hailed as The Clash's masterpiece. It made number 9 in the charts. But it seemed the band had passed their creative highpoint. Musically, they seemed lost. The three-album set *Sandinista!* sold dismally and The Clash got a mauling from the critics, who scoffed at its political posturing.

John Shearlaw wrote in the *Record Mirror*:

The Clash have become a messy conglomerate of present day Don Quixotes. So credible, so concerned and so in control of their output that from behind a mixing desk, they can now tilt at more non-existent windmills than even the Pentagon can.

Melody Maker's Patrick Humphries wrote, 'The odd highlights are lost in a welter of reggae/dub overkill . . . [the album] suggests – in its bewildering aimlessness – that the band are floundering, uncertain of their direction.'

Nick Kent in the *NME*, as usual, cut straight to the chase: 'This record is strong testimony that The Clash have – temporarily at least – lost a grip on their bearings and find themselves parked in a cul-de-sac.'

Commercially, it was a nightmare. The band wanted the retail price for the three-album set fixed at £5.99, but CBS said that if the album sold at that price they would have to sell 200,000 copies in the UK before they would start paying royalties. The band recognised that, as *London Calling* had sold only 180,000 copies in the UK, that target seemed completely unrealistic. There was an air of depression around the band – and then John Lennon was assassinated just as the album was released. It seemed to cast a pall over the whole affair.

Blackhill Enterprises were to be the whipping dog over the *Sandinista!* debacle. In retrospect, the band thought Blackhill were too considered, too straight and unimaginative. Bernie, for all his faults, was now beginning to look like their best hope of survival.

In *Westway to the World*, Paul Simonon says, 'After a couple of years with Blackhill, Joe put his foot down and I'm glad he did. He wanted Bernie back.'

Mick Jones didn't see it the same way and, although Bernie got his old job back in early 1981, a barrier had been forced into Jones's relationship with Joe and, over a period, he became increasingly remote, intractable and difficult to work with. Joe commented, 'Mick was intolerable to work with – no fun at all – like Elizabeth Taylor in a filthy mood.'

In the interim, Bernie had been preoccupied with Vic Godard and the Subway Sect but dropped everything when The Clash gave him the call. It's hard to establish exactly how much effort Bernie put into Vic and his band. The Subway Sect, although barely known by those outside a punk inner circle, were influential and their performances are still treasured memories for many. The pleasantly eccentric Vic, who has worked happily as a postman for years, playing Dylan covers with his band in the evenings, says Subway Sect came about because Malcolm McLaren had spotted him and his distinctively dressed mates at a Sex Pistols gig and asked him if they wanted to play at the 1976 100 Club Punk Festival. 'He arranged for us to use Bernie Rhodes free (as long as The Clash weren't using him),' Vic said in an interview with Keith Rillington on the Punk77 website. 'He didn't put anything into the band musically but did once buy us all red jumpers and he did some good artwork for the sleeves. As for producer, he did work very closely with Mickey Foote on all our tracks during that time, so I always credit them jointly as producer.'

The band released a track called 'Ambition', which went to the top of the indie singles chart, but by then Bernie had sacked them, although he continued to manage Vic. It all fizzled out amid grumblings about unpaid advances and royalties, and Vic has been doing the post ever since. He has recently reformed Subway Sect.

Strummer talked about the reunification with Bernie to Paul Du Noyer at the *NME*:

We fell out with Bernie, he lost control of us, and it's a pity we fell out with him because we made a good team. But he got really funny when The Clash started to happen, and we wouldn't see him from week to week. If he wanted to communicate, he'd just send a minion – inferring he was too busy elsewhere to deal with us. We got the phrase 'Complete Control' off Bernie. I remember him going – he'd obviously been talking to Malcolm [McLaren] and was trying to be the master puppeteer – 'Look, I want COMPLETE CONTROL,' and we were laughing at him.

Bernie immediately announced a European tour, followed by another American tour, with a British tour coming at the end of the year. On the European leg, the band played to 18,000 people in Lyons, but some of the British dates were slow sellers, so Bernie contrived the idea of Joe Strummer 'going missing' to garner some press coverage. Joe duly went off to Paris and the press, as expected, speculated at length about his whereabouts. Bernie issued a statement that read: 'Joe Strummer's personal conflict is, "Where does the socially concerned rock artist stand in the bubblegum environment of today?" I feel he has probably gone away for a serious rethink.'

But then, on the prearranged signal, Joe didn't reappear. It seems he'd had the chance to reassess where the band was and wouldn't follow the script. He had the hump about Topper's worsening addictions, and Mick's lateness for appointments, surliness and general star-trip behaviour.

His no-show threw the management into panic. The British tour would have to be cancelled – but that would require that a $75,000 rebate be paid to the promoters. The only way of getting the money for that was to play a one-off gig in the Netherlands, but the tickets for that weren't selling because nobody thought The Clash would show up. It all went to the wire and Joe was only found when private detectives had been employed – he had grown a beard and had even run in the Paris marathon without anyone spotting him.

The Clash played the gig, raised the requisite cash and cancelled the tour, but Topper's catatonic condition led to the Netherlands gig being his final one, with the band anyway. They had to sack him. He was shocked by his sacking, but unsurprised. 'I fucked up,' he commented.

Weeks later, the album *Combat Rock* was released. Ironically, it was Topper's jaunty contribution to the band's songwriting, 'Rock the Casbah', that would help make the album their most commercially successful yet and provide them with top-ten hits on both sides of the Atlantic. However, Topper would play on no more albums and, though they didn't realise it at the time, neither would Mick Jones.

Meanwhile, flushed with his band's regained success, Bernie began to imagine he had a transatlantic business on his hands and found a New York office that would briefly become Clash Headquarters USA. The Clash had gone global.

Terry Chimes was called up as a replacement for Topper on drums and the new Clash moved up a gear, supporting The Who on a few American dates, which climaxed at the massive Shea Stadium. There was even talk of the Rolling Stones wanting them as support. The gigs passed well and suddenly The Clash were hanging out with the New York scene: Andy Warhol and his entourage were rubbing shoulders with the Camden rockers.

But behind the superficial highs, things weren't good. A suddenly directionless band returned to Britain for a rest that went on and on, and might have continued for months had they not received an offer of $500,000 to play at the US Festival in Los Angeles. This sharply brought into focus the dilemma the 'street' band had before it. The gig had that 'corporate' vibe – the fee put them in a stadium band bracket, something they'd always despised. What were they to be, another version of The Who? Accepting the gig seemed like treason.

Terry Chimes had left, so drummer auditions were held – auditions that initially none of the band attended. The job was delegated and the band only got involved after a shortlist had been drawn up. They were becoming increasingly remote from their fan base; they were losing the common touch and they knew it, on top of which Bernie was still penny pinching despite their hugely improved circumstances. The new drummer, Pete Howard, was only getting paid $300 a gig on the American warm-up tour. Roadies would be given the runaround before Bernie eventually paid them.

The Clash were now in some gloom about what they considered to be their hypocrisy. They hated the idea of playing a huge venue and just taking the money. On the other hand, half a million dollars was hard to turn down – an irreconcilable anti-capitalist/capitalist stance.

Instead of doing the gig in style – taking the money and running, or alternatively refusing to do it altogether – they chose a somewhat snotty middle route. Whether it was all Bernie-the-militant's idea or whoever's, on the day of the gig they (via Bernie) informed the show's organiser, Steve Wozniak, of Apple Computers, that they wouldn't play unless he donated $100,000 to underprivileged children. (Bernie, it has been reported, now claims that it was this idea – his idea, the charity gig event – that would eventually give Bob Geldof the concept for Live Aid.) The day wound on, until finally some kind of deal was reached between an intractable band and the long-suffering organisers, but by then the crowd was bored stiff and the atmosphere was poisonous. The band went on late and when they came off, there was a backstage brawl.

Back in London, relationships in the band deteriorated further. Mick Jones wouldn't show up for rehearsals and when it was decided something should be done, Simonon and Strummer asked him to leave (no doubt helped along with a gentle shove from Bernie).

There, perfectly demonstrated, is the curiosity which was the McLaren/Rhodes axis. While they both had the terrific creativity and energy necessary to build their respective bands, conversely, when it suited them, they also had the spoilt-child compulsion to destroy those bands.

Two new guitarists that no one can remember now took the place of the one. There was another gigantic tour, presciently called the Out of Control tour, during which the roadies were paid £100 a week. Bernie was at the helm, after all – or he thought he was. In fact, he was so in control now that when CBS wanted another album, he had the verve, or was it the nerve, to take the producer's chair alongside Strummer. And he co-wrote it.

In *Passion is a Fashion*, Pat Gilbert argues that, fed up with Jones's 'tortured artist thing', Bernie now desperately wanted to be in the band; perhaps he'd been egged on by his old mentor and fellow non-musician McLaren, who had managed to inveigle his way into the pop charts in his own right. After all, these were the days of the punk ethos – DIY. Sadly for all, the record was slammed.

Then it was all over, apart from the odd gig and tears of recrimination.

Topper Headon now lives quietly in Dover. He did a spell in prison on drugs offences and has been a cab driver. While he is still having drug problems, he plays occasional gigs down the local pub and survives on Clash royalties (including those from Will Smith's 'Will2K', which featured samples from the perennial 'Rock the Casbah').

Paul Simonon, always a talented artist, continues with that work. He did tread the boards again with Havana 3am, which Bernie briefly managed. He is currently playing with Damon Albarn in The Good, The Bad and The Queen.

Strummer is sadly dead but did at least live long enough to see his band The Clash inducted into the Rock and Roll Hall of Fame. Typically, he and Jones were arguing up to the last minute about whether Jones would appear (he did).

Jones had a good run with Big Audio Dynamite and was chuffed to be offered the production job on The Libertines' album *Up the Bracket*. He was recently in a band with his old mate Tony James, called Carbon/Silicon, described by Alan McGee as 'the Stones jamming with a laptop'.

Kosmo Vinyl, Bernie's sidekick, says of his one-time boss in Gilbert's book, 'Bernie was a "true radical", a man with a unique mind. There has never been anyone involved in music that thinks like Bernard. He's always looking at the whole culture, not just part of it. His ideas are completely out of the box. Sometimes he comes at things at such an unexpected angle. It can completely throw you. He is a one-off.'

That may be, but his cultural muddle-headedness and the 'divide and rule' tactics he must surely have picked up from Malcolm McLaren, or that they cooked up between them, always seemed destined to bring about failure. All bands break up, but usually it's of their own volition and not by the hand of their manager – a manager with his cards gripped so close to his chest that he may not have known what they were himself. But, of course, it's impossible to say unless you were there at the time.

In *Westway to the World*, Mick Jones states, 'Bernie was always 100 per cent, but he wouldn't share.'

Towards the end of the same film, Strummer bemoans the break-up of his beloved Clash, regretting the dismemberment of the original line-up, saying words to the effect that when you've got something good, 'Don't mess with it.' Then he adds. 'We learned that bitterly.' He then turns his head from the camera with tears welling up in his eyes.

11

ALAN McGEE

The creative habit is like a drug. The particular obsession changes, but the excitement, the thrill of your creation lasts.

– Henry Moore

I t's amazing and amusing that Alan McGee was ever allowed through the hallowed portals of No. 10. Even though there's been a veritable who's who of despots, mass murderers, insider traders and money launderers trooping in and out since the time it was built, have the august premises ever entertained a Glaswegian speed freak with self-confessed violent tendencies – even allowing for the fifty-grand Party donation?

Whatever, the bastard alignment of pop and politics was unseemly, ugly (the only notable muso allowed in prior to McGee was Andrew Lloyd Webber) and stillborn. A grinning Blair having an ill-conceived crack at trendiness by gladhanding the Scots *enfant terrible* and the Manc musician by his side just left a nasty taste. At least two out of the three looked like stooges.

To be fair, it was the end of 18 years of Tory misrule and there was an air of celebration and expectation. A devoted Labour supporter, McGee was surely there for altruistic reasons and

281

Noel Gallagher had presumably turned up for the craic (Alistair Campbell had apparently kept a wary eye on Noel and Meg in case at any point they headed off to the toilets with a gleam of intent in their eyes), but Blair conspicuously failed to garner the thinnest veneer of cool by schmoozing the donor and talking Fender or Gibson with the king of Britpop. Politicos and popsters could never, and should never, sail into a golden sunset hand in hand. Each is, and needs to be, at opposing ends of the spectrum. The red, white and blue-ensigned barge *Cool Britannia* slid beneath the waves and the only musician prepared to be seen with Tony these days is Cliff Richard.

As Irvine Welsh pointed out in S. Redhead's *Repetitive Beat Generation*, 'You're either right outside society or you're exploited.'

Alan McGee was (is) essentially a fan: the sort of guy you'd more likely find rummaging around in record-shop racks than making the records that go into them. He left school in 1977 with the ubiquitous one O level and a casual friendship with Bobby (Primal Scream) Gillespie. It was a big year for punk. McGee's earliest singles purchases were 'God Save the Queen' and 'Sheena is a Punk Rocker'. While working on a building site and listening to The Jam, he resolved to be a pop star and on answering an audition met Andrew Innes, another future Primal Screamer. Innes convinced McGee that the streets of London were lined with pop gold and the duo headed south to squat in Clapham, Alan to stopgap as a clerk for British Rail.

New Romanticism and pomp pop were everywhere in 1982–3: Spandau Ballet, Duran Duran, Bonnie Tyler and Phil Collins were clogging up the charts. McGee was itching to hear something better/harder/more intense and was forced to start his own club to get it. After a spell of losing money and changing locations, a regular audience and a small but stable income accrued. He was now venturing into territory mere fans rarely ever visit.

Alan was hooked. Driven by an urge to work in music or in the music business on a permanent basis, he also saw that the running of a club was helping him to make friends, as he told Paolo Hewitt in *Alan McGee and the Story of Creation Records*. 'I ended up having tons of pals. And that's how I broke through the media really fast as well. Because if you're on the door of a club that everybody wants to get into, you meet loads of people. I was putting the gigs on, so kids were saying "geezer" and all that stuff.' This is a constant theme in the McGee story: the desire for friends and girlfriends, for appreciation, to be part of the gang. There seems to be an undercurrent of lack of self-esteem and unworthiness – of a yearning for approval.

With the club profits, McGee and his partner, Joe Foster, started the proto-Creation Records (then known as Autonomy) with the release of a single by The Legend. Other acts followed, such as Biff Bang Pow, The Jasmine Minks and then The Jesus and Mary Chain. He found himself at the hub of something.

The Jesus and Mary Chain's 'Upside Down' sold 35,000 singles and topped the indie charts. It made reputations for the band, Creation Records and Alan, who was effectively managing the act, although he says he never took any money from them. (This was because of the legendary 50–50 deals that Creation would do with its artists; basically, the artist and the label would split any profits half and half, and The Jesus and Mary Chain didn't really make any.)

McGee was wearing many hats now. He was in charge of the label, he was running the club nights, he was dabbling with music management and he was also writing and performing in or with some of the bands, including Biff Bang Pow.

Ironically, the DIY punk ethos was never more manifest than in these post-punk days. Nobody had a management contract. Nobody had a record contract. 'It was all handshake deals,' says McGee. Whoever was around was co-opted to help. Bobby Gillespie, who had been acting as a roadie for Altered Images, was soon playing drums for The Jesus and Mary Chain. He also printed the sleeves.

McGee had been a keen observer and admirer of Malcolm

McLaren. 'I was on a massive, massive Pistols trip,' he says. 'I was thinking, "I can't be Johnny Rotten, but I can be Malcolm McLaren."'

Paradoxically, when Malcolm McLaren had wanted a label, he hadn't knocked one up himself, as McGee had done, he'd gone straight to EMI, that most establishment of record companies; however, although McGee had his own label, he was similarly forced to knock on the doors of the loathed majors from time to time – The Jesus and Mary Chain went to Warner Brothers when the band threatened to leave him and later the House of Love went to Phonogram because it made so much financial sense. McGee made big bucks. The DIY deal-maker.

McGee told Paolo Hewitt he saw no problem running a label and managing some of its artists at the same time. 'I've always done it,' he said. 'I think it was quite good for me, managing House of Love. Because the deal [with Phonogram] was huge. It was a £400,000 deal. So I made £80,000 out of it and that funded Creation. The other side of it was that I learned how not to go about things.'

Hewitt went on to ask McGee if he had a management philosophy back then. He agreed he had, albeit a fairly basic one: 'It would probably have been: take as many drugs as the band. Be more rock 'n' roll than the group.'

True to his rock and roll word, when the first-wave ravers brought Ecstasy back to Manchester from Ibiza, McGee was on hand to help them dispose of it – he and Bobby Gillespie, that is. Pretty soon they were shovelling down every E they could get their hands on. Bobby loved the drug so much, he wanted Alan to go into manufacturing it. 'We started taking loads of Ecstasy,' he told pr-inside.com. 'I remember asking Alan McGee to finance an Ecstasy factory . . . The idea was we'd give out the tablets for free. Alan didn't go for it.'

A drug-taking phase turned into a six-year bender for Alan, which led to a mental breakdown, but even when he was running at the fringes of sanity, it didn't seem to blunt his talent-spotting skills. Despite regular mind-altering attendances at the Hacienda

Club and taking to acid house music with the same super-accelerated vigour of a Bez (he even moved into a flat above Factory Records just to be nearer to the centre of it all), when he signed My Bloody Valentine in 1988, paradoxically Alan confirmed his title as the King of Indie. Critically renowned, they were always a 'difficult' band and would later almost cause the crash of Creation. But they certainly weren't house music.

Indeed, McGee objected when it was suggested that Andy Weatherall, a non-producer house DJ, should mix a track for Primal Scream. But surely fortune favours the brave, for when he finally assented he was hugely rewarded when 'Loaded', a pioneering fusion of rock meets club was sent out on white label to the DJs. Weatherall, who'd only ever been involved in mixing one track before, played it at London's Subterrania club and was shaken by the rapturous response.

'I got a call from Andrew Innes at about four in the morning,' Bobby Gillespie said in an interview with *The Guardian*. 'He was saying "I think we've got a hit record on our hands. We played it here and people went nuts!"'

Creation received 7,500 advance orders before the track's release in February 1990. It gave Gillespie and the Primals the hit they had so long awaited – a hit that ironically had little to do with the indie music they had previously been peddling.

Waves of house fever fuelled by Ecstasy hit Creation Records. The label's offices became drug central. Motorcycle messengers were deployed every Friday night to pick up the weekend stash to feed the needs of the staff and whichever band happened to be hanging about. Parties raged all night on the premises. And the fun went international: McGee had caught the drug bug bad and would zoom off to Los Angeles with cohorts, ostensibly to do business deals but there were plenty of drug deals, too, with serious all-night cocaine binges and girl-chasing parties packed into the frenetic schedules.

However, despite good sales in the UK and Germany of *Screamadelica*, Primal Scream's biggest and best album, Creation

Records was going down the pipes and a deal had to be struck with Sony for international distribution.

Alan was simultaneously managing Primal Scream and St Etienne but regular income streams were unreliable. It didn't help when My Bloody Valentine, led by Kevin Shields, locked themselves in the recording studio for more than two years to make an album with Creation footing a bill running at £200,000 and with no prospect of a finish date in sight.

This was McGee's constant inner conflict, the duality of the man: one half an inveterate fan, the other a businessman. Here's a man who says, 'I just want to make good records,' and indulges his artists to the point of bringing his creation, his *Creation*, crashing down around his ears. On more than one occasion, he was left crying down the telephone to Shields, begging him to finish the project 'before you bankrupt the label'. Despite the perilousness of the situation, and long after parting ways with My Bloody Valentine, McGee still has the respect and charity and sheer hero-worship to say of the man who nearly dragged it all down that Shields was 'in the great tradition of the true fucking Irish genius . . . He's the greatest artist, as in "artist", I've ever worked with. No doubt about it.'

McGee: obsessive-compulsive fan to the end.

Despite mounting money worries and a monster appetite for drugs, somehow Alan stayed wobbling along the tightrope. And his persistence eventually paid off, in spades. Back home in Glasgow one night, he wandered into King Tut's club – some say because he wanted to make a date with a girlfriend of his sister, or because he had missed the last train home; others, because he wanted to watch one of his bands, who were playing that night.

The legend goes that the club management didn't want Oasis to play – presumably because they hadn't been booked. It was only when Noel Gallagher pointed out that there were only two bouncers in attendance and that there might be ructions if he announced to his rowdy Manc mates that their favourite combo had been blown out that the manager carved a niche for them in the billing.

It took McGee, who'd never been a slouch at A&R, a mere two numbers to realise that the band – who *The Face* magazine's Cliff Jones was later to describe as 'The Sex Beatles' – would be huge and that he was going to sign them. Creation's publicist Jeff Barrett reinforces the view that his then boss is blessed with powers beyond those of normal men. 'Oasis? I think that it was just perfect, that it was a great moment in time. If there had been another record company at the same gig, they'd have all walked out. And I really believe that. I don't think that anybody else would have got it, believed in it, shouted about it. I mean, he knew straight away and that's Alan McGee.'

If further proof of his faith in his own strong instincts is required, when Gallagher asked if McGee wanted a demo tape, McGee said he didn't need one – surely a first: a record company boss who doesn't demand tape, CD, artwork and video in the first utterance, and a ten-year commitment signed in blood in the second.

As with all Creation's new projects, McGee spent a lot of time with his latest charges and his already hedonistic lifestyle moved on to another level as he tried to keep pace with the roistering Gallaghers. 'There was a lot of partying with girls and stuff like that. Then Oasis came along,' he said. 'There was hardly ever a night off and I'd started getting into things like diet pills. I was also drinking like fuck. So it was like I was just doing drugs, coke, fucking E, Jack Daniels . . .'

The group's first record, *Definitely Maybe*, became the fastest-selling debut in British history, entering the charts at number 1. *(What's The Story) Morning Glory?* shot to number 1 in England, becoming the fastest-selling album in the UK since Michael Jackson's *Bad*. It spent a total of three years in the chart and sold eighteen million copies. Oasis became an international phenomenon. 'Wonderwall' scored highly in the American charts and *Morning Glory* went top ten over there, eventually being certified quintuple platinum. It also went top ten in Europe and Asia.

Oasis became the biggest band of the '90s and Creation Records, so often on the brink of disaster, was suddenly awash with money. But just as it all started happening for the Gallaghers, it started ending for McGee. He entered chemical hell, as he told journalist John Harris of *Select* magazine:

> I nearly lost it completely in August 1993. I was at a party in LA with the Primals and Evan Dando, and I ran back to my hotel with fucking shitloads of drugs, and I mean fucking shitloads. I locked my door and started doing all of them and Evan Dando is knocking on my door and I'm saying "Fuck off, I'm in bed!" I was a total fucking drug addict.

He would also swing a fist if he thought he could get away with it, and get away with it he often did, despite his slender frame. But the Glasgow fighting cock hung up his gloves after a confrontation with the then editor of *Loaded*, James Brown, which led to him receiving a battering.

Loud music, drugs, booze and punch-ups: it's a recipe for disaster, but at least McGee stayed off the heroin. 'I thought it was a dirty drug,' he said. 'Cocaine, Ecstasy, speed, acid, diet pills, fucking Night Nurse cough mixture – I thought these were all OK – but I wouldn't do heroin because it was brown. I was deluded like all drug addicts, thinking I was in control and that everyone else was in trouble.'

A few months later, Alan was taken off a plane after some kind of attack. 'When the plane landed in LA, the paramedics diagnosed me as suffering from nervous exhaustion. My sister put me to bed and I was shaky but all right. I went to see Swervedriver at the Roxy and I was downing Jack and Cokes, just hammering them. I had about 20 and I was absolutely paralytic. I woke up at four in the morning . . . and now everything is getting really fucking bizarre. I think that the blinds are moving and I'm getting utterly freaked out.

'I'm not in control of my body and I'm certainly not in control of my mind, and I feel like I've got a metal pole in the back of my neck, which I realise now is hypertension. We get the paramedics out again, and my blood pressure is 170 when normally it should be 110. They're worried that I'm going to have a blood clot, so they put me into a wheelchair and hook me up to some oxygen, and they're saying, "Don't move." And I suddenly thought, "What the fuck is this all about? If this is rock 'n' roll, just who gives a fuck?"'

There followed years of rehab, which included regression therapy and what he calls 'rebuilding my ego'. He even visited a church (after the visit, he got home to find a message on his answer machine saying that *Definitely Maybe* was number 1). 'There was always a joke after that that I should go to church more often,' he said.

When Oasis did their massive gigs (there were two million ticket applications for their Knebworth concert), a sympathetic Noel Gallagher dedicated 'Live Forever' to his absent manager/ label boss, who was struggling to free himself from the clutches of a mental breakdown.

In the interim, with its founder staring into the abyss, Creation just kept house, servicing its existing bands but signing nothing new. When Alan returned, he found a new regime in place. Sony had installed their own marketing staff, a lot of old Creation faces had moved on and the Friday night drug run had been long curtailed. McGee didn't like the vibe and started making plans to move on himself. As a parting shot, he signed ex-Dexys Midnight Runner ex-vagrant Kevin Rowland, who made a £270,000 album that was accompanied by a suitably expensive marketing campaign featuring Kevin in a blue velvet dress, black pants and stockings. The posters, calculated to scare and repel, had the desired effect and the album sold zilch.

Typically, McGee stands by his man. 'Commercially, we lost money doing that record. But from where I'm sitting in the world, I was part of a Kevin Rowland record and it's a work of genius.'

He didn't manage Rowland, but then who could?

Alan sold off Creation and formed Poptones, a label that would re-establish the ethos he'd had when he started out. It would be 'totally anti-Establishment, anti-music business, totally left-field', and yet despite the radical mission statement, he floated Poptones on the stock exchange and investors rushed to buy. It was an astute move and a masterpiece of timing; he made a fortune, such was the afterglow from the Oasis experience. The label has had a platinum album with The Hives.

Alan kept clean and fit and at some point obviously felt strong enough to take on the management of The Libertines and all that that (Pete Doherty) entailed. Yet again McGee found himself at the epicentre of what was hip and happening in the UK. Of course, it could never last. The Libertines – particularly Doherty – were unstable and inevitably the band broke up. If Alan had been bestowed with more hair in the first place, there would have certainly been none left by this stage.

The fatally flawed Doherty has subsequently had his addictions to crack cocaine and heroin (as well as his love life) splashed across tabloidland. He was dumped from the Libertines tour for being generally flaky and then robbed band member Carl Barat's flat while they were still away gigging. Doherty went into rehab on the advice of *EastEnders'* fag-tilting star Dot Cotton, discharged himself and was then arrested with a flick knife. Narrowly escaping prison, he formed another band, Babyshambles, and rejected McGee's wise and benign managerial influences, as well as his label, in favour of Rough Trade. McGee might well be glad the lad has gone, since it can only end in tears. Doherty was acquitted of blackmail and robbery charges, but his addictions rage on and the press and the law hound him still, maybe unto the grave. Even Bobby Gillespie and the one-time tabloid target Liam Gallagher had been less of a handful.

Yet, despite his frustrating experiences at the coalface of artistic temperament, McGee has talked about managing the troubled Courtney Love. He is still resolutely unable to avoid flying close to the flames. Who knows what Alan McGee will take on next? He has money, vision and a compulsive drive. Watch the headlines because he'll be in them for some time to come.

Alan McGee

A revealing insight into his character comes from Kate Holmes, Alan's wife and the one who nursed him back to health. She agreed with Paolo Hewitt that Alan had an obsessive nature, saying that sometimes he would phone her 15 times a day, and added, 'The first day I met him, I was at his flat and he opened the door and offered me a drink. He had a shelf on the fridge that was filled from the bottom to the top with Purdeys. And that lasted about a month. And after that it was grapes. He'd eat 20 pounds of grapes a day. And then it was oranges. And it was muesli. Then it was rice cakes. Now it's cornflakes and coffee.'

Creation management's recent roster includes The Charlatans, Mogwai and Dirty Pretty Things. Alan has recording studios in Glasgow and London. His publishing company still has Oasis and Primal Scream on its books. He is a band-builder of some distinction, a highly successful record company boss, a promoter, an accomplished mass marketeer and quite possibly the best raw-talent spotter of the past 20 years, but it seems he is not really a manager per se and probably only ended up managing his acts because there was no one else around to do the job adequately for him. 'Alan McGee is a pop entrepreneur in the classic mould,' says Sean O' Hagen. 'Someone who combines barrow-boy flash with an old-fashioned faith in rock music.'

In recent months, Alan has written off the existing record industry as 'pensionable'. 'The whole music business model as we have known it these last 30 years is completely out of date,' he wrote on his MySpace site. 'The only people who are on top of the changes are Apple . . . They should just buy EMI – buy The Beatles and take it from there.' He's also accused Robbie Williams of destroying music.

McGee has returned to clubland. His Death Disco club nights have residencies in London, Inverness, Budapest and New York. Two other London club nights are The Queen is Dead and the wryly named Now We're Off to Rehab. On his MySpace site, he lists his interests as Diet Coke, bananas, iPods, Hungary and Poland, Mexico, 'the greatest country in the world, Scotland' and 'rock 'n' roll till the day I fucking die'. Never to have a real job, he lists his occupation as Situationist.

He's a fan still and he's certainly opted to stay well outside the Establishment that tried in such a high-profile way in the early Blair years to absorb him. As he told Paolo Hewitt: 'I swear to you if they gave me a Sir Alan McGee OBE, MBE or CBE, I'd tell them to stick it up their fucking arse. I hate the Royal Family. I hate the Conservatives. I don't want any fucking honours from the fucking Establishment.'

Alan's sister, Susan McGee, attests to this: 'I mean, you could tell he was going to be rebellious – a temper on him that was unbelievable. Total fiery redhead.'

12

SIMON FULLER

There is something rarer than ability. It is the ability to recognise ability.

— Elbert Hubbard

The statistics are astonishing – and they've come straight from his own website, so they must be true. Simon Fuller has had a hand in the making of 106 number 1 singles and 83 number 1 albums in the UK, along with 'an impressive tally' of 281 top 40 albums and 430 top 40 singles.

'19 Entertainment Ltd is one of the most successful entertainment organisations in the world,' the site reads. 'Simon Fuller became the world's most successful manager – breaking a record set by The Beatles manager Brian Epstein in the 1960s – when three of his artists occupied the number 1, 2 and 3 positions on the US single chart as well as the number 1 position in the album chart.

'He manages Annie Lennox's solo career; he created and managed the Spice Girls, who went on to sell over 45 million albums and became a global phenomenon. Simon also manages Cathy Dennis, the most successful female British songwriter of the last 30 years.'

Wow, that's impressive reading. And there's much, much more

to be impressed by on the 19 Entertainment site: 'Simon also created the most successful TV format of the new millennium – *Pop Idol* (*American Idol* in the US) . . . aired in more than 35 markets . . . generated several multimillion selling acts . . . achieving unprecedented audience records of around 28 million viewers per show . . . highest rated TV show in America . . . 19 is a world leader in the integration of brands with entertainment properties . . .' Phew!

Fuller, at 21, scored his first hit by signing the then unknown song 'Holiday', Madonna's first hit, to Chrysalis Music in the UK. His career as a manager started in 1985, when he set up 19. He created S Club 7 and discovered Will Young; he manages Victoria and David Beckham and he's acquired the global rights to manage Elvis Presley's back catalogue. It's impossible to disagree that Fuller has had a massive effect on pop culture in the world today.

Additionally, Fuller is a one-man media giant who, in TV terms, carries more weight in the USA than any British TV executive has since Lew Grade. One of his recent pilots was an *EastEnders*-style soap for Fox TV called *Southsiders*, based in Chicago. A British company making a soap for the USA about life in an American city? It would have been inconceivable before Simon Fuller came along.

But, of course, it's the Spice Girls phase of his career that is the most interesting even now; especially now, in fact. The more you look back at some of their cringingly awful solo releases, the more remarkable it seems that Mel B, Mel C, Victoria, Emma and Geri ever sold so many records when they were the Spice Girls – 53 million, to be precise(ish). That's a lot of records. It's hard to argue with such a multi-platinumed tribute to Simon Fuller. However, the Spice Girls didn't start with Simon. They were put together by father-and-son management team Bob and Chris Herbert.

The (unfortunately named) Herberts, who had previously nurtured the band Bros before watching them get plucked from under their noses by a new manager as soon as they showed a glimmer of success, were backed by an enigmatic figure known as Chic Murphy, who used to be involved with running the Three Degrees. It was Chic who first saw a niche for a young all-girl group and who first proposed the idea to the Herberts. It was the Herberts who did the recruitment and the auditions and who, having pared the applicants down to the band we knew and loved, put them together with voice coaches, choreographers and all the other 'consultants' the modern wannabe needs.

The Herberts thought they'd keep the girls keen by not immediately giving them management contracts. Big mistake. When the Spice Girls did a wildly successful showcase for the record companies, the boot was on the other foot and they refused to sign anything with the Herberts. Not only that, they retrieved the master tapes of most of the initial recordings they'd done, vacated the house the Herberts had provided for them and moved on.

When Bob Herbert died in a car crash in 1999, the obituaries inevitably said he was the 'unluckiest man in pop'. His son Chris went on to manage Five and Hear'say, and it's a fair bet that those band members have had to sign management contracts the size of phone books before a penny was spent on their behalf.

The girls embarked on a search for a new manager and they went in all guns blazing. One who witnessed their outrageous sales pitch was Martyn Barter of Freedom Management. He recalls being amazed by their audacious presentation, in David Sinclair's book *Wannabe: How the Spice Girls Reinvented Pop Fame*: 'They came through reception downstairs and it was like a whirlwind. Messengers, receptionists and all the people coming and going – everyone was stunned. "What the hell was that?" Then they came into my office and this whole routine unfolded in front of me. They put the track that they'd done with Elliot [Kennedy, one of Barter's managed writers] on the cassette player and they sang along to it karaoke style, with this dance routine going on. The whole thing was completely choreographed to turn me on. I remember Emma Bunton had a short skirt and a blouse on, the school uniform-looking thing, with her hair in bunches and she pulled up a chair opposite me and sat down so I could see up her skirt.'

Paul Conroy, then the president of Virgin Records, told Sinclair, 'The effect they had – from the car-park attendant to the executive boardroom – was certainly something to behold. They were pretty frightening in their level of confidence. It was as though they'd gone to EST or had some sort of training. In their own sort of pop way, there was something quite anarchic, quite punk in the way they physically assaulted an office. They'd turn over your desk. It reminded me of when I used to work at Stiff Records and The Damned would come into the office and just cause chaos.'

The word was out and all the heavy hitters in pop management wanted a piece of this as yet unknown pop sensation; they all knew the girls were going to be mega. One by one, they were rejected.

Simon Fuller is a cute cookie, however, and he outsmarted the Spice Girls. He made them sit and wait until he was good and ready when they came to his offices. He impressed them with his smooth ways, his 'You've been Tango'd' suntan, his Prada wardrobe and a plummy voice that has been compared with that of Nigel Pargetter from *The Archers* (although the twanging accent may have owed more to his father having been an RAF pilot – 'Roger, wilco' and all that). Interestingly, Fuller's grandfather was a music-hall comic and acrobat – perhaps entertainment is in the genes.

Fuller senior was stationed in Cyprus when Simon was born. The family later moved to Ghana where Dad, who had become a teacher, set up schools. Fuller says that the postings abroad and his father's experiences in education ingrained in him a business culture. 'Dad was an entrepreneur at heart,' he says in Sinclair's book. 'He was proud that whenever he bought a car, he sold it at a profit. Even now I feel like I'm doing what he might have wanted to do.'

At secondary school, his father became his headmaster – a situation that might have terrified another child, but Simon seems to have been happy enough. After school, he went to art school in Hastings and ran discos on the side. Fuller landed a job at Chrysalis Music, the music publishing arm of Chrysalis Records, and after a couple of years went into management with the artist Paul Hardcastle, who had a worldwide hit with '19'. The superstitious Fuller kept the song's title as the name for his company (as well as using the number 19 in his office phone number and on his car registration number) and went on to recruit other artists, including Gary Barlow, Annie Lennox and Cathy Dennis, who originally was a performer and who historically went on to write 'Can't Get You Out of My Head' for Kylie Minogue and 'Toxic' for Britney.

However, when Fuller encountered the Spice Girls in early 1995, his life was to change for good, although he was never the Svengali he was subsequently made out to be. Before they met Fuller, the girls had formed and had done many rehearsals; they already had their name and a number of tracks in the can, including 'Wannabe', '2 Become 1' and 'Who Do You Think You Are', all of which would go on to be number ones. The Spice Girls may have been a 'manufactured' band, but it wasn't Fuller who did the manufacturing, and he stayed in the background while the girls did the rounds of the record companies. In the end, all the majors bar one had put in a bid for them, but it would be Virgin who landed the prize and popped the corks on the champagne. During the ensuing celebrations, the story goes that the girls took a cab to a restaurant and Victoria had her knickers ripped off her by her tipsy bandmates, who then threw them out of the cab window – perhaps now the treasured souvenir of an unsuspecting passing lad!

The video for 'Wannabe', although not cheap to make, looked shoddy, but somehow it was pure Spice Girls. The Box video-request channel played it once and within two hours viewers had voted it into the number 1 position. It stayed there for 13 weeks before being displaced by the band's own 'Say You'll Be There'.

It was *Top of the Pops* magazine's Peter Lorraine who handed them the simple sobriquets Posh, Scary, Sporty, Baby and Ginger, thus allowing everyone to pick their own favourite Spice Girl without having to go to the bother of learning their real names. Unwittingly or not, it proved to be a masterstroke; in fact, it became essential that you had a pet Spice Girl, like some walking, talking Tamagotchi.

As 'Wannabe' rose to number 1 in the UK, the girls embarked on a marathon promotional tour of Japan, Germany and Holland. Shortly after, they visited Hong Kong, Korea and Thailand. In between, they filmed the video for 'Say You'll Be There' in the Mojave Desert. Fuller and the girls knew innately that the Spice Girls were an international brand and that they would quickly have to flog it around an international circuit and ram that brand home. They were rewarded for their efforts when 'Wannabe' became number 1 in 31 countries. 'Say You'll Be There', the follow-up, entered the UK charts at number 1.

Girl (next door) Power had been lapped up by tiny tot, pre-teen and teen females from Shanghai to Santiago. And it was cross-gender: it seemed the boys liked the sound of Girl Power, too. Then the parents jumped on the bandwagon. Even white-van men wanted a Spice Girl. Spicemania gripped the world. It was now not only an international brand, it was a cross-generational brand to match even that of the mighty Harry Potter.

There was a concomitant love affair with the press. From day one, of course, the tabloids couldn't get enough of the Spice Girls, but then the heavyweights found all sorts of reasons to write about them, too. When Emma sprained her ankle falling off her four-inch platform shoes, the *Daily Telegraph* reported it. A few weeks after the album *Spice* was released, the high-minded, right-wing *Spectator* magazine interviewed the girls and Geri and Victoria artlessly declared that they were Tories and that Maggie Thatcher was 'the first Spice Girl'. It was a throwaway comment that might have helped to kiss the career of a regular rock band goodbye, but these were the Spice Girls, and instead it had the curious effect of endearing them to the population even more. That issue of *The Spectator* sold 600,000 copies, the biggest-selling issue in its 200-year history.

What you saw was what you got with the Spice Girls: they were artless, daft. They tottered on huge heels and we loved them. *Spice* was the 1996 Christmas number 1 and it settled in at number 1 in the UK charts for nine weeks, selling nearly two million copies.

Such a frenzy of press interest demanded some measure of control from the management, who were eager to stymie as many of the inevitable kiss-and-tells that would come as possible. Fuller appointed a young lawyer named Gerald Tyrell, who had allegedly been known as 'that bastard' by some of the criminal fraternity, to do the job. David Sinclair notes that Tyrell's tactic was to go over the heads of the editors of the various journals and instead talk directly to the senior management. An expert in libel and litigation, Tyrell ably used the carrot-and-stick method to prevent harmful stories entering the press. His message was terse but clear: 'If you print anything libellous, we'll sue you, and you'll get no more access, ever.' Grumbling photographers were forced to sign forms acknowledging that the Spice Girls retained copyright of all their images, a hitherto unprecedented act and one that has now become the norm in the business.

Chris Heath wrote in style bible *The Face*:

> With uncomfortable speed, [the Spice Girls] have become part of the fabric of the world, of our language and of the way we talk and think about ourselves . . . They are talked about in Parliament. They are fought over by our leaders . . . They are the currently favoured metaphor for any kind of high spiritedness or feisty femininity.

Tory MP Kenneth Clarke quoted 'Wannabe' in a keynote speech to the British Retail Consortium: 'I'll tell you what I want/what I really, really want,' he gurned. 'I want to see healthy, sustainable growth and rising living standards for the next five years.' Tony Blair, rather pitifully, listed 'Wannabe' as one of his Desert Island Discs.

Of all of them, Victoria consistently showed the most awareness of the huge potential of the Spice Girls' commercial appeal and branding. 'We want to be as famous as Persil Automatic,' she asserted, a slogan that could have fallen from the lips of Andy Warhol.

When 'Wannabe' was released in the USA, it shot into the charts at number 11, the highest first-week entry since The Beatles 'I Want to Hold Your Hand'. It went to number 1 shortly after. Within weeks, the *Spice* album also topped the US chart. They became the first UK act ever to reach the top of the American album chart with their debut release.

The indefatigable group did endless promotional trips. Label boss Paul Conroy called them 'the hardest-working group in Christendom'. It must have all been one crazy trip for Fuller, but you wouldn't have known it. 'As a manager, there are two options,' he said. 'To steady the ship and steer it through the rough waters ahead, or put the foot down harder and come up with bigger and better things. I'm going for the latter approach.'

His hell-for-leather approach entailed licensing the Spice Girls image all over the planet. Soon they were endorsing more than thirty-five products and had eight sponsorship deals – totalling over £5.5 million – with companies including Asda, Sony PlayStation, Walkers Crisps and Pepsi, who each signed them for £1 million.

Lucian Grainge, then chairman and chief executive of Universal Music UK, told the *Financial Times*:

> [Fuller] has redefined the role of a manager for the twenty-first century. He treats pop acts as brands, to be exploited over different media, rather than performers who make money only by selling records and playing concerts. He's a genius – he makes everyone else look like complete amateurs.

In 1997, the Spice Girls were nominated for four Brit Awards – Best British Group, Best British Newcomer, Best British Single ('Wannabe') and Best British Video ('Say You'll Be There'). The co-writers/producers Absolute (Paul Wilson and Andy Watkins) and Stannard & Rowe were nominated for Best Producers for their work. Stateside, 20,000 Americans voted for the girls in the categories

Favourite New Pop Band and Favourite Band, and made *Spice* Favourite Album at the 25th Annual American Music Awards.

The Brit Awards ceremony was opened by the band, who performed 'Who Do You Think You Are'. It was a triumph. The unforgettable image of Geri, breasts bursting from the top of her Union Jack mini-dress, flashed all around the world. The dress, made on a sewing machine by Geri's sister, Karen, at the last minute, is in *The Guinness Book of Records* as the most expensive piece of pop-star clothing ever sold at auction. The Spice Girls went on to win two of the categories, Best British Single and Best British Video. *Spice*, the album, returned to the number 1 chart position. The Spice Girls epitomised fun and a gaudy Cool Britannia vibe far more than Blur, Oasis or Pulp all rolled together. The Union flag was again a worldwide icon for the first time since the Swinging '60s.

A few weeks later, the Spice Girls released a double A-side single, 'Mama' and 'Say You'll Be There', timed to coincide with Mother's Day. The band donated their royalties to Comic Relief's Red Nose Day – the biggest single donation. The record went straight in at number 1, making the Spice Girls the first band ever to have four number ones with their first four singles.

A live performance of 'Wannabe' and 'Say You'll Be There' on *Saturday Night Live* was watched by more than 20 million Americans, thus providing the oomph to push the *Spice* album to the number 1 position. It stayed there for five weeks – the biggest-selling album of 1997. 'They're certainly singers,' the *New York Daily News* said. 'And they're certainly lookers.'

The girls flew home in triumph and picked up a cool £500,000 for launching Channel Five.

Weeks later, when they appeared in a variety concert for the Prince's Trust at Manchester Opera House, the girls met its patron backstage. Mel B gave the blushing Prince a sloppy kiss on his cheek and Geri pinched his bum. She described it later as 'wobbly'. It was reported by *Rolling Stone* that she had also asked the Prince why he didn't get 'a Prince Albert' – a penis ring.

All they had to do now was stay together and their futures were platinum-plated. Everything seemed supremely harmonious. The girls, closer than ever, would hold hands when doing interviews and finish one another's sentences. It's said that their periods had synchronised.

The merchandising went mad. Fuller pulled in Edward Freedman, whose company, Brand Power, had turned Manchester United into the most powerful brand in world football (Fuller is a Man Utd zealot; it was he who introduced Posh to David at a Chelsea v. Man Utd game). Freedman turned the Spice Girls into the most powerful brand in the history of pop, with a merchandising income that in the short span of the Spice Girls' existence exceeded even that of The Beatles. Here is just some of the Spice Girls truck that seemed suddenly to be everywhere: dolls, chocolate bars, Chupa Chup lollies, bed linen, crockery, cameras, deodorants, crisps, biscuits and balloons, T-shirts, coffee cups, crash-hats, roller skates, BT phone cards, watches, bomber jackets, posters, school bags, calendars, keyrings and pencil cases. There were more product tie-ins with Benetton, Fabergé and Polaroid.

'The sponsorship deals were far more about exposure than the money,' Fuller said. 'A lot of money was made, but my thinking was if we can get Pepsi to spend $40 million basically running what was a commercial for my group, then Hallelujah! . . . It was about using their money to make my group famous and then they'd make lots of money anyway.'

That statement couldn't have been more accurate. The Spice Girls gained exposure in the Far East because of their Pepsi deal and, as a direct result of their association with the band, Pepsi's market share rose by 5 per cent. Walkers Crisps benefited, too, reporting a 6 per cent rise in share prices.

John Toone, a lawyer who had acted for the band when they had been negotiating with Virgin, said, 'No one has more marketability than the Spice Girls. Up to 10 per cent of their income comes from sponsorship, whereas for most artists that figure ranges from 0 to 1 per cent.'

In June 1997, the *Daily Express* reported that the Spice Girls had so far applied for 100 trademarks, adding, 'They are proving ruthlessly determined to exploit the merchandising possibilities of their fame. If you thought their confessed admiration for Thatcherism was just a bit of showbiz PR, think again.'

Two months later, *Forbes* magazine put the band's earnings at $47 million. But, despite the cash in the bank, there was no let-up in the hectic schedule of promotional trips, and now they were working on a second album and a movie as well.

When Simon Fuller needed a scriptwriter for the film, his first thought had been that they should find someone from the Disney realm, but the treatment the mighty Mouse corporation put together was rejected by the girls. Fuller cast around, but all the time the obvious candidate had been staring him in the face: his own brother, Kim Fuller, who had already written sketches for Tracey Ullman and Lennie Henry. Kim's trial scripts met with approval from the girls.

Such was the Spice Girls sensation that normally choosy stars were slavering to get roles in *Spiceworld – The Movie*. Roger Moore played a shadowy management Svengali, with Richard E. Grant as a day-to-day manager (Grant gets to utter the immortal lines: 'They're hot, chief! They've got fire in their eyes, hunger in their bellies . . . and great big shoes on their feet!'). Other parts were played by Elvis Costello, Bob Geldof, Stephen Fry, Jason Flemyng, Jools Holland, Bob Hoskins, Barry Humphries, Jennifer Saunders, Elton John, Hugh Laurie, Meatloaf and Jonathan Ross. Two cast members that the producers might not have booked for the sequel, should there ever have been one, were Michael Barrymore and Gary Glitter. Barrymore made it into the film, but Glitter's performance was erased.

In the movie, Victoria remarks of the Roger Moore figure: 'Life would be even better if it wasn't for that slave-driver bossing us about.' A portent of what was to come in real life, perhaps.

The work was incessant – the girls would be filming all day long then check into the studio to record all evening. As soon as shooting and recording were over, it was determined that the

Spice Girls would do a world tour – playing proper gigs rather than just personal appearances. Fuller rented them a mansion in the south of France for rehearsals. This killed two birds with one stone: it lumped them all together so that they could concentrate on getting ready for the road with no distractions and, by staying out of the country, they could help ameliorate the massive tax bill that they had coming their way.

In the midst of rehearsals, Fuller and Tyrell pulled off their greatest PR stunt. The Spice Girls did a free gig in South Africa and, following in the footsteps of Fidel Castro, Michael Jackson, President Clinton and the BBC's *Ground Force* team, got to meet Nelson Mandela. It's a toss-up who was more impressed with whom.

'They are my heroes,' Mandela gushed to reporters. 'I don't want to be emotional, but this is one of the greatest moments of my life.' Prince Charles, who was also at the event, was asked if this was the greatest moment of his life as well. 'Second greatest,' the smitten Prince replied. 'The first time I met them was the greatest.' Who next? Mother Teresa? The Pope?

During the girls' South Africa trip, Fuller was in the USA having surgery on his back and then convalesced in the UK and Italy. He was away from the girls at a crucial juncture, giving them time to pause, reflect and start grumbling. David Sinclair thinks that there was a lot to talk about. '[Fuller] was keenly aware that the Spice Girls were the one act which could give him a big enough platform on which to build an empire,' he says, 'but he had misjudged the wear and tear . . . inflicted on the vehicle of his good fortune . . . The Girls were being run ragged.'

There had been arguments with the girls, desperate for some time off, and there had been friction between Fuller and the record company, whose interest in selling records didn't always chime comfortably with his plans for some sort of global dominance. While world conquest was certainly in his mind, Fuller was no Napoleon. Rather, some business acquaintances and friends spoke of a soft-spoken character – but a character who was obviously single-minded, driven even.

'When you meet him,' one commented, 'he is perfectly pleasant and agreeable. He will listen and nod and take everything you say on board, then he will very courteously say goodbye and go and do exactly what he intended to do before he met you. He has his own agenda and no one is going to change that.'

However, the five Spicers were now multimillionaires. They'd always made their own decisions about song-writing partners and producers, and they began to think even more independently now. And no matter how risible some might think the Girl Power mantra to have been, the Spice Girls definitely believed in it at some point – well, Geri did, at least – and here they were being dictated to by a man! Most agree it was Geri who first started talking about ridding themselves of the sixth Spice, so, as the other girls shed tears and Simon Fuller lay flat on his back in Italy, she coolly announced, 'The girls have made the ultimate Girl Power move. We want to control our own careers.'

When, on 6 November 1997, Fuller heard from the Spice Girls' accountants that they had been instructed to terminate his contract, he was stunned and refused to believe what he was hearing. That evening, the band won the Best Group award at the MTV Awards. Fuller's name had been ruthlessly removed from the acceptance speech.

The official announcement was made on the 8th, and the following day *Spiceworld* went into the British album charts at number 1. Fuller assuaged his disappointment at his rejection by accepting a reported £10 million severance pay-off.

There was much press speculation about the reasons for the split, and without Gerald Tyrell there to keep a lid on things (he was a Fuller man, after all), the papers could speculate as wildly as they wanted. It was said that the girls hadn't liked the fact that Fuller – on 20 per cent – was earning more than any individual in the band. It was said that Geri and the others had resented the press reports of his alleged affair with Emma. Worse, the press was saying that he'd only gone for Emma because all the others had turned him down. Emma denied it pretty unequivocally to *Sky*

Magazine in 1998: 'I did NOT have an affair with Simon Fuller,' she said. 'Really. No.'

The real reasons for the sacking are shrouded in contractual mystery. Mel B and Geri have hinted that there is a story to be told, but no one is allowed to breathe a word of it under the terms of the deal they did with Fuller, so we are left to speculate.

Geri certainly lived to regret the move, as she related in her book *Geri: Just for the Record*: 'Looking back, Simon was a wonderful manager and I wouldn't be where I am today without him, but, at the time, I believed that we needed a change. For a while it felt great that the girls and I were in control again. It was just like the old days in my Fiat Uno: five girls taking on the world. The downside was that, without Simon, taking on the world was a tiring business. It was ironic that we had sacked him because of our heavy workload, but now we were working twice as hard to prove we didn't need his help.'

Almost immediately things started to go wrong and they would get a lot, lot worse. Suddenly, the girls were outside the cocoon that was 19 Entertainment. The chauffeurs, cars, security guards, stylists and flunkies evaporated. A gig the girls did in Barcelona deteriorated into a near riot. The band had insisted that photographers leave the auditorium before they came on, stating that it had been agreed that they would do so. Most refused to leave and when the girls came on and started miming, they set up a round of booing that was audible over the music.

A number of journalists – particularly those who had been infuriated by Fuller and Tyrell's heavy-handed press control – now turned on the Spice Girls. Matthew Wright in the *Mirror* made vitriolic attacks on a regular basis. The *Daily Telegraph* muttered darkly about poor audiences for the movie and slower sales for the album. Others began calculating the odds on who would be the first Spice Girl to leave the fold, now that the farmer had gone. The mega-marketing of the Spice Girls brand again came under the spotlight, with insinuations that they had gone too far with their endorsements and that they were somehow cheap and vulgar. The backlash was on.

The Spice Girls had gone further faster than any band before or since. They'd made more money in the two years before Fuller was dropped than other major stars make in entire careers. And in that high-octane accelerated existence, their honeymoon was over almost as soon as it had begun. The Slap a Spice Girl website appeared.

However, as *Smash Hits* pointed out, 'It doesn't matter to a ten-year-old fan in Spain or the Philippines that they haven't got a manager.'

But the dust was yet to settle on the sacking. The film company wobbled about the movie's release and talked of issuing it on video only. They shouldn't have worried; when it eventually opened, it became the most profitable film in British movie-making history: it was made for £4 million and took about £50 million worldwide. Kim Fuller, the writer, attended the Royal premiere, but Simon didn't feel able to go along. Kim commented, 'It was the opening of one of the biggest British movies of all time, and the guy who set it all up didn't get to see the film.'

The Spice Girls made attempts to find a new manager – a female manager. They approached Gail Colson, who had looked after Peter Gabriel, and Lisa Anderson, who was later to manage Geri as a solo artist. Both turned them down, which is a shame. It would have been interesting to see a female running a female band – the biggest band in the world at that time. A female did make the team, though, when Nancy Phillips, who'd been involved with The High Llamas and The Undertones, agreed to set up a Spice Girls office and help pull the loose ends together.

In the midst of rehearsals for a new tour – one where the girls would have a proper band and dancers (including one Jimmy Gulzar) – they attended the 1998 Brit Awards. Perhaps the writing was on the wall – pop is, after all, a more fickle business than rock – as they won nothing except a one-off special award, which all assembled regarded as a consolation prize. They were beaten to

Best Video by All Saints and, worse, sat and watched as All Saints took Best Single as well.

The ensuing tour – a tour set up by Fuller (even four months after his departure the band was seemingly still singing from his song sheet) – was a sell-out. However, more cracks were appearing. The girls resented the dominant role that Geri had taken in the running of their affairs. Perhaps the competition for onstage dominance was too intense. Geri also knew that All Saints were a good act who some were setting up as the new queens of pop. She figured that the first Spice Girl to go solo could quite possibly have more of an edge than those who followed. After all, it had worked for Robbie Williams. Geri did her calculations, then jumped. So 5 became 4.

She chose, rather abruptly, to leave at the end of the European leg of their tour, but with a number of North American dates outstanding. The remaining four girls were shocked, riled, but didn't even break their stride. As far as the press was concerned, the loss of Ginger Spice was no problem. They all still loved one another. Their press statement read:

> We are upset and saddened by Geri's departure, but we are very supportive in whatever she wants to do. The Spice Girls are here to stay – see you at the stadiums! We are sorry to all our fans for having to go through all of this.
> All our love, Victoria, Emma, Mel C, Mel B
> Friendship never ends!

Victoria's biography *Learning to Fly* (the bestselling non-fiction book of 2001) tells a different story. 'She was one of my best friends,' she wrote. 'And now she had walked out without a word. What I felt was first anger at the selfishness of it, then betrayed. Total betrayal.'

The gigs were sold out; tickets for Madison Square Garden were being touted for $1,000. The band grossed $60 million for those dates – the big bucks coming from the merchandising yet again.

Spice T-shirts were $30, Spice teddies $25 and rolls of Spice stickers cost $7. Onstage, the fab four coped well in the absence of Geri, haunted, as they were, by her ginger image looming down on them from the giant overhead (pre-recorded) videos and with her mugshot still grinning out from the mugs. The Spice Girl quartet went on, but there was a gradual slide. Geri's departure left a lot of kids confused, inconsolable even.

In the end, Mel B had solo success first (although it was really a duet with Missy Elliott). Likewise, Mel C saw success with the Bryan Adams' song 'When You're Gone'. Posh had met Becks at Fuller's instigation and Brooklyn was on the way, so she was busy with other things. Mel B had met Jimmy Gulzar at her own instigation but was also pregnant.

The girls managed a third Christmas number 1, though, with the appropriately named 'Goodbye'. It would be two years before another Spice Girls song saw the light of day, but in the interim the individuals released twelve hit singles and three albums.

Meanwhile, Simon Fuller had been making other plans. S Club 7 were the first of his TV-centric projects. Following a well-trodden path, he spent more than £1 million searching for three boys and four girls who could sing and dance. The plan was to make an entire comedy-drama television series, like that of the first prefab band The Monkees, to promote their records. It was a resounding success. The group's three television series, *Miami 7*, *LA Seven* and *Hollywood 7*, were seen by 90 million people in 104 countries, while the albums have sold more than 10 million copies worldwide and the group had 11 UK top-five hit singles.

But, despite his success, Fuller is dogged by disregard for all his effort and controversy over his methods. 'He's not really in the music business at all,' complains an industry figure of Fuller in Sinclair's *Wannabe*. 'He's in the TV business. And the things he's involved with clog up the music industry's arteries. There are only so many spots on radio-station playlists, there's only so much space in magazines. His TV-driven projects relegate music to be a spin-off not a core product.'

S Club 7 walked out of a BBC interview after being asked how much they had earned from their four years together.

'It's complicated,' S Club 7's Jo O'Meara said. 'We get royalties and merchandising fees. We're not yet millionaires, but we're certainly richer than most people our age.'

It's been estimated that S Club 7 eventually made about £50 million for Fuller's management company, of which the band themselves pocketed a mere £590,000 each, but figures are not often forthcoming from the inscrutable 19 organisation. In his defence, Fuller says, 'The whole thing was my idea. I came up with the name and the embryonic group.'

It was at this stage that Fuller dropped out of sight. He would give few interviews and avoided being photographed as far as possible. 'There's no upside to fame that I can think of,' he said to Caspar Llewellyn Smith in the *Daily Telegraph*:

> If I have a girlfriend, I want her to be my girlfriend. I don't want the rest of the world to know if we've gone to the shops . . . In the modern world, celebrity is even afforded to business people, executives. To Simon Cowell – for Christ's sake! In an ideal world, it would be great if everyone knew who Simon Fuller was but didn't know what I looked like.

Some see this as the Garbo-esque struggle of a hugely successful man to carve himself a little privacy, while others have voiced the opinion that it is just an artifice of the star-maker.

S Club 7 was followed by the cringeworthy S Club Juniors; *Pop Idol* was followed by *American Idol*, *World Idol* and *American Juniors*. An attempt to form another all-girl group, a 'punk' version of the Spice Girls, or 'a female Slade for the millennium' known as 21st Century Girls, was one of Fuller's rare flops.

19 Entertainment now manages a constellation of dimly twinkling stars, the brightest of which, Will Young and Gareth Gates, were born of TV talent-show formats. 19 Entertainment has become a many-tentacled, all-encompassing media group. It

is said that each of the ten *Pop Idol* finalists was required to enter into agreements exclusively with 19 Records as a recording artist; 19 Merchandising for advertising, endorsements, sponsorships and merchandising; and 19 Management to oversee his or her career. All options naturally rest with the 19 Group.

'Most artists working on the old-fashioned model, how do you keep track of your publisher, your record company, your merchandise, your sponsorship agent, your touring agent? There could be ten different people dealing with different areas of your life,' Fuller commented in the press. 'This is one-stop shopping.'

It has been alleged that contestants were offered management contracts on a 'take it or leave it' basis, were told not to disclose any information about the show's workings or their contracts and would be required to appear in the *World Idol* competition.

The *Pop Idol* judges were Simon Cowell, who was in partnership with Fuller; Nicki Chapman, a long-term employee of 19 who had worked on the Spice Girls; Pete Waterman; and Dr Fox, a prominent DJ on London's Capital radio, who had appeared in *Spiceworld*. The winners signed to S Records, a company owned by Fuller, Cowell (dubbed the 'Vice Chancellor of Musical Mediocrity' by the scurrilous newsletter Holy Moly) and BMG, the record arm of multimedia group Bertelsmann. Bertelsmann owns a share of the *Pop Idol* programme with Fuller through its TV offshoot RTL that in turn owns Thames. Cowell is a director of BMG, the company that handles Britney Spears among others. S Records got the rights to contract the artist not just in the UK but also in any other territory in which the *Pop Idol* show was sold, from Belgium to Beijing.

Fuller reputedly earns far more from *Pop Idol* winners than the conventional management fee. On this point, Fuller has commented, 'If you think of Andrew Lloyd Webber, if he creates *Phantom of the Opera*, he owns it. He hires Michael Crawford to take the lead. Crawford doesn't get a cut of *Phantom of the Opera*, and no one questions that. My deals are the best in the world. I create *Phantom of the Opera* and then say to Michael Crawford, "Let's be 50–50 partners, or 60–40 – whatever the deal is."'

American Idol remains the USA's most-watched show.

That kind of business savvy gets you into the UK's Rich List. It buys you a flat in Los Angeles and a sixteenth-century manor in Sussex. When asked how many houses he has, he once replied, 'Four . . . or is it five?' One of his favourites is a farmhouse with its own olive grove in Provence in France. Callers are offered a bottle of olive oil to take home. The name on the label? 19, of course.

He has had other trinkets: a hand-built $500,000 Mercedes Maybach sedan, Gulfstream 5-SP and Dassault Falcon 900 jets in their hangars; his own African game reserve; a Californian vineyard.

However, relations with Simon Cowell went sour when Fuller sued him, alleging that Cowell had stolen Fuller's idea for a talent show and called it *The X Factor*. They settled out of court and are now happily back in bed together, as they say in business circles, the dispute just a hiccup for the media mogul.

The deals keep on coming.

A while ago, he stated, 'I'm going to change the way we consume music.' He said he had set up deals with Vodafone, AOL and Coca-Cola. The concept was called I Love Music, 'a multi-platform global brand that will sell music to the masses online and through new media'.

He has also talked of starting or finding a 'really exciting angry guitar band, with some punk energy – only no one would be able to know that I was involved, if they are to have any credibility'.

In December 2004, all the Spice Girls bar Melanie Brown attended David and Victoria's party to celebrate the christening of their two children. Simon Fuller, now David's manager as well as hers, was in attendance.

US businessman Bob Sillerman paid nearly $200 million for the 19 Group, which merged with his company CKX. Fuller's production company, and its share of the global TV format *Idols*, brings with it exclusive deals with David and Victoria Beckham, Rachel Stevens, Will Young, Annie Lennox and Emma Bunton.

Fuller, who apparently received £64.5 million in cash and around 1.9 million shares in CKX, has signed a contract with the company and will continue to expand and create entertainment brands. CKX was formed as a result of Sillerman's acquisition of an 85 per cent controlling interest in Elvis Presley Enterprises from Lisa Marie Presley for a reported $100 million.

Paradoxically, the huge payment was less than the market expected and it saw Fuller's position on the Music Rich List drop from a projected £220 million to £75 million. By any stretch of the imagination, that is a huge underestimate. In recent months, he has announced plans for a fashion TV show hosted by Victoria Beckham and a sitcom for Emma Bunton. He apparently masterminded David Beckham's move to Los Angeles.

Fuller estimates that *Pop Idol* may have created more than a 'billion dollars of revenue . . . even two' for Fox TV and the other companies involved in the phenomenon.

Britain's most successful producer, Pete Waterman, had a crack at explaining the *Pop Idol* phenomenon to Caspar Llewellyn Smith in *Pop Life: A Journey by Sofa*. Pete's view was that the show has been such a huge hit essentially 'because we are all overexposed to music'. As Llewellyn Smith notes, 'That was spot on.'

Llewellyn Smith then asks Simon Fuller's sidekick, Nicki Chapman, how she would explain the success of *Pop Idol*: 'It's all that empowerment, isn't it? And there's that side of people wanting to have their say . . . I think people like to be entertained. And they know talent.'

Surely, this is the essence of Fuller's genius: his reading of the zeitgeist. He came from a talent-spotting job. A&R men were, and possibly still are, among the elite of the record industry. It was always the A&R department that had the pick of the company cars, the best office chairs, the grade-A cocaine.

In some way, Fuller has broken this structure down and democratised it. Now we are all in A&R, all in the power seat. We can make or break acts with a telephone call. These days, no clever record company boss signs an act and commits large sums of his company's money on his own initiative. It goes to a committee – and it frequently sounds like it's been to a committee. We get the pop we deserve.

Fuller can't be blamed for this. The homogenisation of pop had already begun and all he has done – brilliantly, it has to be said – is seize the trend and make it his own. What better way of testing a new act on the market than by getting the public to vote on it? Could you get a bigger committee? The programme sells the acts, the acts sell the programmes. The public chooses. It's a marketer's dream.

Simon Fuller is giving us all a master class in twenty-first-century management, and management will never be the same again. Having said that, the artist roster at 19 Management could be considered to be leaning toward the underwhelming (by Fuller's standards) at the moment. But that could change at any moment – that's the beauty of the music business.

'You have to remember, I understand popular entertainment better than anyone,' he told *The Observer* in 2004.

Early in 2007, the world's press got hold of a story that Michael Jackson had asked Fuller to mastermind a career comeback. It's appropriate that the King of Pop should seek help from the most successful manager in the history of the business.

CONCLUSION

The only people for me are the mad ones, the ones who are mad to live, mad to talk, mad to be saved, desirous of everything at the same time, the ones who never yawn or say a commonplace thing but burn, burn, burn like fabulous yellow roman candles exploding like spiders across the stars and in the middle you see the blue centre light pop and everybody goes 'Awwwwwww!'
– Jack Kerouac, *On the Road*

What is so important about British pop success in America? Anything? Nothing? The Asian market is every bit as large as that of the USA these days, despite rampant piracy, and the right band on the right day can make megabucks in either territory or both. If it is important, is it because of our easy/uneasy relationship with the Americans?

We love them because in some distant past they – or at least a great number of them – are of us, and we need their approval like perhaps a mother needs a child's. But yet, like a child, they won't do as they are told so we disapprove of them as well. We look on tutting as they stomp around the world like they own it with their guns and their mangled English language, inflicting on everyone their brash culture. Yet, at the same time, we want to be part of that culture – their culture.

Is it because to make it in the States means everyone knows you've made it, whereas to be big in Japan – well, anyone could claim that and it would pass without much comment around the dinner table? Or could it be because, during the '60s, '70s, '80s and for some of the '90s, British acts bestrode the world, including the USA, like colossi? Is it because we think that if anyone's going to make it big in the States – to repeat that fabulous performance, by virtue of our common language and culture and our illustrious history of success over there – we have a shoe-in and that it is more likely to be a Brit than a Jap or a Frenchman?

Prior to 1964, only two British acts had ever enjoyed number 1 success in the USA. They were Acker Bilk with 'Stranger on the Shore' and Joe Meek's 'Telstar' – both in 1962. After the dam was burst by The Beatles, the top three positions in the Billboard Hot 100 were regularly visited by the Rolling Stones, Herman's Hermits, Manfred Mann, Peter and Gordon, The Animals, The Zombies and Petula Clark. Also hanging around the top end of the charts were The Who, The Kinks, Freddie and the Dreamers, Wayne Fontana and the Mindbenders, the Dave Clark Five, the Troggs, Donovan, Lulu, The Searchers, Arthur Brown and Tom Jones.

Great Britain had become a reliable source of pop and rock for the American market as well as the emerging territories, and held a market share and cultural influence that was way out of proportion to its size and political clout. Over many years, Britain consistently boxed above its weight and, from 1964 onwards, influenced the music of the world from pop/rock through psychedelia, heavy metal, art-rock, punk, new wave and beyond. On stages across the world, presenters would yell, 'Ladies and gentlemen, put your hands together for the greatest rock and roll band in the world . . . It's the Rolling Stones!' Hip journalists would refer to The Clash as 'the only band that matters'.

Zeppelin, the Stones, Phil Collins, Elton John, Depeche Mode,

Conclusion

Duran Duran, ELP, Yes, The Police, ELO, Rod Stewart, The Clash, The Prodigy, Queen, Pink Floyd, the Bee Gees, Bowie, Judas Priest, Def Leppard, Boy George, George Michael, even the Bay City Rollers have kept the British flag flying since, but, despite the fact that those acts look quite impressive when they are all arranged in a sentence like that, there has been a slow, inexorable and some say terminal decline in US market share for UK acts ever since.

Robbie Williams, T. Rex, Slade, Bryan Ferry, The Jam, Squeeze and old rockers Status Quo conspicuously failed to capture the hearts and minds of the great American pop-buying public. Imagine, the Yanks didn't even understand Quo – the band that was quite possibly the model for Spinal Tap.

Barney Hoskyns in *Musician* magazine in July 1996 reckoned that, from this side of the water, only U2 have 'consistently grasped what it is that Americans want in a band: big, anthemic songs; amorphous sentiments; huge self-belief; the willingness to ask, "How ya doin', Cleveland?!!" Rock stars must first of all think like rock stars.'

'It's true that other countries, America in particular, did look to us for guidance,' commented Sting, 'particularly where alternative music was concerned. Now they make their own. The world has changed.'

Bush, a band that hardly a soul in the UK outside of the business has heard of, were the only big-time standard-bearer until Coldplay came along.

Between 1989 and 1999, the share of British music in the US charts declined from 30 per cent to 0.2 per cent, and although stalwarts like Dido and Radiohead have made an incredible impact, the big hitters are thin on the ground.

The house/dance/techno music explosion, which saw British DJs as the highest paid in the world, almost completely passed the Americans by. At their height, the Welsh brigade – Manic Street Preachers, Catatonia, the Stereophonics and Super Furry Animals – found it difficult to get the big push that's necessary to make a dent over the pond. It's an irony that the boybands Take That,

East 17 and Wet Wet Wet, instead of being embraced by our cousins, as they might have been in the past, were merely copied. 'N Sync and the Backstreet Boys were clones. Even king boybander Ronan Keating had to guise himself as a country artist in his fifth attempt at 'breaking America'. Pulp, Blur, Supergrass and especially Oasis have had scant success, despite huge pushes.

The White Stripes had an English sound and even used an English studio packed with '60s-style equipment to capture that gritty British authenticity, but they aren't British.

'Why the Yanks Think Brit Rock Sucks', declared *Mojo* magazine in March 1995.

In the meantime, American pop, rock and particularly hip hop goes from strength to strength, dominating most of the world's charts. The US film, TV, music and video game culture is one of its biggest exports. Maybe we are destined to live, at least in modern music terms, under the Yankee yoke from now on and thoughts of a distinct UK exportable sound have become a pipedream. Maybe there is no British sound left, other than that winsome stuff that The Kinks created, Blur and Pulp promulgated and now only Coldplay can maintain.

Hoskyns, writing in *The Observer* in 2000, rejects the idea that we have become so Americanised that there is little unique UK culture to export:

> A more convincing analysis would be that America has taken what it needs from British pop – style, irreverence, artistic daring – and simply moved on. In a country of 280 million, where Spanish is about to become the dominant language, 'Cool Britannia' has become just another ice-cream flavour. London is calling, but America ain't home.

Pre-Coldplay, the Spice Girls were the last big thing.

Conversely, and most worryingly, there are few UK bands in the UK charts.

Simon Fuller, however, love or loathe what he and Cowell have done to those charts, seems to be at the top of his game. But it has to be said that none of the music artists currently under his wing look like worldbeaters.

There is no easy answer.

Maybe it's just foolish nationalistic tub-thumping to insist that there be a distinct UK presence in any chart anywhere, as we all gradually get strained through the cultural blender. Or is it because we just don't like being ignored – especially by the Americans?

In recent years, the government, via the British Council, has launched an initiative to promote British bands in the USA, putting some (taxpayers') money into a festival in Austin, Texas, where the acts were showcased. Billy Idol and Robert Plant gave masterclasses. *Time* magazine spoke of a new British invasion, saying, 'British rock is back, and even Americans want to listen.'

Although that sounds hideously like Colin Welland standing up at the Oscars and saying 'The British are coming,' hopefully there is a grain of truth in it and possibly bands like Kaiser Chiefs will make an impact because of it. However, the idea that bands need backing from the state to break into the £10 billion American music market makes one wonder what Kit Lambert or Peter Grant might have made of it. Oh, sure, they would have taken the subsidy, but then they would have gone behind the door to piss themselves laughing.

In this most capitalistic of businesses, only the strongest survive – and that was always the case, despite the paradox that most bands harbour a rather limp socialist credo. The concept of an audience relishing the rebel yell of a state-sponsored band is an odd one indeed.

British musicians, DJs, mixers and managers will always have an important role to play in an increasingly amorphous culture, but it's hard not to think that an era has passed, and we are right to pause for a minute of silence to mourn its loss. Could it be because back in the bad old days, when British industries were closing down, when the unions were always on some futile warpath, when Britain was regarded as the 'sick man of Europe', however economically and culturally mediocre the UK appeared, we could cling to the idea that at least we had one of the finest music industries in the world?

And now that's gone.

So, it seems madness, death and after-dinner speaking engagements are the best that can be hoped for by those crazed enough to contemplate a career in rock management.

Of the twelve managers featured in this book, five are dead – all before their time, it could be said – but then folk don't tend to live long in rock and roll. As Jerry Hopkins and Danny Sugerman said in the title of their book about The Doors – *No One Here Gets Out Alive*.

Let's hope the other seven managers live long and prosper – and as only two of them are still actively working as such, they might get away with it. It doesn't seem possible to have a nice quiet, long career managing a massive pop group. It's not that kind of business – unless you manage a band that is anodyne, bland and, in historical terms, unimportant, a band so bloodless that it is incapable of making a pulse race or a heart flutter. By that measure, Simon Fuller will probably live to be 180.

John Peel once bemoaned the state of the music business, saying, 'These days, show me a band and I'll show you a career structure.' By this he meant that kids no longer band together merely for fun, to make a filthy racket and become popular almost by accident; it is all far too serious now, too professional, too slick and, as a consequence, too boring. To a large degree, the great man had a good point. Bands now regard pop music as a viable career option, when years before it was the life choice of the slightly reckless or the unhinged. You see, in the '60s and the '70s, no one thought it would last. No one in their right mind thought that there would still be a burgeoning pop/rock industry at the turn of the millennium, let alone a beast that makes more money than the arms industry and that has metamorphosed into what is, apart from football, perhaps the world's only international language.

Back at the birth of rock and roll, the manager of the band was the one among a group of friends who couldn't play or sing. He would be appointed manager by default mostly, and if he had a driving licence, then he'd likely become the roadie as well. To a great degree, this has all changed – bands have found other ways to get exposure, bypassing the established route of endless motorways, clubs, cafés and lack of cash, demos, drink, drugs and disappointments.

Managers have changed. In the hunt for bucks, it might be said that it is the demands of the new breed of manager that have forced professional homogeneity onto the legions of kids who want to be in the music business. Most managers don't want to spend months nurturing a band, travelling with it, training it, tweaking its membership and its songs, improving its performances incrementally and hoping that some day a label will sign it. Those days are gone. If you do it right, you can have it all now. Become a finalist in *Pop Idol* or *The X Factor* and you can have a top-ten single a few weeks later or maybe a Christmas number 1 – even though you can't play and you've never written a song or done a gig and you weigh fifteen stone. A&R men don't go to clubs any more, they trawl MySpace.

But thankfully, the band wagon rolls on. The old school ways occasionally prevail. There are still bands that have formed themselves – no auditions or fashion parades, just a gang of mates with three chords and a dream. And as long as there's an audience of music-loving kids, earnest students and rowdy boozers who want a Friday night thrash, to get home covered in cider and love bites with their ears ringing and a phone number written on their shirt front, then the show will go on . . . and on.

LAST WORDS TO LOOG OLDHAM

In an interview on dotmusic.com Andrew Loog Oldham was asked by one Shirley Leggitt, who had just started managing a band (and who had no previous experience of management), if he had any advice for her. His reply is right on the button, as you'd expect, and should be printed off by any management aspirant, Blu-tacked to the wall and gazed at daily.

'Thank you, Shirley. No previous experience is probably the best inoculation against despair. Don't fall in love with the act, do fall in love with what they can be. Don't appeal to their dreams except through reason and actual reality as it occurs; let them know what the possibilities are and make them work at every one of them so that a slam-dunk is not an accident but an ability to be and be again. Order a book called *Get It In Writing* by Brian McPherson from www.halleonard.com or Barnes and Noble or Amazon. Make the group read it, and you too, so you all know what you are up against.

'The main change in the game is no change. You are food for a machine. If you don't write, you must learn to or attach yourself to writers who can service and provide the group with songs. You must get some of the publishing, otherwise, even on a million seller, you'll end up broke. Study that book and make sure you can deal with a contract and have it understood by you and your band. A lawyer telling you it's standard or OK is not good enough and irresponsible.

'A few years ago, I picked up an *Ebony* magazine and saw this article on Nat "King" Cole's widow. She had a mansion in Massachusetts and a couple of Rolls-Royces out front. I knew she hadn't got it from her freebasing-at-the-time daughter Natalie. She told the interviewer that during his career Mr Cole had put 50 per cent of every dollar away for tax, saved 25 per cent and spent the rest. That's an admirable achievement that I was not born poor enough to aim for.

'I fell in love with the game. You'll gauge your own cloth. I wish you luck, I wish you fame, in which case the act will have to leave you – it's the nature of the game. Get everything in writing or else it isn't true. Do not work with drug-takers; the world is no longer recreational, it's deadly serious. Depend on the applause in the moment of work as opposed to third-party applause. That is supportive, required but dangerous when taken as the be-all. Enjoy yourself, enjoy each other; it's still the best game I know.'

SOURCES

Chapter 1: Don Arden

Mr Big: Ozzy, Sharon and My Life as the Godfather of Rock by Don
  Arden with Mick Wall (Robson Books, 2004)
All the Rage: A Riotous Romp Through Rock and Roll History by Ian
  McLagan (Macmillan, 1998)
Starmakers and Svengalis: The History of British Pop Management by
  Johnny Rogan (Futura Publications, 1989)

Chapter 2: Brian Epstein

*A Cellarful of Noise: The Autobiography of the Man who Made the
  Beatles* by Brian Epstein (Simon & Schuster, 1998, originally
  published by Souvenir Press)
In My Life: The Brian Epstein Story by Debbie Geller (St Martin's
  Press, 2000)
Revolution in the Head by Ian MacDonald (Fourth Estate, 1997)

Sources

Chapter 3: Andrew Loog Oldham

In My Life by Marianne Faithfull (Penguin, 1994)
Stoned: A Memoir of London in the 1960s by Andrew Loog Oldham
(Secker and Warburg, 2000)
2Stoned by Andrew Loog Oldham (Vintage, 2003)

Chapter 4: Kit Lambert

Awopbopaloobop Alopbamboom: The Golden Age of Rock by Nick Cohn
(Grove Press, 2001)
*Rogues, Villains and Eccentrics: An A–Z of Roguish Britons Through
the Ages* by William Donaldson (Phoenix Press, 2004)
Before I Get Old: The Story of The Who by Dave Marsh (Plexus,
1983)
The Lamberts: George, Constant and Kit by Andrew Motion (Chatto
& Windus, 1995)

Chapter 5: Chas Chandler

Animal Tracks – The Story of The Animals: Newcastle's Rising Sons
by Sean Egan (Helter Skelter Publishing, 2001)
Who's Crazee Now?: My Autobiography by Noddy Holder (Ebury
Press, 1999)
Hendrix: A Biography by Chris Welch (Omnibus Press, 1972)

Chapter 6: Steve O'Rourke

Inside Out: A Personal History of Pink Floyd by Nick Mason (Orion
Books Ltd, 2004)
Lost in the Woods: Syd Barrett and the Pink Floyd by Julian Palacios
(Boxtree/Macmillan, 1997)

Chapter 7: Simon Napier-Bell

Black Vinyl White Powder by Simon Napier-Bell (Ebury Press, 2002)

Chapter 8: Peter Grant

I Used to Be an Animal, But I'm All Right Now by Eric Burdon (Faber & Faber, 1986)

Stairway to Heaven: Led Zeppelin Uncensored by Richard Cole (HarperCollins, 2002)

Peter Grant: The Man Who Led Zeppelin by Chris Welch (Omnibus Press, 2002)

Chapter 9: Malcolm McLaren

The Wicked Ways of Malcolm McLaren by Craig Bromberg (Omnibus Press, 1991)

Money For Nothing: Greed and Exploitation in the Music Industry by Simon Garfield (Faber & Faber, 1986)

Rotten: No Irish, No Blacks, No Dogs by Johnny Rotten (Picador, 1995)

England's Dreaming by Jon Savage (Faber & Faber, 1991)

Vacant: A Diary of the Punk Years 1976–79 by Nils Stevenson (Thames & Hudson, 1999)

Sex Pistols: The Inside Story by Fred Vermorel and Judy Vermorel (Omnibus Press, 1987)

Chapter 10: Bernie Rhodes

Passion is a Fashion – The Real Story of the Clash by Pat Gilbert (Aurum Press Ltd, 2004)

Sources

Chapter 11: Alan McGee

Alan McGee and the Story of Creation Records – This Ecstasy Romance Cannot Last by Paolo Hewitt (Mainstream Publishing, 2000)

Chapter 12: Simon Fuller

Learning to Fly by Victoria Beckham (Penguin, 2001)

Geri: Just for the Record by Geri Halliwell (Ebury Press, 2002)

Pop Life: A Journey by Sofa by Caspar Llewellyn Smith (Sceptre, 2002)

Wannabe: How the Spice Girls Reinvented Pop Fame by David Sinclair (Omnibus Press, 2004)

INDEX

Index

Index

Index